A
BETTER
WAY

A BETTER WAY

REDISCOVERING THE DRAMA
OF GOD-CENTERED WORSHIP

MICHAEL HORTON

BakerBooks
A Division of Baker Book House Co
Grand Rapids, Michigan 49516

Published by Baker Books
a division of Baker Book House Company
P.O. Box 6287, Grand Rapids, MI 49516-6287

Printed in the United States of America

Library of Congress Cataloging-in-Publication Data

Horton, Michael Scott.
    A better way : rediscovering the drama of God-centered worship / Michael Horton.
       p.   cm.
    Includes bibliographical references.
    ISBN 0-8010-1234-1 (cloth)
    1. Public worship. 2. Public worship—Biblical teaching. I. Title.
BV15.H68   2002
264—dc21   2001043968

For current information about all releases from Baker Book House, visit our web site:
http://www.bakerbooks.com

To the Lamb upon the throne,

in memory of James Montgomery Boice—

mentor, partner, and friend

Contents

Acknowledgments   9

Introduction: A Glorious Theater   10

1   Setting the Stage   19

Part 1   "Faith Comes by Hearing": The Ministry of the Word

2   A Dramatic Script   33

3   Casting New Characters   47

4   How Preaching Works   61

5   Discovering the Plot   81

Part 2   Signs and Seals of the Covenant: The Ministry of Baptism and the Lord's Supper

6   Signed, Sealed, and Delivered   93

7   A Table in the Wilderness   111

Part 3   Our Reasonable Service: Getting Involved in the Drama

8   Tasting the Powers of the Age to Come   125

9   What Should Our Service Look Like?   141

10   Is Style Neutral?   163

11   Taking a Break from the Buzz   189

12   Reaching the Lost without Losing the Reached   211

Notes   243

Acknowledgments

There are too many people to thank for whatever might be useful in this volume. Besides, most of them are quite nice people, and I would not want to diminish their credibility by association with my ruminations. However, a few names must be mentioned.

First, thanks to all the people who asked me to write this book, many of whom sent articles that were quite helpful in preparation. Especially to be thanked along these lines are Christ Reformed Church (URC), Anaheim, and Dr. Kim Riddlebarger. I've also learned a great deal about worship from my interaction over the years with Dr. Rod Rosenbladt and Rev. Kenneth Jones. Second, thanks to the students at Westminster Theological Seminary in California for letting me try out some of this material on them. I'm grateful also to Eric Landry for his enormous assistance, as well as that of Steve Moulson. Third, I would like to express appreciation to Baker Book House and particularly to Donald Stephenson and Rodney Clapp.

Saving the best for last, thanks to my wife, Lisa, for putting up with me during the writing and for taking such an active interest in reading and editing the first draft.

INTRODUCTION

A Glorious Theater

The premise of this book is that stated so eloquently by the mid-twentieth-century mystery novelist Dorothy Sayers:

> Official Christianity, of late years, has been having what is known as "a bad press." We are constantly assured that the churches are empty because preachers insist too much upon doctrine—"dull dogma," as people call it. The fact is the precise opposite. It is the neglect of dogma that makes for dullness. The Christian faith is the most exciting drama that ever staggered the imagination of man—and the dogma *is* the drama.[1]

After briefly recapitulating the plot of Scripture as it unites around the person of Christ, Sayers concludes:

> Now, we may call that doctrine exhilarating or we may call it devastating; we may call it revelation or we may call it rubbish; but if we can call it dull, then words have no meaning at all. That God should play the tyrant over man is a dismal story of unrelieved oppression; that man should play the tyrant over man is the usual dreary record of human futility; but that man should play the tyrant over God and find Him a better man than himself is an astonishing drama indeed.[2]

Across the spectrum—liberal and conservative, Reformed, Lutheran, Baptist, Roman Catholic, and Pentecostal—there seems to be a general vagueness about the God we worship and the purpose of worship in the first place. But do we have to settle for either dull routine or perpetual innovation? It is part of this book's burden to demonstrate that there is a better way.

For some reason—many, actually—preaching today has lost its nerve. And so has worship in general, along with its effects: missions, evan-

10

gelism, and diaconal care. On one hand, some approaches to ministry these days reduce the Lord's Day to a lecture; everything else in the service is thrown together, almost randomly on occasion. And if worship is reduced to the sermon, the sermon is often reduced to an exercise in doctrinal and moral exhortation and assent. Others, understandably reacting against this barren intellectualism or moralism, have not only recognized the importance of other aspects of the service (especially heartfelt singing) but have increasingly turned preaching itself into a form of entertainment and emotional expressiveness. Further, whereas the reading material of pastors, elders, church musicians, and informed laypeople used to be quite serious theology, today's bibliographies include, in ranking order, marketing studies of the unchurched, pop psychology, practical management guides by successful CEOs, and peculiar end-times novels. Into this arena come the so-called "worship wars," with both sides amassing their proof-texts that supposedly settle the debate once and for all, resulting in a tragic division of Christ's body into "traditionalist" and "progressive" camps, each with its own Sunday morning service.

There could hardly be a more polarized moment concerning the issues before us. In all of this, however, there does not seem to be enough discussion of the deeper issues—the biblical and theological issues—underlying a distinctively Christian view of worship. With notable exceptions, such as Marva Dawn's *Reaching Out without Dumbing Down* and *A Royal Waste of Time*, there has been a dearth of approaches that move beyond this traditional-contemporary impasse. To be sure, a number of practical books on preaching and music are readily available. But these generally advocate a balancing act between traditional and contemporary styles, a balancing act undergirded by more politics and pragmatism than serious biblical and theological reflection. All of this serves to substantiate the prevailing assumption that how we worship is simply a matter of style, not substance—never mind the second commandment, which prescribes not only whom we worship but how he wants to be worshiped. It seems to me that we need to take a step back and say, "Wait a minute. What is worship anyway? Why do we do it? How do we know when we're doing the right thing?" In both "traditional" and "contemporary" camps, there appear to be numerous assumptions that are never spelled out, and they are usually compelling only to those who already hold them.

There are signs that this is a great time to take a step back and ask some deeper questions than whether we should allow guitars in worship. Both sides in the so-called worship wars have had enough time now to figure out that there are more important questions and are eager to come to some consensus that will stem the tide of division over this issue. As an example of maturing reflection, an article in *Worship Leader*, associated with the contemporary "praise-and-worship" approach, features an interview with some "single adult ministry" experts. I expected the usual hyperbolic rhetoric and pragmatic conclusions. But here is what I discovered instead: "In contrast to an application-oriented church, through the seeker-friendly services" offered at her church, ministry leader Holly Rollins said, "We decided to target this highly intellectual, very well-educated demographic with very deep, philosophical teaching. . . . We spent a significant amount of time studying our demographic before we launched the new ministry. The premise of this was that we're not hitting 80 percent of our target demographic going to church."[3]

Ironically, the same pragmatic marketing criteria are being used to move away from seeker-driven shallowness. The unchurched, especially the younger crowd, are burned out on hype. "That makes Soul Purpose [the single's ministry] probably the most 'ecclesiastical' ministry in our very non-traditional church."[4] Rich Hurst, the other expert interviewed, says of these changes:

> I have a whole different view of ministry. I'm still stuck in a seeker mode and I'm trying to get out of it. That's a big problem with our church world. I find it difficult to say anything positive about the church growth movement. In 1970 there were 10 megachurches, today there are over 400, and yet overall church attendance is off 35 percent. I was in Chicago recently with some pastors. I used to be on the pastoral staff of a seeker church, so I have a pretty good working knowledge of that kind of ministry and what it takes to raise a lot of money. I don't think they have much of a future; they'll wind up being tourist attractions or community colleges because they haven't learned how to reach the next generation. The idea of seeker worship hasn't been the answer to what ails Christianity in America.[5]

Interviewer Sally Morgenthaler adds, "That's the difference between self-help and transformation. It is a whole different worldview if you believe in [human] depravity," to which Rich Hurst replies, "Churches influenced by the seeker-church movement have just become big self-help places, sort of a Parks and Recreation Department for the middle class." In the next article, Jeff Peabody writes, "Many good books and gifted speakers have prompted me to rethink my concept of worship and worship leading. I have become increasingly aware that worship is more profound than what typically occurs on any given Sunday morning. We breeze through our worship, without giving it the theological reflection it deserves." He thinks we need to start asking of worship leaders, "Do they show any theological understanding of their role, or are they musically gifted but biblically illiterate?"[6] These criticisms by insiders reveal that the debate is over theology after all and that the claim to stylistic neutrality (and therefore relativism with respect to it) has for too long gone unchallenged.

Many advocates of traditional worship have also realized that they have not thought too deeply about the principles that guide their reflection. Recognizing that their flock is as likely as a neighboring seeker church to be inarticulate about why certain things are done in worship while others are not, these pastors are opening up to criticisms of the ingrown churches. Accomplished musicians among them are teaching some of these pastors that they may take advantage of instruments other than the organ without putting a praise band or choir up front. There are encouraging signs of greater convergence that does not necessarily involve settling for a "blended" service that will cater to consumer tastes. Of course, not everybody is moving in this direction. And a ministry based on pragmatism is built on sand regardless of whether it is more traditional or contemporary. Furthermore, it will take an entire generation of reeducation in the substance of Christian faith and practice for us to attain linguistic competence again.

This book is an attempt to take a breath and develop some biblical foundations for our understanding of worship. We cannot simply defend positions with either the this-is-the-way-we've-always-done-it assumption or the new-is-better assumption. Even if the practice of the past is correct, each successive generation needs to rediscover that for itself. On the other hand, dismissing the past by slavishly embracing the culture of modernity can lead in the end only to something other than Christianity. Neither assumption is faithful; neither assumption can restore our unity as the people of God from all nations and generations in the presence of God.

Scripture is so rich in delineating the meaning of worship that we could have taken any number of metaphors or paradigms as the way into our subject. I have gone with the model of drama or theater, not because it's an obvious biblical motif but because this appears to be one of the richest ways of reading the Bible.[7] I am persuaded that one of the reasons why so many churches have gone to drama and other theatrical arts in worship is because the sermon and the larger liturgical setting have failed to provide the sense that something important and dramatic is happening here, now, as we gather before God. Divine and human action easily become "choreographed" by the culture when we do not sense that it is occurring at all. The clamor for "more excitement" and "more drama" can lead to two simplistic solutions: a retrenchment of intellectualism or adding our own dramatic gimmicks to God's worship. The goal of this book, however, is to recover the sense of redemp-

tive drama that we not only see illustrated in Scripture but that the Word
and Spirit actually bring into our communal gathering.

Every great revival of worship, including the creation of new hymns
and more faithful as well as understandable liturgies, has come on the
heels of a great reformation in church proclamation and teaching. When
God's people understand who God is, who they are in his presence, and
what is happening to them when they come into his presence, not only
their minds but their hearts are transformed. These great periods always
involve two things that seem contradictory at first: a massive clash with
the world and a worldly church, *and* a renewed sense of the immense
relevance of forgotten truths and practices in a new setting.

And each of these reformations has understood that when God's people gather for worship, a drama is already set in motion that makes our
attempts at staging religious and moral drama silly by comparison. One
thinks, for instance, of the descent of the Spirit at Pentecost, which is
followed not by a B-minor mass or a praise song but by a lengthy sermon (Acts 2:14–36). And what a sermon! Peter begins by announcing to
the astonished and incredulous crowd that they are witnessing the fulfillment of Joel's prophecy and then draws both this prophecy and all
of Scripture around Jesus of Nazareth. He was delivered up to death,
both by the Father's predetermined plan and yet through the personal
choices of wicked men, Peter relates, citing more Old Testament passages that anticipated this climax to the thickening plot. David, he says,
longed for this Son who would sit on his throne forever. "This Jesus God
has raised up, of which we are all witnesses," he declares. "Therefore
being exalted to the right hand of God, and having received from the
Father the promise of the Holy Spirit, he poured out this which you now
see and hear" (vv. 32–33 NKJV). After quoting David one last time, Peter
reaches the "application" part of the sermon: "Therefore let all the house
of Israel know assuredly that God has made this Jesus, whom you crucified, both Lord and Christ" (v. 36 NKJV).

But the drama doesn't stop with the sermon:

> Now when they heard this, they were cut to the heart, and said to Peter
> and the rest of the apostles, "Men and brethren, what shall we do?" Then
> Peter said to them, "Repent, and let every one of you be baptized in the
> name of Jesus Christ for the remission of sins; and you shall receive the
> gift of the Holy Spirit. For the promise is to you and to your children, and
> to all who are afar off, as many as the Lord our God will call."
>
> verses 37–39 NKJV

Now that's drama! At Pentecost the Holy Spirit descends to empower
the proclamation of his Word and to bring about the acceptance of it

by sinners who were otherwise hostile to it. Then he sweeps them into that pentecostal reality through baptism into Christ and the plot that connects us to those who played their parts before us and who now cheer us on from the stands.

Another notable reformation of new covenant worship occurred with the Reformation of the sixteenth century. The gospel having been eclipsed by humanly devised doctrines and practices, the Reformers knew that the power was in the preaching of the gospel—not only in the sermon but in the entire service. The service, they recognized, was not primarily about human action but centered on divine action. God was not only central as an object of worship but also as a subject—an actor, who reconstitutes strangers and aliens as his own redeemed people each week.

As at Pentecost, the encounter with God was seen by the Reformers to occur only because God had descended—in the incarnation, obedience, death, and resurrection of Christ, and in the descent of the Spirit. The apostles did not program a "revival" but were led by the direct commands of the ascended Christ, who gave them not only salvation as a free gift but also the gift of being made witnesses to Christ.

The medieval church had accumulated many innovations in both doctrine and worship, and the average layperson knew little about the Scriptures. Worship services introduced morality plays, stirring music to excite a sense of mystery and majesty, and relied on images, "the 'books' for the unlearned," as the saying went. The Heidelberg Catechism of the Reformed Churches thundered back, "No, we should not try to be wiser than God. He wants his people instructed by the living preaching of his Word—not by idols that cannot even talk."[8] If the people were not up to speed in their biblical maturity, the answer was to get them up to speed, not to accommodate to a degenerating condition. Calvin called worship, as he called creation and redemption, "the marvelous theater" in which God descends to act before a watching world. As many writers have observed, this stands in contrast to much of worship today, whether it takes its cue from high culture or popular culture. It is that presence of the Spirit through his ordained means that makes the worship service a theater of grace in which Christ and all his benefits are communicated to those who were once "not a people"—living aimlessly without any definable plot to make sense of or give a sense of significance to their fragmented lives.

As our age, commonly labeled "postmodern," furthers and even celebrates this fragmentation and the loss of any stabilizing identity, our response must be neither one of mindless conservatism nor an equally mindless accommodation. Scottish minister P. T. Forsyth issued the following warning just after the turn of the twentieth century:

There are few dangers threatening the religious future more serious than the slow shallowing of the religious mind. . . . Our safety is in the deep. The lazy cry for simplicity is a great danger. It indicates a frame of mind which is only appalled at the great things of God, and a senility of faith which fears that which is high. Men complain that they are jaded and cannot rise to such matters. That may mean that the matters of the world absorb all the energies of the great side of the soul, that Divine things are no more than a comfort. And, if so, it means much for the future of religion, and much which is ominous. And the poverty of our worship amid its very refinements, its lack of solemnity . . . is the fatal index of the peril.[9]

Part of this peril, of course, is due to a changing view of the church's relationship to the world. It was once the conviction of most churches, both Roman Catholic and Protestant, that the church was a mother who cared for her children. Now, it is increasingly the case that churches across the denominational landscape regard themselves as department stores in a shopping mall that must sell a product to choice-obsessed consumers.

A growing chorus of secular commentators has indicated the remarkable shift that has taken place over the last two centuries in this regard. Feminist historian Ann Douglas observes, "Nothing could show better the late nineteenth-century Protestant Church's altered identity as an eager participant in the emerging consumer society than its obsession with popularity and its increasing disregard of intellectual issues."[10] In his best-seller *The Triumph of the Therapeutic,* Philip Rieff describes the role of the churches in lending credibility to a fundamentally non-Christian paradigm: "Christian man was born to be saved; psychological man is born to be pleased."[11] Are our market-determined, therapeutic, and entertainment-shaped views of worship parallel in some ways to the clamor of Israel in its moments of apostasy for the gods of the nations? Even if they are nothing more than the attempt to make worship relevant for those who no longer understand the Bible "straight-up," will they end up reaching the lost or losing the reached?

Of one thing we can be certain: God has given us the greatest show on earth, a drama full of intrigue that is not only interesting but actually brings us up onto the stage, writing us into the script as actors in the ongoing production. It gives us a role that contrasts sharply with those one-dimensional characters and shallow story lines of this present age. And because it is more than a play, "putting on Christ" involves a lot more than trying on different costumes and masks. Let's go into the Scriptures, then, to better discover both its plot and our own in its light, once more following the advice of one of England's favorite twentieth-century playwrights:

Let us, in Heaven's name, drag out the Divine Drama from under the dreadful accumulation of slipshod thinking and trashy sentiment heaped upon it, and set it on an open stage to startle the world into some sort of vigorous reaction. If the pious are the first to be shocked, so much the worse for the pious—others will pass into the Kingdom of Heaven before them. If all men are offended because of Christ, let them be offended; but where is the sense of their being offended at something that is not Christ and is nothing like Him? . . . Surely it is not the business of the Church to adapt Christ to men, but to adapt men to Christ. It is the dogma that is the drama—not beautiful phrases, nor comforting sentiments, nor vague aspirations to loving-kindness and uplift, nor the promise of something nice after death—but the terrifying assertion that the same God who made the world lived in the world and passed through the grave and gate of death. Show that to the heathen, and they may not believe it; but at least they may realize that here is something that a man might be glad to believe.[12]

ONE

Setting the Stage

Imagine the worship service as a magnificent theater of divine action. There is the pulpit, lofty and grand—this is God's balcony from which he conducts the drama. Beneath it is the baptismal font, where the announcement, "The promise is for you and for your children" is fulfilled. Also prominent is the communion table, where weak and disturbed consciences "taste and see that the Lord is good." That which God has done to, for, and within his people in the past eras of biblical history he is doing here, now, for us, sweeping us into the tide of his gracious plan.

This chapter briefly sketches the backdrop or stage for this divine production, taking the covenant renewal theme in Scripture as the starting point. What are we doing on the Lord's Day, especially when we are gathered as God's people in church? How do we understand Christian growth and discipleship—as chiefly corporate or individual, as nourished by the preached Word and the divinely instituted sacraments or by self-approved "means of grace"? Would an outsider coming into our worship services be immediately impressed with the centrality of preaching, baptism, and the Supper, or would he or she be more likely to notice the importance given to other performances, whatever the style?

The Covenant Renewal Ceremony

Central to a biblical understanding of worship is the notion of *covenant*. As biblical scholarship has shown in recent decades, the Old Testament is largely in the form of a treaty, with the great king or emperor promising to protect smaller nations that could not generate their own standing army. In exchange, the great king would receive loy-

19

alty from his vassals. They would not turn to other kings for security but would uphold the treaty.[1] A covenant always involved three things: a historical prologue that gave the narrative rationale for the covenant, a list of commands and prohibitions, and a list of sanctions—the benefits for those who fulfill the treaty's terms, the penalty for violating them. To understand the context of worship, we need to do a bit of spadework with respect to this covenant motif.

In Eden, Adam was created by God to be the federal head of the human race. In him, humanity would either be confirmed in righteousness if Adam fully obeyed and endured the time of testing, or humanity would be judged in Adam, should he violate the terms of the covenant of works, also called the covenant of creation. "Do this and you shall live" was (and remains) the principle of this covenant. But this is, happily, not the only covenant in Scripture. There is the covenant of grace. We can trace the steps of this covenant of grace in the following brief summary.

Even after the fall, God promised Eve a son who would crush the serpent's head, and although Cain murdered Abel, God provided another son, Seth. While Cain's descendants were building their own proud city of rebellion (Gen. 4:15–24), "Seth also had a son, and he named him Enosh. At that time men began to call on the name of the Lord" (v. 26). Thus, the two cities (God's kingdom and the world's cultures), fully integrated in creation, were now divided, and they pursued two separate ends through distinct means. Jesus' warning that the world will hate his disciples and Paul's contrast between the wisdom of this world (works-righteousness) and the wisdom of God (the righteousness that comes by faith) are not born out of any hostility toward the world per se. Rather, it is the world in its sinful rebellion that the biblical writers have in mind.

After calling Abram out of Ur, God commanded a ritual sacrifice as a way of making the covenant. In fact, the Hebrew phrase is *to cut a covenant.* In ancient Near Eastern politics and law, a suzerain (i.e., great king or emperor) would enter into a treaty with a vassal (i.e., the king or ruler of a smaller territory) by cutting various animals in half. Then, walking together between the halves, both partners agreed to perform all the conditions of the treaty with the following sanction: If I should be unfaithful for my part, may the same end befall me as has befallen these animals.

In Genesis 15, when God makes his covenant with Abraham and his descendants, this ancient Near Eastern treaty is the pattern:

> But Abram said, "O Sovereign Lord, how can I know that I will gain possession of it?" So the Lord said to him, "Bring me a heifer, a goat and a ram, each three years old, along with a dove and a young pigeon." Abram

brought all these to him, cut them in two and arranged the halves opposite each other. . . . As the sun was setting, Abram fell into a deep sleep,
and a thick and dreadful darkness came over him. Then the LORD said to
him, "Know for certain that your descendants will be strangers in a country not their own, and they will be enslaved and mistreated four hundred
years. But I will punish the nation they serve as slaves, and afterward they
will come out with great possessions." . . . When the sun had set and darkness had fallen, a smoking firepot with a blazing torch appeared and passed
between the pieces. On that day the LORD made a covenant with Abram.

verses 8–10, 12–14, 17–18

Two sorts of things are promised by God in this covenant: a holy land
(Canaan, the earthly Jerusalem) and everlasting life (the heavenly Jerusalem). What especially distinguishes this treaty is the fact that although
God and Abram are covenant partners, the Lord (appearing as a smoking firepot with a blazing torch) walks alone through this path, placing
on his own head all the sanctions and assuming on his own shoulders
the curses that he himself has imposed should the treaty be violated.
Then in chapter 17 there is another cutting ceremony:

Abram fell facedown, and God said to him, "As for me, this is my covenant
with you. . . . I will establish my covenant as an everlasting covenant
between me and you and your descendants after you for the generations
to come, to be your God and the God of your descendants after you. . . .
This is my covenant with you and your descendants after you, the covenant
you are to keep: Every male among you shall be circumcised. You are to
undergo circumcision, and it will be the sign of the covenant between me
and you."

verses 3–4, 7, 10–11

Signifying the cutting away of uncleanness, especially of original
sin, which is passed on from Adam through every subsequent father,
circumcision was a bloody rite of consecration. But here, instead of
the knife being plunged into the body to bring down the curses of the
transgressors, it is used to cut away the sin so that the recipient may
live.

Eventually, God's promise was fulfilled: Israel did inherit the land.
As mentioned above, God promised a holy land and everlasting life. As
becomes clearer with the progress of redemption, the former was (like
Adam's enjoyment of Eden) dependent on works—the obedience of the
Israelites. The Mosaic covenant, with its ceremonial and civil as well as
moral laws, promised blessing for obedience and judgment for disobedience. Once again, God would fight for his people and give them a new

Eden, a land flowing with milk and honey. God would be present among his people in the temple as long as they were righteous. Along with Adam, the earthly Israel as a typological kingdom was in league with God on the basis of the works principle: "Do this and you shall live." But (also like Adam) Israel failed and in its rebellion violated the treaty with the great king, provoking God to enact the sanctions of this works covenant. The lush garden of God became a wasteland of thorns and thistles, as God withdrew his kingdom back up into heaven, the children of Israel being carted off to Babylonian exile. "Like Adam, they have broken the covenant" (Hosea 6:7).

After these years of exile, a remnant returned to rebuild Jerusalem. Ezra and Nehemiah report this remarkable event and the tragic infidelity and infighting that went along with it. Despite human sinfulness, under Nehemiah's leadership the remnant rebuilt the walls of Jerusalem and its magnificent temple, which God's evacuation had left desolate and ransacked by invaders. The poor were cared for again. But the centerpiece of this event appears when the Torah is rediscovered for a generation of Israelites that had never read or heard the Scriptures read except perhaps from their grandparents' memory:

> When the seventh month came and the Israelites had settled in their town, all the people assembled as one man in the square before the Water Gate. They told Ezra the scribe to bring out the Book of the Law of Moses, which the LORD had commanded for Israel. So on the first day of the seventh month Ezra the priest brought the Law before the assembly, which was made up of men and women and all who were able to understand. He read it aloud from daybreak till noon as he faced the square before the Water Gate in the presence of the men, women and others who could understand. And all the people listened attentively to the Book of the Law. Ezra the scribe stood on a high wooden platform built for the occasion. . . . Ezra opened the book. All the people could see him because he was standing above them; and as he opened it, the people all stood up. Ezra praised the LORD, the great God; and all the people lifted their hands and responded, "Amen! Amen!" Then they bowed down and worshiped the LORD with their faces to the ground.
>
> Nehemiah 8:1–6

Even during their exile the Israelites were reminded by Jeremiah's prophecy of the divine promise—not to restore ethnic Israelites to the geopolitical territory of Palestine as God's kingdom on earth but to save a remnant from both Israel and the nations of the world. Although the *Mosaic* covenant had been thoroughly violated, God, you will recall, was still carrying the entire burden for the fulfillment of the *Abrahamic* covenant of grace. Thus, again and again in the prophets we read, "Not for your sakes, but for the sake of the promise made to Abraham, Isaac, and Jacob . . ." So through Jeremiah God declares:

> "The time is coming," declares the LORD, "when I will make a new covenant with the house of Israel and with the house of Judah. It will not be like the covenant I made with their forefathers when I took them by the hand to lead them out of Egypt, because they broke my covenant, though I was a husband to them," declares the LORD. "This is the covenant I will make with the house of Israel after that time," declares the LORD. "I will put my law in their minds and write it on their hearts. I will be their God and they will be my people. . . . For I will forgive their wickedness and will remember their sins no more."
>
> Jeremiah 31:31–34

This new covenant "will not be like the covenant I made with their forefathers" under Moses, says the Lord, but will be an everlasting and unbreakable covenant. It will be based not on the national election of Israel and their existence in the land by their collective obedience but on the eternal election of individuals whom the Son redeemed: ". . . and with your blood you purchased men for God from every tribe and language and people and nation. You have made them to be a kingdom and priests to serve our God, and they will reign on the earth" (Rev. 5:9–10).

The Sabbath rest that Israel forfeited in the Holy Land because of disobedience is now freely given to sinners, Jew and Gentile, just as it was to Israelites in the old covenant (Heb. 4:1–10). Even Joshua, Moses' lieutenant who led the Israelites into the land, was looking for a greater land, a more excellent kingdom, with a firm and unshakable foundation: "For if Joshua had given them rest, God would not have spoken later about another day. There remains, then, a Sabbath-rest for the people of God; for anyone who enters God's rest also rests from his own work, just as God did from his" (Heb. 4:8). Thus, the New Testament gospel is identical to that which Abraham believed when he was credited with the perfect righteousness of Christ through faith alone, apart from works (Gen. 15:6; Rom. 9:8; Gal. 3:6–14). This is not the Mosaic covenant, an administration based on *our* faithfulness, but the Abrahamic covenant, an administration of *God's* faithfulness and grace. Works are witnesses to, not the basis of, our right standing before God. And yet, we cannot be justified merely by being forgiven: That would still leave us without the perfect righteousness that God's justice requires. In Christ, the greater Adam and the true Israel, God's justice is fully satisfied. Our Lord's thirty-three years of loving his Father with all his heart, soul, mind, and strength, and his neighbor as himself, is the basis for our acceptance before God. So in a real sense, we are saved by works—but by our covenant head's works, not ours. Because he fulfilled the covenant of works, we inherit salvation through a covenant of grace.

It is in this context that we talk about the "covenant renewal ceremony." Whenever we gather for public worship, it is because we have been summoned. That is what "church" means: *ekklesia,* "called out." It is not a voluntary society of those whose chief concern is to share, to build community, to enjoy fellowship, to have moral instruction for their children, and so forth. Rather, it is a society of those who have been chosen, redeemed, called, justified, and are being sanctified until one day they will finally be glorified in heaven. We gather each Lord's Day not merely out of habit, social custom, or felt needs but because God has chosen this weekly festival as a foretaste of the everlasting Sabbath day that will be enjoyed fully at the marriage supper of the Lamb. God has called us out of the world and into his marvelous light: That is why we gather.

But we also gather to receive God's gifts. And this is where the emphasis falls—or should fall. Throughout Scripture, the service is seen chiefly as God's action. This is where God walks along through the severed halves—not of animals this time but through the true temple's torn curtain—Jesus' body—on Good Friday. On the cross, God's glory is hidden under the form of its opposite: shame and dereliction, the true and faithful Israel being abandoned to exile, the judge becoming the judged in our place. The one who brought us up out of the land of Egypt and made us his people takes the initiative in salvation and throughout the Christian life. The shadows of Christ in the Mosaic covenant, most obviously the detailed legislation for the sacrifices, are fulfilled in the advent of the Messiah. Therefore, we do not worship in an earthly sanctuary but in the heavenly sanctuary where we are seated with Christ in heavenly places; hence, Jesus' statement to the Samaritan woman in John 4: True worship comes from the Jews but is no longer attached to any earthly sanctuary, including the temple in Jerusalem. Our earthly buildings, however marvelously built and maintained, are no longer divine sanctuaries in their own right—something far more amazing occurs in our services in the new covenant. Here we are living stones being built up together into the heavenly temple, which is nothing less than Jesus Christ himself. While the earthly temple was a holy place, our earthly buildings are common rather than holy. It is the presence of the holy *God* by his Spirit that creates through the means of grace a holy *people.*

Notice what Jesus is *not* saying here. He is not saying that the Jews were not God's chosen people—that the Samaritans' worship had his approval as well. Nor is he saying that there had not been a right place—namely, the earthly sanctuary in Jerusalem—to worship. What he is say-

ing is that "the time is coming and now is" when these things won't matter. That is because God's temple-dwelling among his people is no longer
a temporary building on earth but the indestructible person of Jesus
Christ himself. As God's typological kingdom, the Jewish theocracy was
literally "heaven on earth," but it was always temporary (like Adam's
probation) and witnessed to the faithful Adam in the future who would
fulfill the probation, earning the right for himself and his spiritual heirs
to finally eat from the Tree of Life.

The Book of Hebrews was written to warn Jewish Christians against
turning back again to the shadows that merely pointed to the reality.
Arguments about worship in our day, therefore, cannot be based on the
nature of worship in the old covenant. Christ has come and Moses has
stepped aside, pointing away from himself as John the Baptist did, to
declare, "Behold, the Lamb of God who takes away the sin of the world!"
While we do not turn back to the shadows of the law, we do inherit the
same covenant of grace that God made with Abraham and his seed. As
in the vision of the smoking firepot with a blazing torch, God walks
down the middle of the aisle in our worship service, assuming the judgment that his own justice requires and his own mercy satisfies. He cir-
cumcises our hearts.

God's Work and Our Response

When we think of "God's work," we immediately think of the cross
and resurrection—and for good reason. There God's purposes in history
are seen, the mystery is revealed, and Jesus Christ is publicly held forth
as the substitute for sinners. But as central as God's past works are in
redemptive history, we should realize that he works his wonders among
us today just as he did in the past. To be sure, there are no more burning bushes, no more atoning sacrifices or redemption-securing resur-
rections. Pentecost is an event in the past as well. However, God still
works through signs and wonders. The difference is that these modern
signs and wonders are ordinary rather than extraordinary works. Ordinary preaching raises the spiritually dead to life, while ordinary water,
bread, and wine are taken up by God as signs and seals of God's saving
presence. That which God has done once and for all in the past is applied
in the present. Thus, God's work during the service is not just talk about
God and the wonders he has wrought; it is yet another opportunity for
God to work among us through the means he has ordained.

As in all covenants, there are two parties to the covenant of grace.
God speaks and delivers; we respond in faith and repentance. And yet,

faith and repentance do not constitute "our part" in this covenant in the sense of providing some of the grounds for our participation in it. God even grants faith and repentance. And yet God does call us to respond, to grow in grace, and to persevere to the end. The triumphant indicative concerning God's action in Christ establishes a safe foundation on which to stand as we seek to obey the divine imperatives. That's why worship is dialogical: God speaks and we respond.

That is the form we find in the psalms: God's wondrous works in creation, preservation, judgment, and redemption are extolled, and it is only then that it makes sense to respond, whether in confession, praise, thanksgiving, lament, or whatever else might be appropriate to the divine activity that is announced. Unlike the psalms themselves, many of the hymns and praise choruses of the last century and a half have become increasingly human-centered. This is why I am always somewhat nervous when people argue for the "old hymns" as opposed to the "new choruses." Often, "old hymns" means romantic gospel songs written between 1850 and 1950, songs that exchanged object-centered praise (God and his saving work in Christ) for subject-centered praise (we and our spiritual activity). A classic example is "In the Garden," in which the pattern of the psalms (concentration on God's wondrous works on behalf of his people) is exchanged for sentimental individualism. Shifting attention from the objective person and work of Christ to the subjective person and work of individual believers, many of these hymns that can still be found in abundance in evangelical hymnals could be sung with gusto by a Unitarian, and some of the most loved were in fact written by Unitarians.

Even with contemporary praise choruses that versify or paraphrase a psalm, the *response* section of the text is often separated out from the *indicative* section, which proclaims who God is and what he has done. Thus, the focus of worship these days seems to be on what we are doing, how we are feeling, and how we intend to respond: "I just want to praise you"; "We will lift you up"; "Let's just praise the Lord"; "I am joyful," etc. But this is to separate the law from the gospel, the imperative (what we are to do) from the indicative (what God has already done, is doing, and will complete for us in Christ). Vagueness about the object of our praise inevitably leads to making our own praise the object. Praise therefore becomes an end in itself, and we are caught up in our own "worship experience" rather than in the God whose character and acts are the only proper focus.

The same is true for preaching and the other elements of the service. If worship is a covenant renewal ceremony, the service must reflect the divine initiative in the covenant itself. There must be response—and there will be response, if there is something to which we are inclined to respond. At the same time, there should be an emphasis here on God's work: God renews the covenant with us, assuring us of that which we easily lose sight of unless Christ is publicly placarded before our eyes each week. God meets his people in Christ as the Holy Spirit works through the liturgy: confession of sin, declaration of forgiveness, songs of praise, confession of the faith, the preaching, the prayers, and the sacraments. It is the person and work of this Triune God that must be front and center, as this God actually confronts us just as he did in the assembly when Ezra read God's Word. It is the Word, not Israel's response to the Word, that is central in that account, and yet the report does not fail to inform us that "all the people listened attentively" (Neh. 8:3) and, later, even "lifted their hands and responded, 'Amen! Amen!'" and then bowed down "with their faces to the ground" as they wept because of their sense of their own sinfulness and God's amazing grace (vv. 6, 9).

No wonder, then, that at Pentecost a similar event occurs as Peter preaches. Out of this preaching the new covenant church was established. And what was the pattern of this weekly covenant renewal ceremony? "They devoted themselves to the apostles' teaching and to the fellowship, to the breaking of bread and to the prayers" (Acts 2:42, author's translation).

It is a new and better covenant, with Christ himself rather than Moses as its mediator. The Lord's Supper is neither a mere memorial of Christ's death nor a re-sacrificing of Christ (as if we preferred the shadows of Moses to the reality in Christ). Rather, it is a participation in the very body and blood of Christ Jesus (1 Cor. 10:16). "This cup is the new covenant in my blood," we read in the words of the institution. No wonder the writer who so strongly urges believers to recognize the superiority of the new covenant also charges us not to give up the covenant renewal ceremony that God enacts not once but each Lord's Day:

> Therefore, brothers, since we have confidence to enter the Most Holy Place by the blood of Jesus, by a new and living way opened for us through the curtain, that is, his body, and since we have a great priest over the house of God, let us draw near to God with a sincere heart in full assurance of faith, having our hearts sprinkled to cleanse us from a guilty conscience and having our bodies washed with pure water. Let us hold unswervingly to the hope we profess, for he who promised is faithful. And let us consider how we may spur one another on toward love and good deeds. Let us not give up meeting together, as some are in the habit of doing, but let us encourage one another—all the more as you see the Day approaching.
>
> Hebrews 10:19–25

More than Music

We are repeatedly told these days that music is the most important thing we do in worship. In fact, "worship" usually means singing or enjoying the singing of others. "Let's just take some time now to worship" is roughly translated, "Cue the praise band." In preparing for a talk recently, I picked up an issue of *Worship Leader*, a publication of CCM Communications. In one of the articles, a minister reminds us of how important music is as our "heart language." "The function of music is to give persons access to their heart language so that they might worship more fully," he writes. Even more, "music can be spiritually generative." "Spiritually generative events are things that 'connect' people with God and have a self reproducing quality." But there is more to learn concerning things spiritually generative:

> In antiquity we see this concept in the conversion of Celts in Ireland during the sixth century. Celtic orbs, knots and images about the Creation were incorporated into what we know as the Celtic cross. . . . At the same time, the orb and knots were christianized. To look at the cross was to see Christ. To look at Celtic art was to think of the cross, wherever one might be. This is a good example of a spiritually generative event.[2]

But couldn't it rather be a good example of what the prophets and apostles might well have regarded as idolatry—the violation of the second commandment, which prohibits the creation of images of the true God? Even if one were to accept that such art were an acceptable form of education, surely critics of any representation of God will feel somewhat vindicated when these images are cited as examples of "a spiritually generative event."

In the author's church, he tells us, "we pluck our themes right off of alternative and Top 40 radio. We are hoping for a spiritually generative result." The subtitle of the article is "Music as Medium to Connect Us to God." Can music really connect us to God? Not the Word as it is sung but the music itself? In a generation that views music (especially pop music) as the lifeline to selfhood and the world, it is not surprising that it would be regarded as the best bridge to God.

Lest I be suspected of overstating my case, I want to say that I do not regard alternative and Top 40 songs as inherently sinful or idolatrous. Similar examples could be taken from "high culture" appropriations, as when a traditional church eliminates congregational singing in favor of professional choirs and musicians. But in worship we are talking about something different. Here it is not the culture—whichever slice of it one might prefer—that determines the shape of things. What we do on the

Lord's Day is already determined by God: preaching of the Word, the sacraments, and prayer (Acts 2:42). How can we blithely "pluck our themes right off of alternative and Top 40 radio" when we have been sent out on someone else's mission?

The assumption these days often seems to be that God has not said anything about how we should worship him. For instance, some have argued that a weekly service need not include the preaching of the Word, as God can speak his Word through a variety of other instruments: drama, liturgical dance, poetry, and so on. Repeatedly, worship is reduced to a matter of consumer tastes. One person prefers guitars, another prefers organs: Isn't that all this debate is about? It might seem so at first glance, but as the theme develops, I hope we will see that it's not just about taste, much less about guitars versus organs. I will argue the case that style is never neutral and that whether we sing "Shine, Jesus, Shine!" or "O Sacred Head Now Wounded" or, for that matter, Psalm 23, style is never merely a matter of preference. Nevertheless, we have to develop a theology of worship that avoids biblicism on one hand (i.e., the tendency to "free" oneself of the theology of Scripture by limiting its normativity to explicit proof-texts) and on the other a dogmatic traditionalism that justifies its positions by saying, "That's the way we've always done it."

Our Jealous God

Idolatry is a loaded term and should not be hurled about indiscriminately. And yet, it is a perennial temptation even for us as believers. To view worship as a covenant renewal ceremony in which God summons us and acts in word and deed for our good is to recognize that *how* we worship (the second commandment) is as much God's prerogative to define as *whom* we worship (the first commandment). This chapter launches the thesis that will run throughout the rest of the book. That thesis is this: *God has promised to save and keep his people through the means he has appointed and through no others; the ordinary means of grace are limited to the preached Word and the administered sacraments; God's rationale for these means is made explicit in Scripture.* There are many other things that are essential for Christian growth: prayer, Bible study, service to others. However, these are not, properly speaking, means of grace but means of discipleship.

In this wilderness epoch between the two comings of our Savior, God is savingly present among us through Word and sacrament. We need props to strengthen our faith, but we dare not invent our own, as Israel did at Mount Sinai, when Aaron's lame excuse for the golden calf was, "You know how the people are." Only in glory will we no longer need faith, since hope will dissolve into sight. There will be no more promises, no more anticipation. But for now God has given us his means of grace to ensure that the method of delivery as well as the method of redemption itself is his alone. Here in the wilderness God has given us both the preached Word and the visible Word (baptism and the Supper). Here is God's drama, the liturgy of life, in which God acts in saving grace and we respond in faith and repentance. Even our architecture is to be conscious of this mission to proclaim God's method of grace alone, through faith alone, because of Christ alone, delivered in the church alone, through the means of grace alone. Donald Bruggink and Carl Droppers offer a charge that could apply to any Reformation church: "To set forth the God-ordained means by which Christ comes to his people, the Reformed must give visual expression to the importance of both Word and Sacraments. Any architecture worthy of scriptural teaching must start with the Christ who calls men unto himself through the Word and Sacraments."[3] In the divine drama, the "set" is not insignificant.

Through this drama of the weekly covenant renewal ceremony, we are not merely playacting. It is for real: Christ here exercises his threefold office as prophet, priest, and king. As our prophet, he pronounces his judgment and announces his salvation through his ambassadors. As our priest, he stands between us and the just wrath that divine holiness entails in relation to rebels like us. Beyond mediating, he, the judge, assumes our judgment. As risen king, he has conquered sin and death for us and now rules in his church so that no alien ruler can conquer us.

It is by grace alone that we are redeemed and by grace alone that we stand in this redemption. The logic of the message controls the logic of the method, rendering both unbridled "enthusiasm" and "dead orthodoxy" false alternatives. But the logic of both leads to Paul's doxological conclusion in Romans 11: "For from him and through him and to him are all things. To him be the glory forever! Amen" (v. 36). Having set the stage for this divine drama, in the remaining chapters we will try to unpack the wonder and wisdom of this God who, in this covenant renewal ceremony, gives us "every spiritual blessing in Christ Jesus" and eagerly receives our gifts of praise.

Part 1

"Faith Comes by Hearing": The Ministry of the Word

TWO

A Dramatic Script

One of the interesting by-products of living in Southern California is having a handful of friends who work in Hollywood, particularly on scripts. One thing I have heard my friends say repeatedly is how many flat, one-dimensional, go-nowhere scripts they have to read in order to find a single decent one. The scripts that lack a compelling plot are the most likely candidates for playing to "the lust of the flesh, the lust of the eyes, and the pride of life" (1 John 2:16 NKJV).

So too the scripts of our own lives. By nature children of Adam—rebels, wanderers, strangers to God—we have no plot, except the explicitly "plotless" postmodern plot. There is nothing to make sense of our lives as a whole. For many people, hours, days, and years are "doomed" to an ocean of meaningless obscurity and random meaninglessness. That is not unduly pessimistic but an entirely appropriate and mature assessment of life "under the sun," where "everything is meaningless" (Eccles. 12:8). To be sure, God upholds even his rebellious creation with common grace, giving pleasure in labor, family, milestones in one's life and career. But upon further assessment, the life of presumed independence from God is one-dimensional, flat, one trivial success or failure after another. It lacks a narrative or plot that unifies the events, characters, and setting and puts them in motion as part of a larger story.

But the problem is not only one of lacking a compelling script but of having no script at all. It's all impromptu dialogue—or rather, monologue, in a one-man show. And however much they clamor for community, most Americans will easily surrender it for more individual choice and autonomy. Neal Gabler has provided a riveting account of how entertainment has conquered reality by making each person think of himself or herself as the star of his or her own show. His title is *Life the Movie, Starring Everyone.* "An ever-growing segment of the American economy," says Gabler, "is devoted to designing, building and then dressing the sets in which we live, work, shop and play; to creating our costumes; to making our hair shine and our faces glow; to slenderizing our bodies; to supplying our props—all so that we can appropriate the trappings of celebrity, if not the actuality of it, for the life movie." Drama coaches such as Martha Stewart help us achieve this approximation of ourselves to the image that we have of ourselves in our life movie.[1] It is precisely this process of being scripted by the world (Rom. 12:2) that this chapter challenges.

Before we can be rescripted, we have to take a step back. While today our identities are more the scattered clippings of ideal images packaged and marketed to us in a barrage of advertising masquerading as entertainment, the "self" who is rendered in the biblical drama of redemption is a solid self only because he or she belongs to a story that is much larger than oneself. In the former, the identities of others (usually celebrities) are consumed and made a part of my life and identity. In the latter, the real identities (not images) of the many biblical characters become the context in which my life makes sense. It is here where strangers and aliens finally belong to God and become part of his family throughout history. In the former, even God himself is "appropriated," drawn into our script, ending in futility, while in the latter, even the most villainous character can be drawn into the divine drama by the director as a new character.

Unlike most plays, which simply entertain or evoke various responses, the divine drama actually incorporates the audience in the overarching plot. "Faith comes by hearing the Word of God." How is it that by hearing this script and story as it proclaims God's judging and saving action, skeptical spectators become new characters in the play? Why hearing? Is preaching the only way of creating faith in the hearts of unbelievers? Finally, how can we recover a sense of the dramatic in preaching?

The Logic of Grace: Way of Salvation and Way of Saving

For answers to these questions, we turn now to Romans 10. First, there is the well-known lament concerning the offense of the cross—a lament because so many of Paul's flesh and blood stumble over the Rock. But the Rock cannot be moved. It cannot be softened, broken into pieces, or absorbed into the environment. It's just there—in the way, inconvenient, offensive. God demands a perfect righteousness, which some of the Jews he addresses seek by their own works rather than by faith in Christ alone. Paul works out the logic of grace quite clearly throughout this epistle, but especially beginning at Romans 8:29 it becomes a tight logical argument: "Those God foreknew he also predestined to be conformed to the likeness of his Son. . . . And those he predestined, he also called; those he called, he also justified; those he justified, he also glorified. What, then, shall we say in response to this? If God is for us, who can be against us?" (vv. 29–31). And then Paul further adds that the "righteousness that is of the law" leads to conclusions that are antithetical to those reached by the "righteousness that is by faith." This is most succinctly stated finally in chapter 11: "If by grace, then it is no longer by works; if it were, grace would no longer be grace" (v. 6). That's the logic of the gospel.

This summary is familiar enough to many of us. To be sure, there are two ways of salvation: our way, which leads to death, and God's way, which leads to life everlasting. Each road has its own destiny and its own method of redemption (works or grace). But what may not be so familiar is Paul's argument in Romans 10; namely, that each road not only has its own destiny and method of redemption but also its own *means of attaining or receiving* that redemption. It is possible to accept the logic of the message ("salvation by grace alone through faith alone because of Christ alone") while missing the logic of the method (*receiving* this by grace alone). Note Paul's argument closely:

> Moses describes in this way the righteousness that is by the law: "The man who does these things will live by them." But the righteousness that is by faith says: "Do not say in your heart, 'Who will ascend into heaven?'" (that is, to bring Christ down) "or 'Who will descend into the deep?'" (that is, to bring Christ up from the dead). But what does it say? "The word is near you; it is in your mouth and in your heart," that is, the word of faith we are proclaiming . . . for, "Everyone who calls on the name of the Lord will be saved." How, then, can they call on the one they have not believed in? And how can they believe in the one of whom they have not heard? And how can they hear without someone preaching to them? And how can they preach unless they are sent? . . . Consequently, faith comes from hearing the message, and the message is heard through the word of Christ.

> Romans 10:5–8, 13–15, 17

Do you see the logic of the method that Paul outlines here? Paul is saying that grace has its own method. The spirit of works-righteousness says, "How can I climb up to God and bring Christ down to me, where I am, in my own experience?" Like Ulysses crossing the expansive seas to conquer dragons and finally to arrive at his reward, the logic of works-righteousness conceives of salvation in terms of a personal conquest. Martin Luther would talk about ladders that people climb in order to make it into God's presence: Mysticism, merit, and speculation were the ladders he had in mind. These same ladders are plentiful today. Scores of methods abound for pulling God down out of heaven, to manipulate him into doing what we want him to do when we want him to do it. Just know the right techniques and spiritual principles. Just do the right thing. Just find the right spiritual leader or movement to join. Just travel to the latest shrine of reportedly divine activity. This, of course, is what the Israelites attempted in the wilderness. While God was giving his redeemed people a written and preached Word through his servant Moses at the top of the mountain, they were busy fashioning a golden calf that they could see and touch—and control.

Today people still want to see, touch, and control God. They will do almost anything to be where the "action" is, where God has been conjured down out of heaven, whether it is flying to Toronto, Pensacola, or even Lourdes. Not content with hearing God's Word, they want to see God's glory. But God warned Moses, "No man may see me and live" (Exod. 33:20). In fact, it was during this episode, just after God agreed not to destroy his idolatrous people, that Moses pleaded with God to see his glory. Informing Moses that this would spell the prophet's doom rather than delight, God did agree to allow his goodness rather than his glory to pass by. And he did this by preaching a little sermon: "I will have mercy on whom I will have mercy" was the introduction, body, and conclusion.

Throughout the history of Israel, idolatry was the Big Sin. It was not adultery or fornication, greed or theft, even murder or being disobedient to one's parents. These were all-important, each with its own sanction under the Mosaic civil code. Nevertheless, idolatry was the sin from which all else was seen to flow. The Canaanites and other nations in the region were much more culturally sophisticated and technologically advanced than the children of Israel. Furthermore, they credited their prosperity to their own efforts and the approval of the gods. Each of these gods they could see: There were visible manifestations or points of contact with these deities in the form of huge statues and altars raised up on the highest points on the horizon. Israel was tired of hearing, which corresponds to patient waiting for God's timetable in hope. Instead, Israel wanted to see, which corresponds to the reality itself: "Seeing is believing." And that really is true for us as fallen creatures, born untrusting and cynical. But as Paul reminds us, "For in this hope we were saved. But hope that is seen is no hope at all. Who hopes for what he already has? But if we hope for what we do not yet have, we wait for it patiently" (Rom. 8:24–25).

Therefore, there is a correlation in biblical faith between faith, hope, and a promise announced (hearing) on the one hand, and vision, sight, and a reality fully experienced on the other. Those who demand the vision of God here and now will be particularly susceptible to idolatry, whereas they would likely not be as inclined to it if they were patient in waiting for the salvation that they have in Christ as it is mediated through the broken and not so spectacular vessels of human messengers and the most common elements (water, bread, and wine). Why are these effective means of grace? Not because of the minister or the elements themselves but because of God's *promise*. God has promised to deliver his grace through these humble venues. It is not that we get one sort of grace in the preaching, another in baptism, and another in the Supper. Rather, in these divinely instituted means, God offers and gives the same grace: forgiveness and new life. The revival down the street may promise the vision, but God's Spirit calms us down and says, "Give ear to my words." The logic of the righteousness that is by works may attract us to a forty-day fast as a method of gaining victory over all known sin, but the logic of the righteousness that is by faith says that we don't have to cross the seas to find God and "appropriate" his power. Rather, he is as near as the means of grace—in this passage specifically, as near as the preaching of the gospel.

This is great news! It means that God has not only *saved* us by grace in sending his Son two thousand years ago, but he has also *applied* this grace *by grace alone*. He did this by sending his Spirit down to us here and now and his witnesses out to the ends of the earth, to make his preached gospel and his administered sacraments means of grace, creating faith and confirming it until the end.

One proponent of "contemporary" worship says, "Those that [sic] champion the cognitive suggest that worship should center upon the proclamation of the Word."[2] This is a typical assumption today, and it works not only because of our increasingly anti-intellectual culture but also because so many Word-centered churches are in fact identified by dry, lecture-style discourses about God instead of being treated as the means through which God summons his people and judges and justifies them in his presence. The preference for the cognitive is emphatically not why the proclamation of the Word should be central. Despite the fact that a great deal of conservative preaching is excessively didactic, treating Scripture as if it were primarily a manual for doctrine or principles for living, the argument Paul makes here (and could be made elsewhere, especially in Ezekiel 37) is quite different. For the biblical writers, as for the Reformers, "the preached Word of God is the Word of God" *(Second Helvetic Confession)*. It is not chiefly an event of instruction, motivation, encouragement, inspiration, or exhortation. All of these may be involved, depending on the passage, but the preached Word is primarily *a means of grace*. That is what Paul argues especially here in Romans 10 but also elsewhere in various forms (viz., that the gospel is "the power of God unto salvation"). We have to be careful here, of course. There can be no saving encounter with God's Word apart from the communication of certain truths. The preaching of the law cannot slay and the preaching of the gospel cannot create faith if there is no content. So it is ill-advised to pit knowing certain things about God against knowing God himself ("not a proposition but a person!"). We cannot know anybody without knowing certain things about them. But the point is that too often preaching is primarily conceived as an event in which God is the topic but not the actor!

Doctrinal lectures and inspirational how-to motivational talks dominate both traditional and contemporary approaches, but both tend to undermine the event-character of the service. It is one thing to talk about the doctrines of sin and grace and another to actually be faced with God in judgment and justification. It is one thing to hear exhortations to victory and quite another to actually experience the power of being drawn into the plotline of God's victory over our enemies (the world, the flesh, and the devil). Doctrine and exhortation will be involved in all good preaching of Scripture, but preaching can never be reduced to either. If that happens, it is no wonder that people eventually sense the loss of God's active presence and look for other means of grace, other sources of "bringing Christ down" into our daily experience that is threatened by meaninglessness and triviality.

Preaching is not merely the minister's talk *about* God but *God's* talk—and not just any talk. It's the kind of talk that produces a new people. It is the encounter through which God himself takes the judge's bench, arraigns us as sinners by the standard of perfect justice, and then finds a way, in Jesus Christ, to be both just and the justifier of the ungodly. All of this happens to us before our very ears. It is worked upon us and in us by the Holy Spirit as the Word is preached (and is confirmed visibly for us by the sacraments). And it is preached, Paul says as he continues his argument, by one who is *authorized* to speak on God's behalf: "How can they preach unless they are sent?" (Rom. 10:15). It is not a free-for-all, a daytime talk show in which people share their own religious experience and opinions on things. One does not become qualified to represent God officially in this capacity because of charisma, a stirring testimony, or remarkable administrative and people skills. As Earl Lautenslager writes, "A minister without theology is like an engineer without physics or a doctor without anatomy. He'll kill you."[3] God has appointed officers in the church to protect his sheep from this sort of danger. Even in establishing an ordained ministry God was seeking to protect the delivery system of the gospel.

In this way, God makes sure not only that the good news is preserved but that it remains good news in the way in which it is delivered. Just as faith is the sole instrument of justification, so too "faith comes by hearing the Word of God." The ears are organs of *reception*, not of *attainment*. This is so important at a time when we seem to think that what we do in the worship service is really up to us, just a matter of style, preference, tradition—and that, consequently, what worked in other periods may not work for ours. Preaching is necessary not because it's a magic but because God has ordained it for the justification and sanctification of sinners. To many, this sort of approach can sound only legalistic. This is the "Have it your way" generation, and we must not let even God himself get in the way of "kingdom work." But people need to realize that this is the opposite of legalism: God is sparing his people from hucksters, from the whims of self-appointed crusaders and the cleverness of the human religious imagination, which is, as Calvin rightly said, "an idol factory." He wants to save us and not leave us to the subtle distractions that would send us down rabbit trails rather than to the one who is the Way, the Truth, and the Life. He wills to save us his way, so that it may be entirely of grace and so that he may receive all the glory. Paul's logic is not legalism but grace—God's discovery of sinners and his attainment of their salvation, not our discovery of God and our successful striving.

There is too much talk today of God "manifesting" himself to us. It is not that this is a bad thing, or that God has not manifested himself in some ways. Rather, manifesting is already heavily weighted toward vision and controlling rather than hearing and hoping. Philosopher Paul Ricoeur is therefore quite correct in emphasizing the priority of proclamation over manifestation in biblical religion. It is what God *says*, after all, and not what God *is* in the hiddenness and overwhelming majesty of divine existence, that is of concern to mortal (and sinful) pilgrims. According to the manifestation model, says Ricoeur, "the sacred" is central and seeing is the key. Everything is sacred and miraculous. The world is shot through with divinity and nearly everything and every experience is an opportunity to touch and see God's face.

This is the typical line of thought in pagan religion, including today's widely held versions. But this is precisely what Israel was commanded to avoid. While the ungodly religious outlook sees everything as basically sacred and miraculous, the proclamation model of biblical faith is quite different, says Ricoeur.

Indeed, one cannot fail to be struck by the constant, obstinate struggle against the Canaanite cults—against the idols Baal and Astarte, against the myths about vegetation and agriculture, and in general against any natural and cosmic sacredness—as expressed in the writings of the Hebrew prophets. . . . I will say first of all that with the Hebraic faith the word outweighs the numinous [ineffable sacredness]. Of course, the numinous is not absent from, say, the burning bush or the revelation at Sinai. But the numinous is just the underlying canvas from which the word detaches itself. . . . A theology of the Name is opposed to any hierophany of an idol. . . . Hearing the word has taken the place of a vision of signs. Certainly there is still a sacred space (a temple) and a sacred time (the festivals). But the general tendency, even though it did not entirely or enduringly prevail over its rival, is fundamentally ethical and not aesthetic. To meditate on the commandments wins out over venerating idols.[4]

Not only is the ministry of the Word sometimes challenged by a preference for visual and aural stimulation in our day, but there are also other cultural factors at work. One of the most typical defenses of seeker-driven services is what I have called generational narcissism. As with race, nationality, college or professional football teams, and denominations, it is also true that with marketing the church there can be an embarrassing degree of group arrogance. People today do not have a long attention span, we are told, and are impatient with sermons that are not relevant (often "relevant" here means sermons that focus on us and our practical improvement rather than focusing on God and his works). Hearing profound sermons and participating in the liturgy as actors rather than as spectators may have worked for the "cloud of witnesses" from Abraham to Warfield, but not for us. Ours is, after all, a unique generation, and we must be catered to by those who are sufficiently sensitive to our niche market needs.

But, of course, this generational narcissism, in which the sociological "is" determines the theological or practical "ought," is nothing new at all. Nor is the visual dominance unique to our day, as we've noted with respect to the Reformation's response to medieval worship, where visually stimulating ceremonies, pictures, and statues had supplanted preaching. The history of idolatry is largely the history of visual consumerism. We may easily observe the Hebraic suspicions—not of art but of imagining God or the sacred in art; not of ritual but of creating our own rituals, our own method of worship; not of music but of a captivity to music that undermines the liturgy, preaching, and sacrament. Ricoeur is right, then, to contrast Hebraic and pagan attitudes here. While the pagan could be as eclectic and innovative as possible within one's range of creativity, the Israelite had to turn away from the impersonal "sacredness of everything," which was represented by the idols as visual aids, to embrace the very definite infinite-personal God who spoke through the patriarchs and prophets. The Israelites were free to exercise their imaginative creativity with respect to the visible things of God's world but not with respect to the heavenly. God's people recounted the stories of the redemptive acts of God in Israel's history, and the very definiteness of this God and his self-revelation demanded that he be worshiped in no way other than he had commanded. God did not reveal himself everywhere, and he was not Joseph Campbell's "hero of a thousand faces." It was the particularity of biblical faith that frustrated paganism: *this* God, *this* elect people, in *this* time and place.

The typical pagan would (and still does) find such a restriction on sacred manifestation offensive. Still scandalous is the notion that God reveals himself as our Savior in the history of redemption through Jesus Christ and not just anywhere we happen to look for him. While the law (God's justice, holiness, majesty, sovereignty, and power) is known to us by nature and clearly seen through what has been made, the gospel (God's mercy and grace in Christ) is not present in nature or creation. This good news comes after creation, after the fall, as an announcement of a surprising turn of events that we could not otherwise have known or expected. This orientation is at some distance from that line of an otherwise good hymn, "My Father's World": "In the rustling grass I hear him pass, he speaks to me everywhere." While God is revealed as our Creator through the creation, we can only know him as our Redeemer in the Scripture passages that focus on the announcement of Christ's person and work.

Some will reply, yes, that was true of Israel, but isn't Jesus Christ the icon (*eikōn*) of the invisible God? And doesn't that mean that our worship should be *incarnational* (a term that is used more often to refer to us and our ministry than Jesus and his)? But to use the incarnation as a cipher for smuggling "sacredness" into the Christian community is especially dangerous. To be sure, God has become flesh in the person of Jesus Christ. God was preserving a people from idolatry precisely for that event. But here we are two thousand years later. We cannot see Christ, but we can see the bread and the wine that in the sacramental union become sacred by virtue of the Word and the Spirit, because through it God's people receive the reality itself. And as Christ is preached each week, through the whole service as well as the sermon, he is as truly present and active by the Holy Spirit as if he were present physically. There are not three gods but one, so that the presence of the Spirit is the presence of the Son who sent him.

This is why Paul can speak as if his preaching is a visual drama: "Before your very eyes Jesus Christ was clearly portrayed [literally, 'placarded' or 'posted up on a billboard'] as crucified" (Gal. 3:1). And here again he contrasts works-righteousness with whether or not "you *believe* what you *heard*" (v. 5). Even the sacraments have their efficacy through the Spirit only by the Word. God has graciously given us the visible Word alongside his preached Word.

So Paul's logic becomes clearer: The method of salvation that is by grace requires a method of delivery that is executed by God's gracious work and not dependent on human decision or effort for its success. Notice the irony in saying that the message we proclaim is that sinners are saved by grace alone because of Christ's merits alone, and then adding (perhaps in the fine print) that this supposedly free gift was actually attainable only by our discovering, striving, dragging it down from heaven, or descending into the seas to obtain it. In the incarnation, God made the trip across the great expanse and has come all the way. But that was still not enough. In order to unite us here and now to that event "then and there," he sent a minister—an ambassador—carrying his official treaty along with its seals. And that concludes the logic of Paul's argument: "How can they hear without someone preaching to them? And how can they preach unless they are sent?" (Rom. 10:14–15).

There are many today who believe that the gospel is a message of salvation by grace but that the way they receive grace is by grasping, taking a long trip across the sea, or, quite literally, across the country, by trying this fad and then another. And in line with this logic, they believe that nearly anybody can qualify as a "minister" and anything as a "ministry." One need not be "sent," as Paul says here, but may send oneself. (And, by the way, Paul clearly understood "sent" to mean sent by the church through its appointed officers, as his insistence on the laying on of hands reminds us.) An Old Testament parallel is Jeremiah 23, where the "false prophets" are judged by God for proclaiming their own word rather than God's. "I did not send these prophets, yet they have run with their message. I did not speak to them, yet they have prophesied" (v. 21). To protect the ministry of the gospel and the integrity of its content, Christ the King reigns in the church through the officers whom he has commissioned. In this way, the congregation may know that they are recipients of the message that God himself has authorized, since through his church he has sent (authorized) the messengers.

This is why the method of grace's delivery cannot be separated from its content. If it is by grace alone, salvation must be delivered by a medium in which the sinner is a *receiver*. That medium is preaching (as well as sacrament). A service in which the congregation is almost exclusively active (for instance, in singing, especially in singing about what they are doing and will do) abruptly interrupts this Pauline logic. There is a time for the involvement of the people, of course—but that is not a means of grace; it is a means of responding to the grace that has been delivered by God alone. No, Paul singles out preaching—and not just any preaching but a certain kind of preaching: "that is, the word of *faith* we are proclaiming" (Rom. 10:8), "the word of *Christ*" (v. 17). It is the preaching of God's commands that brings conviction, while the proclamation of Christ in the gospel creates and keeps on creating faith and its fruit. This is the miracle that occurs through the fragile instrument of preaching: God is not only the object; he is also the subject who himself judges and justifies, humbles and lifts up, kills and makes alive as the sermon unfolds.

So many people hear the good news when it comes to Jesus' saving work: It's by grace, not by works. But the trouble comes when they discover how many gimmicks, techniques, methods, and means there are out there for climbing up to God and experiencing a vision of his glory, a touch of his power, a glimpse of his majesty. When they get burned out on this sort of religion, they will be ready either for atheism or the theology of the cross and resurrection. This theology of the cross is weakness, not power—and yet, because of the resurrection of Christ, it is "the power of God for the salvation of everyone who believes" (Rom. 1:16). It is foolishness, not wisdom, in the eyes of the world (and a worldly church)—and yet, "the foolishness of God is wiser than man's wisdom" (1 Cor. 1:25).

God Has Already Made the Message Relevant

The weak things of God have become not so much despised as ignored in much of contemporary Christianity. Instead, we look for the powerful things of the world. And then we wonder why we get worldly results: consumers rather than disciples. But traditionalism shouldn't get off easily either. If believers are looking for an exciting encounter with God apart from the Word, we must ask why this is. Is it just because our age is like the Middle Ages, visual rather than verbal? Or could it also be that many of us have turned the service into a dry, purely rational and yet unreflective routine? None of us gets off easily when it comes to the contemporary state of worship.

If people are not clearly hearing Christ preached as good news to believers who are still sinful and weak in faith, then it is no wonder that preaching has lost its power. The power is in the preaching of Christ, not in the medium itself—a medium that Paul calls "foolish" and "weak." More than good acting, good sound, good staging and lighting, what we need most is a good script. We have that in God's Word—and the extent to which we are confident in the power of that weakness, we will be faithful as preachers and hearers of God's good news. If people are hankering after drama, perhaps it is because we are not demonstrating to them the wonder of the divine drama. The Reformation spirit—more importantly, the apostolic spirit—is not one of conservatism any more than progressivism. It strives to faithfully bring God's means of grace to each new generation—without breaking the intergenerational chain that is part and parcel of the covenant of grace. "The promise is for you and for your children," Peter declared at Pentecost. And if many of our folks want to turn our church into an aerobics class or a situation comedy, then instead of merely resisting and retrenching, perhaps we should ask ourselves some tough questions. Are we really ministering God's means of grace? If the preaching of Christ and the place of the sacraments are unclear, it should be no surprise that people set up golden calves—their own means of grace, whether in the form of musical extravagance, emotional hype, visual drama, or any number of methods that they think will help them climb into the presence of One who instead seeks and finds us.

Furthermore, God has provided baptism and the Supper as means of strengthening our faith in Christ, assuring us, and delivering his blessings. They are not merely illustrations, as stage dramas in church are, but actually convey the promised deliverance. God has accommodated to our weakness already: in Word and sacrament. First, he accommodated in the form that his self-revelation took throughout the history of Israel. Scripture itself is "accommodated to our weakness," as Calvin frequently emphasized, comparing it to baby talk. Writing as common people, in their own idiom and style, the human authors of Scripture were moved by the Spirit to draw on everyday analogies.

God accommodated to our weakness in the incarnation. He came down all the way to us, saved us by the death and resurrection of his Son, and continues to provide for our temporal and eternal welfare. But that's not all: After this he still accommodates, coming all the way down to us again here and now as he uses the most everyday and common elements that are familiar to both the uneducated and the academic: water, bread, and wine. Here God even accommodates to our weakness by allowing us to "taste and see that the Lord is good," to catch a glimpse of his goodness as he passes by. The writer to the Hebrews calls it tasting of "the powers of the coming age" (Heb. 6:5). Isn't it a bit arrogant, therefore, for us to respond to this gracious condescension by asking, "But what about the teenagers? How can we make the gospel relevant to people *today?*"

The apostle Paul outlined in Romans 10 the argument for preaching as God's means of condescending to our weakness, making certain that the delivery system of God's good news is as determined by the logic of grace as the message itself. Methods are not neutral; they are always indicative of a particular set of beliefs. One may hold tenaciously to the view that God alone saves and that he saves by grace alone, through faith alone, in Christ alone, and yet attempt to climb up into God's presence or bring him down through the techniques and programs that promise a divine encounter. Paul's logic here should warn us against separating the message from the methods.

But this raises a question: If the "dramatic script" is truly the chief means of divine action in our lives, where is the role of the Holy Spirit? The next chapter addresses that question as we see what it takes for God to cast new characters.

THREE

Casting New Characters

According to Greek mythology, Proteus was a deity who could change into a dragon, fire, or flood at will. Endowed with a singular gift of prophesying the future, he could easily elude those charmers who attempted to wrestle their destinies from his lips. Only one thing could force Proteus to do their bidding: He had to be seized and chained. Only then would he be incapable of changing his slippery form to elude his captors and be forced to tell all.

Psychologist Robert Jay Lifton refers to the "protean style" that dominates the emerging psyche of our time.[1] What used to be called multiple personalities disorder, Lifton says, is no longer regarded as pathological but as the normal key in which the score of postmodern life is played.[2] For such people, there is no "home" identity, and the actor attempts in vain to remove the mask to reveal himself or herself. This is the Beatles' "Nowhere Man," "making all his nowhere plans for nobody. Doesn't have a point of view, knows not where he's going to. Isn't he a bit like you and me?" The multiple masks just are the "reality," such as it is. How does this play out in concrete experience? In the past, people used to convert to other religions or even political parties with great inner turmoil. Even consumer products were marketed on the assumption of brand loyalty. But today, one is *expected* to morph many times within a given lifetime.

Sociologist Peter Berger has appealed to the notion of heresy to describe this widespread phenomenon:

> The English word "heresy" comes from the Greek verb hairein, which means "to choose." A hairesis originally meant, quite simply, the taking of a choice. . . . Thus, in Galatians 5:20 the Apostle Paul lists "party spirit" (hairesis) along with such evils as strife, selfishness, envy, and drunkenness among the "works of the flesh." . . . The heretic denied . . . authority,

47

refused to accept the tradition in toto. Instead, he picked and chose from the contents of the tradition, and from these pickings and choosings constructed his own deviant opinion.[3]

The problem today, says Berger, is that there is no sense of an overarching authority that would measure deviance. In this environment in which personal choice reigns, heresy—cutting one's own path apart from everyone else—is now normal. Accepting the authority of someone else, even God, is abnormal. "Modernity creates a new situation in which picking and choosing becomes an imperative."[4] Everyone has to be eccentric, and every successful enterprise, including the church, must cater to each person's (or at least generation's) eccentricities. Why should we "postmoderns" be expected to think and worship in continuity with "premoderns"? A nation that gets its nose out of shape when someone suggests changing the rules of baseball ("It won't be *baseball* anymore!") takes it for granted that God must get over his own personal tastes in order to accommodate ours—and that his church must either surrender or be left for dead. (The only real apostasy is being left behind in the sweep of progress.)

Interestingly, in the 1950s, radio and TV advertising emphasized intergenerational continuity at least to some degree: "It was good enough for your grandmother." Far from brand loyalty, marketing now plays to the pretense of individuality: "This is not your father's Oldsmobile." The protean self hungers for ideas and meaning, but at the same time insists on eclecticism and is incapable of embracing one identity or community. While earlier Christians saw their lives in terms of "pilgrim's progress" to the Celestial City, most of our post-MTV contemporaries see themselves in terms of "aimless drifting" from booth to booth at Vanity Fair. According to the former, the divine drama plotted a life from death in Adam to life in Christ, and progress was defined not in terms of secular achievements, however great they may be in their own way, but in terms of their growth in Christ and the resurrection of their body at the last. By contrast, the secular drama leaves the self alienated from God, community, tradition, time, and place. Change has no *telos*, no goal, and the feverishness of its pace is the fatal indicator of that consciousness. In theological terms, it is a form of gnosticism.

Guilt, according to Lifton, offers a prime example of the "protean style":

> I suggested before that Protean man was not free of guilt. He indeed suffers from it considerably, but often without awareness of what is causing his suffering. For his is a form of hidden guilt; a vague but persistent kind of self-condemnation related to the symbolic disharmonies I have described,

a sense of having no outlet for his loyalties and no symbolic structure for his achievements. . . . Rather than a clear feeling of evil or sinfulness, it takes the form of a nagging sense of unworthiness all the more troublesome for its lack of clear origin.[5]

The anxieties are never-ending, as the protean self longs both for constant self-transformation and arrival at some mythical past of wholeness and restoration. Pulled both ways by novelty and nostalgia, this self of ever-changing surfaces requires a "youth culture," due to "his never-ceasing quest for imagery of rebirth. He seeks such imagery of rebirth from all sources, from ideas, techniques, religions, and political systems, from mass movements and of course from drugs, or from special individuals of his own kind—that is, from fellow Protean voyagers—whom he sees possessing that problematic gift of his namesake, the gift of prophecy."[6]

Religion, of course, fits in along with everything else as a "mask." Unlike the convinced atheist or apathetic infidel of yesteryear, today's unbeliever is not a disbeliever; in fact, he or she believes in just about anything and everything—simultaneously. Although the notion of a "grand narrative" explaining all of reality is anathema to the postmodern mind, one of its own grand narratives is the abolition of self. Like "truth," the "self" is a construction of one's own will and simultaneously, if contradictorily, of culture: It is made, not discovered. Surrounded by a consumer culture of nearly infinite choices, we can be whoever we want to be . . . today—and become someone else tomorrow. Anyone who has shopped at Nordstrom over the last year or so may have noticed their slogan, "Reinvent Yourself."

Reinvent yourself. We cannot miss here the foundational assumption: human autonomy and sufficiency. It denies God as Creator of selves and as Redeemer of those very selves who constantly reinvent themselves in distorted and self-defeating ways. We might call it "Protean Pelagianism," the latter term referring to the belief that human beings are basically good, self-sufficient, and can save themselves. It is in the consumer's hands to decide what he or she will be and what communities will have the pleasure of his or her company. Freedom of choice is salvation—with or without a particular goal. As Alisdair MacIntyre and others have shown, modernity has unhinged the notion of freedom from the notion of nature. Once upon a time people thought that freedom for a bird was flying, freedom for a fish was swimming, and freedom for human beings was actually experiencing what one was created to be. Today, however, freedom just means *absolute* liberty of choice—the ability to choose from over two thousand channels even if one will never use over forty. The first question of the Westminster Shorter Catechism,

"What is the chief end of man?" is irrelevant to the quest for selfhood and freedom.

No wonder, then, that a *Newsweek* cover story on "The Search for the Sacred" observed that today's spiritual seekers insist on eclectic combination and refuse to submit to the discipline of becoming one thing or another. A cottage industry of studies on seekers has underscored repeatedly that we are dealing here with a widespread fascination with spirituality (consistent with mix-and-match self-creation) alongside a rejection of religion (understood as bounded by particular and relatively stable beliefs, rituals, practices, and communities). Church growth gurus frequently take this as a requirement that we simply have to meet. Brand loyalty is a thing of the past, so out with the old and in with the new.

The presupposition that the church must simply accept and even cater to the statistics about declining brand loyalty is rarely questioned. "In a mobile society that shows little loyalty to product brands or even to other people," George Barna allows, "it is reasonable to assume that people might visit a variety of churches rather than select and support a single church."[7] He cites polling data to support this obvious trend. But is that due to a superficial understanding of this protean phenomenon, and, furthermore, is it in the long-term best interest of the seekers themselves to simply cater to "where they are"? So what if people today can't seem to commit to things or to other people. That is not something we just have to get used to if we want success; it is something that reveals the tremendous need for a real proclamation of God's Word that can bring selfish sinners like us to the foot of the cross. Isn't it possible that the church that grows as a result of catering to such market trends (i.e., selfishness) would be a "church" that Jesus would not even recognize on the last day (Matt. 25:31–46)? However we answer that question, there should be no doubt that the protean style dominates contemporary religion as well as every other enterprise these days.

Too often, we Christians are not as critical of ourselves as we are of the secular culture. And our criticism of the latter is largely simplistic and superficial, so that it does not sweep *us* into its scope. For instance, one can hear numerous sermons or pick up any number of Christian manuals on debt and materialism but then buy into marketing as a legitimate norm for our evangelism, pop entertainment as a legitimate norm for an exciting "worship experience," pop psychology as a legitimate norm for preaching, and management techniques as a legitimate norm of our covenantal nurture. We can preach "family values" throughout the land, but it is increasingly the case that children raised in churches and in Christian homes today are remarkably ignorant of God's Word and separated from the faith of their fathers and mothers. And then we wonder why our churches are enfeebled by a sort of immune-deficiency disorder, even after unrelenting bombardment with "practical" and "morally relevant" sermonizing. Richard Lints describes the challenge:

> Compare the sermon seventy-five million Americans hear each Sunday morning with the daily bombardment of television commercials to which they are exposed, or the "do this or get fired" pressures they experience at work. Put a few thousand dollars in their pocket and send a young couple out to make a down payment on a new car: How much is some vague religious teaching about stewardship going to matter, compared with arguments about sportiness and acceleration?[8]

Today's so-called practical preaching often turns out to be not very practical after all. Recently, a woman took a break from her megachurch to visit ours. "The preacher's starting a twelve-week series on tips for marriage," she sighed, "and I know that what I need most—even for my marriage—is a greater grasp of God's truth in his Word." Being revolutionized in our understanding of God, ourselves, our world, and our time and place in the light of God's work would actually help us stand up to the pressures of life.

What we need in this day is precisely what God has supplied his church in every age, what Stanley Hauerwas has called "the capacity for dissent."[9] It's the capacity to resist the attractive but destructive narratives at hand because "you died, and your life is now hidden with Christ in God" (Col. 3:3). We know the great periods in which the Holy Spirit empowered a fresh proclamation of Christ by the people's marked capacity for dissent. At the heart of that capacity is the overwhelming power of the Christian story to transform the story of our life. This alone renders the dominant alternatives not simply wrong but uncompelling by comparison.

These days the world waits for the church to deliver something important—even if it's a slap in the face. Not something big and flashy, mind you, but something important. Everybody has pretty much already said just about everything—over and over again, in this culture of bland, aphoristic sound bites and spin. People have been sold just about everything and are less happy than their grandparents, who lived through the depression. They aren't waiting for another "March for Jesus" but for an arresting announcement that makes them stop in their tracks and reevaluate everything. The writer John Updike writes, "Mop up spilt religion! Let us have it in its original stony jars or not at all!" That's something we're not quite as likely to hear from our pulpits by the person who is actually paid to say things like that on God's behalf.[10]

The Scripted Self

Even if we are lifelong Christians, we forget why we came to church this Sunday until it all happens again: We come in with our shallow scripts that are formed out of the clippings in our imaginations from the ads and celebrities of the last week, only to be reintroduced to our real script and to find ourselves by losing ourselves all over again. It is not merely as we entertain the possibility of being a character in this story, or some other purely subjective strategy, that this narrative has the dramatic power to reconstitute us. Rather, it is as God the Spirit works on us through the proclamation of the Word that we are re-scripted: our lives, purpose, identities, and hopes conformed to that "new world" into which the Word and Spirit give us new birth—instead of the other way around. Instead of our remaking God and his Word in terms of our experience and reason, we end up being remade—caught in the action of the divine drama. When it happens, it happens before we know it.

My interest in this chapter is not in analyzing this protean phenomenon further, nor in critiquing the church's capitulation to it. Rather, my main concern is to suggest biblical worship as the alternative to this dis-ease and loss of a solid sense of self.

As Alisdair MacIntyre and so many other writers today have argued, the self is not a stable substance, a certain "stuff" that could be identified with a CAT scan. Nor is it exactly the same thing as a soul. Our "self" or "selves" *are*, at least in part, constructed identities. And the means of constructing self-identity is chiefly community-shaping stories.[11] It's one reason why people join movements, so that at the end of their life they can interpret the bits of their lives in some grand scheme of meaning, something larger than their own birth, marriage, parenthood, retirement, and death. For some, it is their family histories; for others, their role in developing a business empire; for still others, it is the story of African origins and American slavery, the struggle for civil rights, and the continuing challenges of urbanization and discrimination. Some just can't stop talking about shopping, while others can't keep from telling stories about their role in the air campaign over Germany in World War II. That is just who they are.

Protean as they may be, our contemporaries are searching frantically for a narrative large enough to give some purpose to their lives, so that (ironically) the more we cater to their immediate cravings, the less we actually contribute to what they're hoping to find: some meaningful and enduring sense of who they are and where they fit into something larger than themselves. And do not underestimate the power of narratives. A narrative of conquest creates one sort of identity and consequent actions, while a narrative of oppression forms another. We are "storied" people and cannot help but think of ourselves as somehow characters in a plot. Worldviews are, in fact, storied plots: the story of America, the story of political liberation, the story of global capitalism, the story of alienation (existentialism), the story of progress (modernism), the story of no-story-but-only-stories (postmodernism).

Even if it's a postmodern (allegedly) plotless plot, as in the movie *Pulp Fiction*, it is a narrative. In fact, to commit the cardinal postmodern sin, we can even say that it's a worldview, a metanarrative (the story behind every story). So too is the Bible, and the metanarrative of "this passing evil age" and that of "the age to come" are locked in mortal combat, so that it is impossible to adapt one to the other. Like the "great chasm fixed" between Lazarus and the rich man in Jesus' parable (Luke 16), the final separation begins here and now in terms of the plot that controls our imagination and, therefore, our lives. The reality of this contest may be recognized more clearly by some hostile critics of Christianity than by us. Drawing on Friedrich Nietzsche, Mark C. Taylor has in recent decades attacked biblical religion as being responsible for the entire notion of history and a grand narrative, with the "tick" of Genesis and the "tock" of Revelation imposing on civilization a false sense of meaning and purpose. By contrast, all we are, says Taylor, is "aimless drifters," always "erring," "straying," "transgressing."[12]

But let's return for a moment to Robert Jay Lifton's suggestion that the protean self has not been able to escape from the experience of guilt and in fact has only intensified it by denying any origin or objective source—just "a nagging sense of unworthiness." In this situation, one could dress their wound lightly, saying "'Peace, peace,' . . . when there is no peace" (Jer. 6:14)—and view religion and preaching as merely a form of therapeutic reassurance or self-esteem. Or one could finally capture and chain Proteus and force him to confess his own identity as a "child of wrath" in Adam who can only be liberated from the source of guilt and bondage to sin by becoming a "child of God" in Christ, the Second Adam.

These then are the two grand narratives: "in Adam" and "in Christ." One is a narrative of pointless rebellion against a good God and his creation, leading only to frustration and death; the other is a narrative of redemption and reconciliation, consummated in everlasting life with the Triune God in a restored cosmos. The bad news is that if there is a true self, then it (or rather, he or she) is objectively guilty (hence, the nagging subjective sense of it) and will stand trial. Many, like the rich young ruler, will at this point go away sad and try to cope with things the way they are. But the good news is that God is in the business of baptism: submerging sinful selves in Christ's death and then raising them up with Christ in newness of life. Thus, Proteus is chained so that he may be freed.

The "postmodern experience" described here by Lifton and so many others is nothing other than a script that has us playing the role of your "empty way of life handed down to you from your forefathers" (1 Peter 1:18). Just as modernity set out to make the self a sovereign creator instead of a humble servant, postmodernity is the witness to the inevitable disillusionment that Adam and his posterity have always experienced when they wanted to be "as God." Losing confidence in the external world as providing a narrative plot, moderns turned inward, and when they couldn't find anything inside to make any sense of their lives, they became aimless wanderers, seekers who are "always learning but never able to acknowledge the truth" (2 Tim. 3:7).

But as we proclaim the biblical script, from Genesis to Revelation, a unity emerges not only within its pages, nor only within the community of Christ, but also within us individually as we are incorporated into it. It doesn't happen all at once, at least in our experience. Gradually, we find ourselves identified, chained, and instead of prophesying we find ourselves prophesied to by God himself, addressed as sinners, enemies of God, "aliens and strangers to the promises of God." That particular, concrete drama of God and Israel becomes our story, our plot. We begin to know ourselves as we come to see how we fit into that drama. To Gentiles as well as Jews who are thus rescripted by this story, Peter declares, "But you are a chosen people, a royal priesthood, a holy nation"—the very role that earlier in the story is restricted to the nation of Israel—"a people belonging to God, that you may declare the praises of him who called you out of darkness into his wonderful light. Once you were not a people, but now you are the people of God; once you had not received mercy, but now you have received mercy" (1 Peter 2:9–10).

As skeptical spectators become cautious inquirers, the play continues to unfold. To those who have heard the story of Israel and Jesus (promise and fulfillment), "the mystery that has been kept hidden for ages and generations, but is now disclosed to the saints," is announced— "the glorious riches of this mystery, which is Christ in you, the hope of glory" (Col. 1:26–27). The "in Adam" role is exchanged for the exalted position of being "in Christ," home at last. Or one better: home at last to the place that we never dreamed of calling home. The apostle Paul declares:

> Blessed be the God and Father of our Lord Jesus Christ, who has blessed us with every spiritual blessing in the heavenly places in Christ, just as he chose us in him before the foundation of the world, that we should be holy

and without blame before him in love, having predestined us to adoption as sons by Jesus Christ to himself, according to the good pleasure of his will, to the praise of the glory of his grace, by which he made us accepted in the Beloved. In him we have redemption through his blood, the forgiveness of sins, according to the riches of his grace which he made to abound toward us in all wisdom and prudence, having made known to us the mystery of his will, according to his good pleasure which he purposed in himself, that in the dispensation of the fullness of the times he might gather together in one all things in Christ, both which are in heaven and which are on earth—in him.

Ephesians 1:3–10 NKJV

And now cautious inquirers become actors on the stage. They may not be able to put their finger on when it happened, but there they are, up on the stage, in the drama of redemption. That is the new identity they trade for aimless drifting and self-creating.

Notice that this passage in Ephesians gives us a place in God's own heart. His intimate and eternal love for his Son means that all who are "in Christ" are therefore included in that intimate and eternal love that each person of the Godhead has for each other. By being recast in this way, our new story actually begins not simply with our conversion here and now but with a plot that began before the world was created. Our identity is rooted not in the changing fashions of today, nor even simply in the history of Israel, but in God's purpose from all eternity that he has worked out in time, until the faithful and eternal Son of God became the faithful and incarnate Son of Adam and Son of David. We learn that in God's electing purpose we were written into the script from the very beginning.

The story gets even better as the plot thickens:

And you he made alive, who were dead in trespasses and sins, in which you once walked according to the course of this world, according to the prince of the power of the air, the spirit who now works in the sons of disobedience, among whom also we all once conducted ourselves in the lusts of our flesh, fulfilling the desires of the flesh and of the mind, and were by nature children of wrath, just as the others. But God, who is rich in mercy, because his great love with which he loved us, even when we were dead in trespasses, made us alive together with Christ (by grace you have been saved), and raised us up together, and made us sit together in the heavenly places in Christ Jesus, that in the ages to come he might show the exceeding riches of his grace in his kindness toward us in Christ Jesus.

Ephesians 2:1–7 NKJV

Again, none of this is possible because of our capacity for imagining a new existence, or because of our clever methods at "soul-winning," but because of God's relentless imagination and skill:

> Whom he predestined, these he also called; whom he called, these he also justified [declared righteous]; and whom he justified, these he also glorified. What then shall we say to these things? If God is for us, who can be against us? He who did not spare his own Son, but delivered him up for us all, how shall he not with him also freely give us all things? Who shall bring a charge against God's elect? It is God who justifies. Who is he who condemns? It is Christ who died, and furthermore is also risen, who is even at the right hand of God, who also makes intercession for us.

> Romans 8:30–34 NKJV

This is why we are told repeatedly to "put on Christ" or to "clothe" ourselves with Christ. This is the costume of our new character. Instead of the fig leaves that, as children of Adam and Eve, we used to cover up our shame, God has provided the sacrificial clothing of Jesus Christ and his perfect righteousness, foreshadowed when he clothed Adam and Eve. This is the answer to the protean self's nagging sense of guilt without clear origin. Tell the story of Adam's creation as the representative of the whole human race and of his fall as the source of sin until guilt-ridden drifters recognize Adam's face as they look in the mirror themselves. The protean self is involved in constant self-transformation not because he or she really doesn't believe in the existence of a stable self but because he or she has not yet recognized in the mirror an acceptable self, despite all the masks.

Here, where God judges and justifies, we are captured and chained, named as who we really are, and then rescripted as new characters with a new role in the drama of redemption that will finally include not only us as individuals but the whole natural world as well (Rom. 8:18–25). Jesus is raised as "the firstfruits" of the full harvest, and when that point arrives in the play when believers are physically raised to everlasting life, the creation itself will be carried with us into newness of life.

This means that we must be careful not to reduce the drama of redemption to our own individual salvation. There is a kind of pietistic individualism that, though faithful enough in proclaiming the believer's sin and redemption, fails to place that marvelous reality in the wider context of God's plan of redemption. Christians, too, in that sort of scheme, can lack the coordinates that give a larger purpose and meaning to their lives. Like Hamlet's "play within a play," our story and its re-emplotment take place only within the context of the whole play itself. We find the coordinates of our identity and role by belonging to a story and a plot that is larger than any one of us. In fact, our identity could not reach any narrative unity apart from being coordinated with a larger narrative plot, which is given in the history of Israel and Jesus. Through twists and turns, it narrates and enacts God's victory over the devil and his designs. Always, the "story behind the story" is this battle between "the seed of the woman," leading ultimately to the Messiah, and "the seed of the serpent," incorporating all those characters in the chorus who ally themselves with Satan's mutiny "against the LORD and against his Anointed One" (Ps. 2:2).

It might help to think in terms of concentric circles: The outer ring is the narrative of redemptive history as a whole; the next ring is the narrative of the people of God within that historical drama; while the inside ring is our own individual life's emplotment in the context of those two outer rings.

Read in this way, the purpose of preaching is not primarily to inform or instruct (though this is clearly involved), nor to exhort and get people to do something (although this is not absent), and certainly not to find helpful tips for using God to make our lives a little less miserable. God does not get incorporated into our play but we into his. This narrative is not there to give us some additional help in constructing our own life movie but to judge it and us with it, so we can finally give up on it and become a character in the drama of redemption. Our purpose in preaching is to chain Proteus and to prophesy his death and resurrection in Christ. Our reference point is no longer endless choice but Jesus Christ, to whose image we are being conformed.

The goal is to rescript our hearers, to give them another plot that draws together all their own personal histories as well as the world's into a meaningful whole that transforms even the parts. Our goal is not to accommodate the Christian plot to the shallow and destructive plots of "the contemporary context" but to accommodate ourselves and our hearers to the real drama of history. Jesus Christ and the drama of redemption that begins, climaxes, and is consummated in him is the real world, the real setting of our life's play. And because the final act is settled firmly in God's purpose, we're not just playacting. This one is for real. Our identity inevitably changes over the course of our life, yet it does not have to be random, pointless change. In Adam, "change" means endless choice made in random freedom. In Christ, "change" means growth in Christ as we are transformed through perpetual immersion in Scripture as the story of our life. It is by the truth and being in the truth that we are free at last.

It is still through the foolishness of preaching that God gives repentance and faith. Jesus still calls us to drop our nets, to leave our past identities as unscrupulous tax collectors, "the Samaritan woman with five husbands," the son who squandered his inheritance, the Pharisee trusting in his own righteousness, the religious devotee too busy serving the Lord to learn from him, and to become rescripted as children of God and agents of reconciliation in the world. Claimed by the world, believers return to the divine assembly to recall their baptism as they attend to the preaching of the Word that constantly reclaims them from the world. We no longer hear the sermon or the service as detached spectators; rather, we see ourselves as participants, actors on the stage— even when we are being acted upon by the master of the stage.

The Gospel according to Whom?

Many well-meaning Christians insist that the story of redemption cannot be compromised. We cannot just preach anything we desire. But, they say, we have to express the gospel in ways that can be easily understood in our time and place. We will discuss this concern more fully in another place. But it does raise an interesting question at this point: Is it possible for the message to remain what it is if we must make it immediately intelligible to those who are currently "strangers and aliens" to it? And if the message is made something other than that gospel which is "the power of God unto salvation," are we doing anybody any favors by trying to make it as inoffensive to and indistinguishable from their present existence "under the sun"?

Part of the problem here may be the tendency of some to separate the message itself from its proclamation. The idea is that there is an objective body of truth that is so stable and untouched by language and culture that it is immune to contamination, whatever diverse ways in which we might accommodate its presentation to our culture. But is there such a thing as a message that is not already shaped by language and culture? The real question, it seems to me, is whether the cultural and linguistic forms we use to present the gospel are themselves shaped by the gospel.

H. Richard Niebuhr contrasted "outer" and "inner" history—one as told by a supposedly objective bystander, the other by a participant in that history:

> Lincoln's Gettysburg Address begins with history: "Fourscore and seven years ago our fathers brought forth on this continent, a new nation, conceived in Liberty, and dedicated to the proposition that all men are created equal." The same event is described in the Cambridge Modern History in the following fashion: "On July 4, 1776, Congress passed the resolution which made the colonies independent communities, issuing at the same time the well-known Declaratio.. of Independence. If we regard

the Declaration as the assertion of an abstract political theory, criticism and condemnation are easy. It sets out with a general proposition so vague as to be practically useless. The doctrine of the equality of men, unless it be qualified and conditioned by reference to special circumstances, is either a barren truism or a delusion."[13]

It hardly seems that Lincoln and the *Cambridge Modern History* were describing the same event. "Hence," Niebuhr adds, "we may call internal history dramatic and its truth dramatic truth, though drama in this case does not mean fiction."[14] We cannot approach the preaching of the Word as if we were merely describing its doctrinal or moral content; it must be preached as indeed it was written—namely, as the dramatic, developing story of God's creative and redemptive work in Jesus Christ as God's true and faithful Israel. Doctrine and practical instruction will be driven home in our hearts as they are embedded in the dramatic telling and retelling of every biblical story in the light of its overarching story centering on Jesus Christ. If *that* isn't practical, then nothing is! My story has become part of his story, without either losing its own distinct character. I have been written into the script, joined the cast of players, and now am running the race to the cheering throngs of glorified saints. One day, I too will join those satisfied spectators in the stands cheering on the cast below (Heb. 12:1–2).

Jesus Christ is called the "firstfruits" of the whole harvest (1 Cor. 15:20). Those whose lives revolved around agriculture knew how the harvest would turn out that year by examining the firstfruits. Our Lord's resurrection, ascension, and present intercession at God's right hand not only guarantee the consummation but already *inaugurate* the new heavens and new earth that will reach their fulfillment when the full harvest appears.

Because we know the plot and stand at a point in redemptive history that has seen the fulfillment *in principle* of God's saving purposes in Christ's life, death, resurrection, and ascension, we can rest assured that our story is no longer "a tale told by an idiot, full of sound and fury, signifying nothing" (Shakespeare's melancholic *Macbeth*). We are like those who are trapped in a deep, dark cave and cannot find our way out—until, in our wandering, a shaft of light reaches us *from outside*. As the writer to the Hebrews reminds us, "The powers of the coming age" (Heb. 6:5) are breaking in on us as we gather together in the Triune name to invoke God's presence, come clean on who we really are, and turn ourselves in to God as his prisoners, only to watch him turn around and make us his adopted heirs together with Christ Jesus.

No longer a spectator to this remarkable drama, suddenly I—Gentile, outsider, "nowhere man living in his nowhere land, making all his nowhere plans for nobody"—get written into the elevated story of chosen Israel, of which Jesus Christ is the "chief cornerstone." Or, to change metaphors, I become a living branch of the life-giving Vine, a vital part of the body whose head is Christ. The outcast gets rescripted as a privileged one. "In Christ," and with his whole body, I am elect and precious, redeemed, justified, sanctified, bodily raised on the last day, and glorified forever. That is the stable part of my identity, regardless of how I might change over the years. And this identity is covenantal: Christ as the federal head of the covenant of grace, the people of God through the ages as the covenant people, and myself as a living member of that covenant together with Abraham and Sarah. It is why worship is a covenant renewal ceremony, as that divine treaty is not only rehearsed but its reality reenacted, re-ratified, and made effectual.

Now we can no longer settle for those sermons in which we were bored or amused with the preacher's own wit, wisdom, and autobiography. We are no longer impressed by "practical" sermons whose goal seems to be to win us by ignoring the real drama going on in the text, conforming Scripture to the protean flux and plotless vanity that derives from our worldly satisfaction with present arrangements. We cannot be rescripted until we are chained down and are addressed by God. "God is in his holy temple: Let all the earth keep silent." He comes not to offer banal support to our sagging self-confidence or to fix the unpleasantness of our daily existence—in other words, he doesn't come to fit in with our already established patterns of thought and life. He comes to dash our silly hopes and to expose our felt needs as trivial, in order to give us new ones that are far greater, and then to satisfy those beyond our wildest dreams.

FOUR

How Preaching Works

It all seems so simple. Surrounded by gimmicks and slick marketing, we assume that evangelism, church growth, and worship are subject to the same rules of persuasion as anything else. If we believe that salvation is essentially in our hands, it follows that it is up to us to determine the most effective strategy for reaching the lost. This has quite a history in American evangelicalism.

One View: "Excitements Sufficient to Induce Repentance"

In the nineteenth century, revivalism spread like wildfire across the American landscape. Often called "protracted meetings," these gatherings took place in huge wooden tabernacles or canvas tents. They elicited excitement and were often as much alternative entertainment as they were serious religious services. (Not surprisingly, they were often funded by business barons, and Barnum and Bailey, of circus fame, contributed the tents on numerous occasions.)

Departing from the architecture and furniture of the average church, these revival centers took their cue from the emerging popular culture—complete with a stage, a choir front-and-center, and folksy gospel songs that borrowed the style of the saloon while decrying its vices. But beneath Charles Finney's methodological pragmatism was his theological departure from classical understandings of God, human nature, and salvation.[1] Then, as now, the message could not be separated from the methods.

For Jonathan Edwards, George Whitefield, and most leaders of the Great Awakening in the mid-eighteenth century, a revival was a surprising work of God, and it was God's extraordinary blessing of his ordinary means (preaching). Finney, however, said of this earlier perspective, "No doctrine is more dangerous than this to the prosperity of the Church, and nothing more absurd."[2] "A revival is not a miracle," Finney declared. In fact, "There is nothing in religion beyond the ordinary powers of nature. It consists entirely in the right exercise of the powers of nature. It is just that, and nothing else. . . . It is a purely philosophical result of the right use of the constituted means—as much so as any other effect produced by the application of means."[3] Find the most exciting method, and you have a revival.

As conversion and revival did not depend on supernatural grace, neither did the methods require a divine mandate. "God Has Established No Particular Measures" is the subheading of one of Finney's chapters in his *Systematic Theology*. So just as conversion and revival were dependent on human agency (both the preacher and the hearer), the methods could be tailored by human preachers and hearers according to "excitements sufficient to induce conversion." "A revival will decline and cease," he warned, "unless Christians are frequently re-converted."[4] Finney's "new measures" triumphed, and eventually churches had to adopt the innovations of the "protracted meetings" or lose members to the revivalists.

The Pelagianizing tendency of Finney's theology legitimized his disregard for God's ordained means in favor of his own innovations. As with many movements that come and go with great fanfare, many "converts" from these new measures sprouted quickly only to be as quickly withered by the afternoon sun. Toward the end of his ministry, Finney himself bewailed the state of religion and wondered aloud if his new measures had unleashed a craving for "excitements" that would never be satisfied.[5] In fact, a much-studied area of American religious history is the "burned-over" district of upstate New York, where the centers of Finney's revivals soon yielded to atheism or esoteric cults.[6]

No clearer example exists to contrast with the logic of Paul's argument in Romans 10. With Finney and the revivalistic tradition more generally, salvation was held out as a goal to strive toward through a variety of methods calculated for success, methods executed by a person who may or may not be sent (i.e., educated and ordained) by the church. Revivals did in fact give the impression that the whole business was about climbing up to heaven, to pull God down. As excitement and sudden conversions and reconversions displaced covenantal nurture over the long haul, various messages at odds with the gospel were equally tolerated, as long as one could demonstrate numerical success. Now it was believed that salvation could therefore be attained by scaling the heavenly walls of "excitements" to bring Christ down or to bring him again from the dead. A few then and now regard it as a religion of works-righteousness, a theology of glory, rather than "the righteousness that is by faith," a theology of the cross. This human-centered theology and practice still guides much of our worship today, at least implicitly—even where Finney's explicit theology is not officially embraced.

Consumerism, the triumph of the therapeutic, and other particularly modern challenges have made this American Pelagianism (theology of self-salvation) all the more palatable. Just as there are many "identities" to be consumed by our voracious appetite for imitation and self-expression, there are many means to be employed. It doesn't matter how one is brought to Christ, evangelists have often said, so long as they get there.

What we desperately need to hear in our day of teeming methods and techniques for "inducing" revival is that the Holy Spirit does not work apart from the ordinary means that he has established in his freedom. The Holy Spirit is not "appropriated" as one might use the energy from an electrical outlet, or as in B. B. Warfield's criticism of the "victorious Christian life" movement, we do not engage the Spirit "(as we engage, say, a carpenter) to do work for us."[7] Whatever "excitements" or "new measures" we might envision as being more powerful than preaching, sacrament, and covenantal nurture, God has only promised to bless the latter as means of grace. He knows that they are weak and foolish in the eyes of the world, which is why he chose them, so that the credit would not go to the clever evangelists or their methods but to him.

By the turn of the twentieth century, Harvard philosopher William James championed religious pragmatism as part of his general philosophy: "God is not known, he is used," he said. "On pragmatistic principles, if the hypothesis of God works satisfactorily in the widest sense of the word, it is true."[8] Today's evangelism, church growth, and worship are deeply indebted to this American pragmatism, and one of the most tragic results is that God is often treated merely as a means to the end of self-fulfillment.

This, of course, is nothing new. Paul noted this role of religion among Jews and Greeks: For the former, the cross was a sign of weakness, not miraculous power, and to the Greeks it hardly appeared to provide the sort of philosophical and moral wisdom that secular thought had attained. How could this gospel hope to compete in a marketplace of "excitements"?

Still, then and now, it has. The Holy Spirit still honors his ordinary means. Scripture itself clearly identifies those means: the preached Word and the administered sacraments (i.e., baptism and the Lord's Supper). While there may be other supports for the Christian life, "faith comes by hearing the preached Word," says Paul. While the Spirit is free to work apart from these means, he has *promised* to work effectually through them alone. We must resist the temptation to associate the work of the Spirit with numbers and noise, or we will inevitably miss the magnitude of what the Spirit is doing every week in the *ordinary* ministry of the means that he has appointed. God works savingly then and there because he has promised to meet us then and there.

Why Is Preaching Effective?

It is important for us to realize that preaching is effective not because of the minister or the people, the music, the staging and lighting, dramas, or other means that we might consider more effective than "the foolishness of preaching." It is effective because God has promised to dispense his saving grace then and there by his Spirit, and it grows organically out of the logic of the message itself because it is an *announcement* of something that has been accomplished by God, rather than an *incentive* to get sinners to save themselves by sheer force of will or effort. It is good *news*, not good advice, good production value, or good ideas.

Suppose a poor person with no insurance were dying, and a philanthropist called him with some good news: If the poor man—we'll call him Bill—will meet him at a coffee shop on the corner of Fifth and Walnut, then and there the rich man will write him a check for a procedure he needs to save his life. Off the hopeful recipient goes, looking for this coffee shop. After searching, the only thing he finds is a dingy café with a rusty sign missing several letters. What Bill finds inside is no more promising: greasy counters with chipped cups and half-washed plates. The people are not friendly and the service is considerably lacking. It's hardly the place where a wealthy person would be expected to frequent. And, after all, there are so many fine restaurants in the town center on the better side of town. But just as the poor man reaches the door to look for more likely meeting spots, he is met at the door. "Are you Bill?" a poorly dressed man inquires. "Yes," Bill replies with some hesitation. Then the two gentlemen find a table, and Bill leaves with the money for his life-saving operation. It was not the circumstances in which Bill expected such a meeting, but it was where it all happened.

Similarly, even the apostolic ministry, says Paul, depended not on the trappings of glory, excitement, or powers of persuasion but on the gospel proclaimed: "But we have this treasure in earthen vessels, that the excellence of the power may be of God and not of us" (2 Cor. 4:7 NKJV). In fact, our situation is worse than Bill's, since we are not dying but "dead in trespasses and sins" (Eph. 2:1 NKJV). Often, God is not present where we would expect to find him. But we can always count on God being where he has promised to meet us, amid the chipped cups, half-washed plates, and all. The power of the Spirit is linked to a promise; namely, a promise that faith comes by hearing the gospel preached (Rom. 10:8, 17).

We may not feel God's presence in every instance, and we may not experience his grace in the same measure each week, but the power is in God's objective promise, not in our subjective apprehension. As we sit there and are ourselves declared righteous by God in the gospel, we recognize that we are objectively accepted by God even though our experience often seems to tell us otherwise. While I may not detect "that peaceful, easy feeling," I can be confident in this: "Therefore, *having been* justified by faith, we *have* peace with God through our Lord Jesus Christ, through whom also we have access by faith into this grace in which we stand, and rejoice in hope of the glory of God" (Rom. 5:1 NKJV, emphasis added). It is not the minister or his methods but God and his ordained means that make preaching different from anything else that we might think more creative, relevant, and exciting. "For the word of God is living and powerful, and sharper than any two-edged sword, piercing even to the division of soul and spirit, and of joints and marrow, and is a discerner of the thoughts and intents of the heart. And there is no creature hidden from his sight, but all things are naked and open to the eyes of him to whom we must give an account" (Heb. 4:12–13 NKJV).

Word and Spirit

The unity of Word and Spirit is well attested in Scripture. One conspicuous Old Testament example is Ezekiel 37. Along with most of Jerusalem's population, the prophet Ezekiel was carted off to Babylon in 597 B.C. While false prophets promised peace and prosperity, Ezekiel (like Jeremiah) told the truth, no matter what it cost, the bad news as well as the good:

> The hand of the LORD came upon me and brought me out in the Spirit of the LORD, and set me down in the midst of the valley; and it was full of bones. Then he caused me to pass by them all around, and behold, there were very many in the open valley; and indeed they were very dry. And he said to me, "Son of man, can these bones live?" So I answered, "O Lord GOD, you know." Again he said to me, "Prophesy to these bones, and say to them, 'O dry bones, hear the word of the LORD! Thus says the Lord GOD to these bones: "Surely I will cause breath to enter into you, and you shall live. I will put sinews on you and bring flesh upon you, cover you with skin and put breath in you; and you shall live. Then you shall know that I am the LORD."'"

verses 1–6 NKJV

Especially in the prophets, God's Word comes as a two-edged sword: law and gospel. "The Churches of the Reformation from the very beginning," writes Reformed theologian Louis Berkhof, "distinguished between the law and the gospel as the two parts of the Word of God as the means of grace":

> The law comprises everything in Scripture which is a revelation of God's will in the form of command or prohibition, while the gospel embraces everything, whether it be in the Old Testament or the New, that pertains to the work of reconciliation and that proclaims the seeking and redeeming love of God in Christ Jesus.[9]

By means of this two-edged sword, both death and life proceed. Through the preaching of the law, the Holy Spirit slays us, leaving us utterly destitute and helpless to save ourselves, and through the preaching of the gospel, he raises us up and seats us with Christ in heavenly places. Notice that I did not say that through this preaching God merely describes our fate apart from Christ, or that he thereby explains what we need to do if we would be saved. Preaching is a lot more than that: Through it God actually accomplishes what is threatened in the law and announced in the gospel. Through these two edges of the one sword, that double action essential for our "rescription" occurs: judgment and justification. Hence, Paul contrasts the ministry of Moses and the law with that of the Spirit and the gospel (2 Cor. 3:1–4:6). "For the letter kills, but the Spirit gives life" (3:6). Both are needed, so that we lose confidence in our own resources and throw ourselves wholly on Jesus Christ as "our righteousness, holiness and redemption" (1 Cor. 1:30).

We have to be careful of reductionism here, of course. Texts are not frozen into categories of either "law" or "gospel." Often, the same verse could be either, depending on how we take it. For instance, God's love and goodness can even become a judgment of the meagerness of my love and goodness. In marriage, I find that sometimes I will be stewing over something that was said or done by my wife, only to find a "makeup" card at the bathroom sink. The sweetness and integrity of my wife's action can hit me as "law," in that her generosity condemns my pride. It can also be "gospel," in that it holds out forgiveness and reconciliation. Scripture is like that: The same verse may strike one as a threat and then also as a consolation. That is because the Bible is not simply a book of objective, timeless propositions but a means of encounter with the Triune God. Through preaching, God addresses us, and, as in any relationship or confrontation with another person, our existential situation before the one who addresses us is never excluded from the event of being addressed. While the grammatical meaning of the text is the same, it is variously applied by the Spirit to each person.

Think of the substitutes we have devised for the ordinary preaching of the law in our day: Every gimmick, slogan, or event that can possibly shift the focus from the sinner's peril to some behavioral change. Often, when the very thing a seeker needs is to be brought to the end of his or her rope with no way of escape but Christ and his righteousness, we trade in this harsh reality for gentle encouragement to greater effort in the future. Personal testimonies of changed lives, while not wrong in themselves, constitute neither law nor gospel, for they are neither a serious word of condemnation (not merely for particular sins but for our sinful condition) nor of redemption (not merely from sinful patterns of behavior but from the wrath of God). They constitute our speech about ourselves, while preaching constitutes (or should constitute) God's speech about himself and us. Furthermore, while changed lives may attract unbelievers to church, they are not in themselves the content of the gospel, and we may risk preaching ourselves rather than Christ. After all, what religion or self-help group doesn't offer extraordinary testimonials to changed lives? We need to really hear the law in all its threatening power, and then we will be prepared to flee to Christ for safety.

But in Ezekiel 37, that word of judgment has already been pronounced upon Israel. That is why they are in exile. Now God has his Word of grace to pronounce through his prophet in the vision of death valley. There could hardly be a starker image of the human condition. Just as Ephesians 2:1–5 defines our situation "in Adam" as being "dead in trespasses and sins," here there is a valley floor littered with the skeletal remains of a vast army. In this vision, the Holy Spirit inquires of Ezekiel, "Can these bones live?" to which the prophet wisely replies, "O Sovereign LORD, only you know." So the Spirit commands Ezekiel to preach to the bones. But notice the kind of preaching occurring here. No one needs to be slain: Death is already taken for granted. It is "gospel" that is now required.

And notice what Ezekiel is supposed to say to the bones—or rather, what he is *not* supposed to say. He is not told to exhort the bones, to encourage them, to coach them out of their lethargy, or to identify himself with them in sympathetic feeling. He is not told to win them through his personal charisma or exciting methods. He is simply told, "Prophesy to these bones, and say to them, 'O dry bones, hear the word of the LORD!'" (v. 4 NKJV).

This is what, in speech-act theory, is called an *illocutionary* speech act. In such acts, one does one thing by doing another. The same occurs in a wedding, when in saying "I do" in a duly constituted ceremony, a bride and groom actually wed. In this instance, I did one thing (took

Lisa to be my wife) by doing something else (uttering the words "I do"). Such utterances, in the right context, do not merely represent the act of marriage but effect it. Or, when I am in the proper context (viz., a witness chair in a court of law with a judge presiding) and take an oath to tell the truth, I am actually doing something other than speaking: I am actually promising and in that act become a witness. In doing one thing (saying something), something else happens.

Ezekiel is told by God to preach to the dead army, the valley of dry bones, and in preaching to them something else is actually going to be done: They are raised to life. There is, of course, nothing inherently vivifying about uttering certain words: There is no magic here. Nor is Ezekiel sprinkled with magic dust to render him superhuman. But God tells Ezekiel to do one very simple and unspectacular thing (preach to the bones), and God does something else thereby (raises them to life). This connection between the sign (words uttered) and the thing signified (regeneration effected) is so close that Scripture can frequently refer to the preaching of the gospel itself as causing the new birth (Luke 8:11; John 6:63; Eph. 5:26; Heb. 1:3; 4:12; James 1:21; 1 Peter 1:23; 2 Peter 3:5). And this is exhibited throughout the conversion narratives in Acts.

Ezekiel's command on earth is God's command in heaven; hence, our Lord's commission to the apostles: "Whatever you bind on earth will be bound in heaven, and whatever you loose on earth will be loosed in heaven" (Matt. 16:19). Through the preaching that he has commissioned, God commands life to enter those who are "dead in trespasses and sins" just as God commanded life to enter Adam in the beginning, commanded life to enter Lazarus at his tomb, and will one day raise the dead on the last day. God himself issues this command through Ezekiel's command. It is through the speaking, and not through something else that the speaking encourages or somehow "sparks" in the dry bones, that the Holy Spirit creates saving faith. Ezekiel does not merely instruct the bones or exhort them to do something that will bring them to life. He knows that they can do nothing. As God's command brought the world into existence *ex nihilo,* out of nothing, so too his pronouncement of new creation life.

Do we have this sort of confidence in the power of the Spirit working through his ordinary means? If not, it may be because our shepherds are increasingly giving the impression that we should have come to hear them rather than God. We need nothing less than the power of God's Spirit working through his Word.

"The *words that I speak to you* are spirit," Jesus said, "and they are life" (John 6:63 NKJV, emphasis added). As a receiving instrument, faith comes by hearing, while idolatry is engendered by the impatient demand for that which is seen and experienced directly by the senses. This is why in religion the appeal to extraordinary visions almost always trumps the preaching of a promise and inevitably leads to idolatry. Is it not remarkable that even during a period in which Jesus was performing signs of his extraordinary ministry, he himself declared, "An evil and adulterous [idolatrous] generation seeks after a sign" (Matt. 12:39 NKJV), as the history of the church in both testaments demonstrates.

Thus far in this chapter we have emphasized preaching as God's work—and rightly so. However, this may be understood by some to give license to laziness on the part of preachers: "Let go and let God." It may also be understood to justify poorly planned and executed services in general. However, the opposite is intended. Karl Barth wrote about the trepidation that should ordinarily accompany pastors as they climb the steps to the exalted pulpit.

> This does not mean that when pastors speak officially, then with their words they enjoy a sense of papal infallibility. On the contrary, they know fear and trembling whenever they mount the pulpit. They are crushed by the feeling of being poor human beings who are probably more unworthy than all those who sit before them. Nevertheless, precisely then it is still a matter of God's Word. The Word of God that they have to proclaim is what judges them, but this does not alter the fact—indeed, it means— that they have to proclaim it.[10]

If we really appreciated this fact more fully, both as hearers and preachers, said Barth, we would all be in a better position to repent of our laziness and receive God's benefits through this means of grace. When we really grasp what is going on in the pulpit, we can hardly approach the task as hearers with our demands as to what should and should not be said in view of our "felt needs." And as pastors, we would know better than to approach the pulpit with casual familiarity or a sense of self-confidence. If our words are to be used by God as his words, they must be the product of hours in the study involving close attention to Scripture (preferably in the original languages), doctrine, and the history of interpretation. There must be a knowledge of the congregation, and this involves pastoral participation in the lives of parishoners: teaching the children, visiting shut-ins, prisoners, the sick, overseeing the flock's spiritual health. Our thirst for truth and a passion for our own godliness and that of our people will never be equal to the task. However, when we are convinced that our role is that of speaking for God and not merely passing along helpful information, when, in other words, it hits us that through our speaking God is actually killing and making alive those who hear us, we cannot esteem this task lightly. Consequently, both preachers and hearers would prepare earnestly for this central event each week.

Genuinely Practical Preaching

William James said that religious claims must be tested in terms of "their cash-value in experiential terms."[11] In other words, what gives one the biggest bang for the buck? What is most likely to improve one's life—or perhaps even society? We have our own stories, our own plots, and our own self-crafted characters. We buy into the American Dream or some other secular promise of the kingdoms of this world that our culture offers here and now. Who wants to buy into that other narrative, of the humiliated servant whose only response to such an offer is, "Man does not live on bread alone, but on every word that comes from the mouth of God" (Matt. 4:4)? Of course, we all see ourselves as the King Lear in our own play, and others—friends, family, coworkers, neighbors, and perhaps even God—are somehow situated somewhere in the cast as characters we draw around our central character.

This is one of the reasons that we hear the cry for "more practical sermons." As we have indicated above, Scripture itself distinguishes its own material in terms of "law" and "gospel," the former commanding without leniency and without giving the power to obey, while the latter promises without threat and without resting those promises on our obedience. Often, this cry for more practical preaching is the call of the old Adam for more self-help. The law, after all, is in us by nature, as Paul reminds us in the first three chapters of Romans; the gospel is not in us at all by nature, nor in the creation at large, and is in fact at odds with every common assumption about how things work between God and us. Gospel words are strange words, as Jesus frequently recognized when he proclaimed the gospel to bewildered crowds. And today it is as likely to be the churches as the secular culture that follow the sentiment expressed in a *Wall Street Journal* headline: "To Hell with Sin: When 'Being a Good Person' Excuses Everything."[12]

At Mount Sinai, when God delivered the Ten Commandments and shook the area with his voice, we read that the people were terrified and begged Moses, "You speak to us, and we will listen; but do not let God speak to us, or we will die" (Exod. 20:19 NRSV). They said this, we read, "because they could not bear what was commanded" (Heb. 12:20). A strange thing happens when God himself addresses his people, and we know that we have heard from God and not simply from a morally and spiritually sensitive coach. When God speaks, we are thrown off balance. At first we thought that we were doing fairly well—could do better, of course, with a few tips. But when God actually addresses us, we know that we are undone just as surely as did Peter when he saw Jesus calming the sea and walking upon it as if it were glass: "Go away from me, Lord; I am a sinful man!" (Luke 5:8). Now there is no golden calf, no controlled environment where God can be used instead of worshiped. Suddenly he is not at our disposal, but we are at his. A faint glimpse of his blinding majesty and holiness sends us running for shelter, like Adam and Eve after their sin had been discovered, or those on the last day who call for the rocks to hide them, but there is nowhere to hide. This can be a traumatic experience.

This is what happens when people really encounter God at the foot of his holy hill. Stripped of their pretenses, they are then clothed in the righteousness of the obedient Son, Jesus Christ, and are then ushered into the very Holy of Holies, the intimate presence of the living God. This pattern of law-and-gospel, or judgment-and-justification, is not a onetime experience for new believers; it is, or should be, a constant routine in our spiritual life. As individuals and as a community, we must experience the reenactment of this drama, "dying daily" and being raised in newness of life. Though clearly distinguished, sanctification is not separated from the new birth and justification but utterly dependent on both.

Too often, we assume that the gospel of free salvation in Jesus Christ, apart from our own efforts, is good news for unbelievers but that believers no longer need it. They "got saved," after all, and now what they need are exhortations to live for Jesus. Sanctification, then, becomes unhinged from justification and the new birth, so that we easily confuse our performance in the Christian life with the gospel. Instead, sanctification must be seen as the outworking of our justification and union with Christ. Obedience is often difficult and demanding—it doesn't just happen to us but is something that we work out with fear and trembling. As essential as this new obedience is to Christian identity, if our acceptance before God were founded on it there could be absolutely no hope.

Indicative-Imperative

Another way of putting the law-gospel distinction together is by appealing to the distinction that is drawn by Paul's use of two Greek moods: the *indicative* and the *imperative*. Imagine a veteran surgeon supervising a freshly minted physician as she performs her first operation. Trembling with nervousness, the neophyte is unsure whether she is ready. It was so much easier in the textbook or on a cadaver than it is in real life. Eventually the senior physician stills his junior's shaking hands and says, "You are a doctor now, Jones. Now perform the operation." "You are a doctor now" corresponds to the indicative—it tells Jones what she is already right now, definitively, once and for all. "Now perform the operation" is the imperative, or command, that issues from the indicative.

This is Paul's customary approach: You were this in Adam, but you are now this in Christ. You are declared righteous right now, apart from your own attainments even in sanctification (Romans 4–5); in your baptism, once and for all, you "were baptized into his death" and raised with him in his resurrection—raised first spiritually, and on the last day, physically. There is no going back now, so be who you are. On the basis of Christ's resurrection, through the faith that comes through hearing the gospel, you were declared righteous and were made victors with him over the powers of darkness, including death itself. The reign of sin and death is broken. "*Therefore* do not let sin reign in your mortal body so that you obey its evil desires," Paul says (Rom. 6:12). Notice that in Paul's preaching, the power for the Christian life comes not from the question, "What would Jesus do?" but from the more genuinely practical question, "What has Jesus done?"

Too much of contemporary preaching today assumes that the church is a public square, where everybody gathers, and in this way we no longer preach to the baptized, to the covenant community, to those about whom all of these marvelous things are said to be true. Slipping from our imagination is the sense that we are part of that drama of a covenant community that has lost its way, gathered beneath the great pulpit constructed in Jerusalem as the returning exiles hear God's rediscovered Word proclaimed once more, breaking them and remaking them in God's image (Nehemiah 8–9). So we try to coax people into becoming better by accepting Christ or, if they are already professing Christians, to emphasize the imperatives without adequate anchoring in the indicatives. We are barraged by appeals to the will to make a choice between products or lifestyles, and here is just one more pitch, one more thing to incorporate into our own life movie. Unbelievers need to hear what God has done in Christ for our salvation, we easily assume, but enlisted men and women just need the rules: That is too often the naïve logic we use. But the indicative is as essential for us now as believers as it was in the beginning. Who we are in Christ has already determined our conduct in the world! That is the apostolic "good news." We no longer belong to that narrative over there, of death, aimless existence, rebellion, self-rule, and finally divine wrath, but have, as believers, already been judged—

drowned in the waters of baptism so that sin *cannot* reign over us. Since it cannot, why live as though it did in fact still reign over us?

That is the method of apostolic preaching. The form of life that dominates the unbelieving world (Romans 1–2) is generated by one set of indicatives—dead in sin, children of wrath, enemies of God—while the form of life that dominates the believing world (Romans 3–11) is generated by another set of indicatives centering in the resurrection of our Lord. No wonder, then, Paul launches his practical instructions in Romans with the transition, "Therefore, I urge you, brothers, in *view of God's mercy*, to offer your bodies as living sacrifices" (Rom. 12:1, emphasis added). Since the law (imperatives) comes to us fairly naturally (we do usually know right from wrong), while the gospel cuts against our grain, we must always have the indicative (who we are in Christ) posted before us. Otherwise, the imperatives become ways into the indicative, instead of a life lived out of it. Once we have this order straight, the imperatives (i.e., the law's guidance in the Christian life) become our *"reasonable* service" (Rom. 12:1).

Imagine that you own a grand sailboat, equipped with the most sophisticated navigational gadgetry. Filled with favorable winds, the tall sails carry you miles off the coast until you finally come to rest for a while and enjoy your lunch. An hour passes and you are now ready to begin heading back to the harbor before an approaching storm arrives. There is only one problem: There is absolutely no wind—a dead calm has fallen upon the water. Since there is no motor, you are at the mercy of the wind. In this instance, the size of the sails and the sophisticated navigational equipment are of no assistance in moving the sailboat back to safety. You are thoroughly apprised of your location and direction, you know where to go, but you have no power.

This is how things often go in the Christian life and, specifically, in our experience of preaching over the years. At first, things appear to be going so well: "Amazing grace, how sweet the sound, that saved a wretch like me!" Furthermore, God's law has provided the wisest direction imaginable. But now, through temptation, sin, hardship, and other challenges—perhaps even the ordinary wear and tear of life—we have lost our passion for the Lord and find ourselves out in the middle of life dead in the water. If we would tell the honest truth, God bores us, no matter how we try to get that "first love" back into our system. We want to know and experience God in greater ways, but the more we try, the more we fail. At this point, there are many teachers of the law, and perhaps not even God's law, but purveyors of their own principles and techniques for victorious Christian living. If you will only follow their directions and consistently apply their principles, you can sail safely back into the harbor.

The problem is that apart from the gospel (indicative), the law (imperative) cannot actually accomplish anything in us but death and despair, "because law brings wrath" (Rom. 4:15). "What shall we say then? Is the law sin? Certainly not! Indeed, I would not have known what sin was except through the law" (Rom. 7:7). John Murray observed, "What was the question that aroused the apostle [Paul] to such passionate zeal and holy indignation . . . ? In a word it was the relation of law and gospel."[13]

What law as law cannot do is implicit in what we have found to be the utmost of its potency. (1) Law can do nothing to justify the person who in any particular has violated its sanctity and come under its curse. Law, as law, has no expiatory provision; it exercises no forgiving grace; and it has no power of enablement to the fulfillment of its own demand. It knows no clemency for the remission of guilt; it provides no righteousness to meet our iniquity; it exerts no constraining power to reclaim our waywardness; it knows no mercy to melt our hearts in penitence and new obedience. (2) It can do nothing to relieve the bondage of sin; it accentuates and confirms that bondage. . . . The purity and integrity of the gospel stand or fall with the absoluteness of the antithesis between the function and potency of law, on the one hand, and the function and potency of grace, on the other. But while all this is true it does not by any means follow that the antithesis eliminates all relevance of the law to the believer as believer.[14]

So what is genuinely practical preaching anyway? In view of the preceding, it would appear that it has to do first and foremost with who God is, who we are in his presence, and what he has done in the history of redemption, and in our own personal history, to save sinners. As a generation nursed on a philosophy of "the customer is king," practical preaching will usually mean horizontal preaching: helpful hints for life that can help us with our life project without upsetting our goals, priorities, assessment of the situation, and ideas of abundant life. But those who have heard the real thing know that this is trivial compared to the riches of being addressed by God and told the truth for a change. The definition of "practical" depends on that encounter and whether we have faced the real problem and met its genuine solution.

Avoiding Bad "Law" Preaching

Temptations attract us to subvert the biblical use of the law in driving us to Christ. The first is what is popularly known as "hellfire and brimstone" preaching. To be sure, the harvest of sin is the second death—the last judgment in which unbelievers are condemned. While all sorts of evasions have been constructed in the history of preaching to dull this sharp edge, its reality runs from Genesis to Revelation. There is no escape from the last judgment or from hell as an everlasting destiny for the unrepentant, and this clear announcement of God's verdict is an essential part of our message.

However, a bad preaching of the judgment to come depersonalizes the matter. In many popular end-times scenarios, the fear of being left behind or of what the "one world government" led by the Antichrist will be like is the motivation for repentance and faith. Saying yes to Jesus is regarded as fire insurance, a way of escaping difficult end-times circumstances or even hell. But is this the way that final judgment is described in Scripture? If we were to list the most relevant passages, we would notice that they are all connected not to tribulation, punishment, death, or even hell as ends in themselves but to God's personal reign in power against offenders. It is not that God stands aloof, merely allowing bad things to happen to people, but that he is actually executing a personal judgment on individuals and empires. We speak of hell as separation from God, but this is far from the biblical representation. The Scriptures know nothing of a hell in which God is absent from unbelievers, but only of a hell that is hell precisely because God is present forever in his wrath. He does not merely let the wheels of justice do their thing, while he wrings his hands in disappointment and frustration, but exercises vengeance, with the zeal of a righteous judge who will right every wrong and cleanse his world from sin, suffering, evil, and pain. Typical "hellfire and brimstone" preaching, therefore, makes a place and not a person the object of fear, and it is no wonder that converts to this sort of preaching rarely persevere. Having misunderstood the problem, they often misunderstand the solution.

It is essential that we see Jesus Christ as the divine rescuer who saves us from divine wrath! That is why the good news is so good. It is not that God is inherently unloving or full of wrath but that he is inherently just and full of righteousness. Furthermore, it is God who "so loved the world that he gave his one and only Son, that whoever believes in him shall not perish but have eternal life" (John 3:16). God is not the world's enemy who must be placated by Jesus. Rather, "God was reconciling the world to himself in Christ" (2 Cor. 5:19). The offended One and the propitiator are both God. Before the world was ever created, God had already planned a rescue for those whom he had chosen and given to Christ as a people. A biblical preaching of the law, then, will relate the coming wrath to God himself, as difficult as that is for us in any age but especially in ours.

Many who were raised on "hellfire and brimstone" have reacted by preaching "soft" law, as if Jesus were a kinder, gentler Moses, who replaces rules against dancing with encouraging, practical direction. In an effort to escape the stern preaching with which one may have been raised, many pastors today do not recognize that sentimental moralism (viz., "If you follow God's principles for success in life, you will be happy") is actually just another way of confusing the law with the gospel in a manner that dilutes the seriousness of one and the sweetness of the other. A sentimentalized law proclaimed as gospel is disastrous. Reacting against a bad preaching of the bad news leads to a bad preaching of the good news as, "If you do this, life will go a lot better for you." It's not as demanding as the law (as if the divine requirement were "Thou shalt be happy"), but it is also not as comforting as the gospel (as if the "good news" was that this life will be more bearable, rather than the announcement of reconciliation with God through Jesus Christ). This sort of preaching will not only engender shallow conversions, it will also gradually erode the theological structure of lifelong believers—that very structure that stirred their hearts to praise and to grateful obedience in the world. Ironically, both forms of bad law preaching share in common the neglect of the vertical dimension. In other words, whether one is afraid of hell or is afraid of low self-esteem, the real issue at stake—namely, being an offender against God's personal holiness—is left untouched. As a result, either sort of preaching of the law leaves people without having to actually stand in the presence of God naked and ashamed. God is left out of the picture at the most crucial point.

Those who have tried just about everything to find happiness and even peace with God do not need more encouragement to try just a little bit harder. They need to give up altogether and cast themselves on the mercy of a God who requires an absolute, inherent holiness and has found that only in his Son. Only when we are found clad in those garments of salvation—Christ's righteousness imputed to us apart from anything in us or done by us—can we have peace with God.

As the sailboat's failure to turn back to the harbor was not the fault of the navigational equipment, our failure to keep God's revealed will is not the fault of the law. It is the result of our own sin. And we would not have even come to realize our real problem unless the law had clearly revealed our sinfulness. This is why, for instance, the Heidelberg Catechism answers the question, "Where does true faith come from?" with the response, "The Holy Spirit creates faith in our hearts by the preaching of the holy gospel and confirms it through the use of his holy sacraments." Notice that faith is said to be produced and confirmed not simply by the Word of God as a whole but by the gospel. Calvin observed, "Faith is not produced by every part of the Word of God, for the warnings, admonitions and threatened judgments will not instill the confidence and peace requisite for true faith." Thus, faith must have unconditional promises to take hold of:

> For a conditional promise that sends us back to our own works does not promise life unless we discern its presence in ourselves. Therefore, if we would not have our faith tremble and waver, we must buttress it with the promise of salvation, which is willingly and freely offered to us by the Lord in consideration of our misery rather than our deserts. The apostle, therefore, bears this witness to the gospel: that it is the word of faith [Rom. 10:8]. He distinguishes the gospel both from the precepts of the law and from the promises, since there is nothing that can establish faith except that generous embassy by which God reconciles the world to himself. . . . Therefore, when we say that faith must rest upon a freely given promise, we do not deny that believers embrace and grasp the Word of God in every respect: but we point out the promise of mercy as the proper goal of faith.[15]

Yes, this is all true enough, some will say, but Paul is talking about becoming a Christian. After we are saved by God's grace, our relationship to the law changes. The law becomes sweet to the believer. And indeed this response is amply confirmed by the Scriptures, so that the believer can exclaim with the psalmist, "I delight in your commands because I love them" (Ps. 119:47). Having executed its just sentence once and for all on the obedient Son, the law cannot condemn those who are forever safe in Christ from its curses. The law continues to guide the believer, even though its curse has been spent on Christ in our place. But this fact does not mean that the believer does not fall into sin and therefore experience God's displeasure—in other words, a guilty conscience and terror of God's law.

Drawing on his own experience, Paul laments that even though he loves the law and wants to obey it, he finds his own continuing sinfulness present alongside this desire. "For what I do is not the good I want to do; no, the evil I do not want to do—this I keep on doing. . . . What a wretched man I am!" (Rom. 7:19, 24). This leads Paul to look for deliverance, but where now can he turn? To the law and its glorious precepts? To a renewed inner resolve to obey it? That is where he finds himself condemned, apart from Christ. So he immediately turns elsewhere, back to the indicative: "Thanks be to God—through Jesus Christ our Lord! . . . Therefore, there is now no condemnation for those who are in Christ Jesus" (Rom. 7:25–8:1). The law can tell us what obedience looks like and can chart our course for it, but it cannot give what it commands, and this is as true for Christians as it is for unbelievers. Only the good news of what God has done for us can empower us for service.

To return to our illustration, then, one can move forward in the Christian life with full sails only if there is a strong wind. And Christians can overcome their unbelief and sin only by hearing the gospel, that external and objective announcement that despite whatever is going on inside of us, this is what God has done for us, outside of us, in his Son. Only then can the law have a positive role in our lives, as it navigates, charting our course with perfect wisdom. Even so, the gospel remains "the power of God unto salvation" not only when one becomes a believer but throughout the Christian life.

There is never a "higher life" than this, a better way, a superior method of moving us along as pilgrims in this world. More quiet times, a newly discovered prayer technique, rededication at summer camp, a "second blessing"—none of these avenues can create faith in Christ. If faith creates works and faith is created by the preaching of the gospel, a renewed appreciation for God's history of redemption is surely the key to transformed communities.

God the Preacher

In short, God enters the room, just as he did at Sinai, a room filled with chattering, demanding, pleading, complaining, sovereign selves, and the announcement rings through the hall, "The Lord is in his holy temple! Let all the earth keep silence before him!" He comes to expose us for the scam artists that we are, to reverse the spin that we have put on our lives, and to leave us with absolutely no foundation and no hope apart from the Son with whom he is well pleased, "who has become for us wisdom from God—that is, our righteousness, holiness and redemption. Therefore, as it is written: 'Let him who boasts boast in the Lord'" (1 Cor. 1:30).

Preaching is the Ellis Island of God's kingdom, the port of entry for "strangers and aliens," through which we must constantly pass again and again throughout our lives. We come in with our own scripts, our own storied selves, and instead of editing them here and there, God rewrites them entirely in the light of his own plot. As Calvin reminds us, "Christ the Lord promises to his followers today no other 'Kingdom of Heaven' than that in which they may 'sit at table with Abraham, Isaac, and Jacob' [Matt. 8:11]."[16] The point is not to find a place for God in our story but to receive the good news that God has found a place for us in his. There is a seat for us at the table of Abraham, Isaac, and Jacob, even though we didn't even belong in the same neighborhood.

Viewed in this sense, preaching does not exist to brighten up the looks of "this passing evil age," like New York City's ill-fated proposal to paint geraniums and white curtains in the boarded windows of burned-out buildings lining the freeway. Instead, it exists to make desolate the plans of those who have set up their reign in opposition to God and to bring "the age to come" into the present in the power of the Spirit. And if not now, then in the last act, Proteus will be chained and will have to finally face the truth. There will be no new transformation, no new mask, no new character or plot to adopt as a way of escape, so that "at the name of Jesus every knee should bow, in heaven and on earth and under the earth, and every tongue confess that Jesus Christ is Lord, to the glory of God the Father" (Phil. 2:10–11).

FIVE

Discovering the Plot

Meeting up with two downcast disciples on the road to Emmaus, the newly risen Jesus encouraged them by opening the Scriptures: "And beginning with Moses and all the Prophets, he explained to them what was said in all the Scriptures concerning himself" (Luke 24:27). This chapter attempts to provide a biblical case for reading Scripture in terms of God's unfolding mystery of redemption, not as a collection of superior moral insights, empowering thoughts for each day, an end-times handbook, or a blueprint for a new social order—indeed, not even chiefly as a repository of doctrine. While Scripture does, from time to time, address all of these issues, and certainly makes clear propositional assertions of both a doctrinal and ethical nature, all of this serves a larger purpose. In explaining the criteria of selection for his Gospel, John the Evangelist speaks for the Scriptures as a whole when he concludes, "Jesus did many other miraculous signs in the presence of his disciples, which are not recorded in this book. But these are written that you may believe that Jesus is the Christ, the Son of God, and that by believing you may have life in his name" (John 20:30–31).

We have already touched on the dramatic encounter with God that occurs through the preaching of the law and the gospel. Here, I want to take a look at an approach to biblical interpretation and preaching that is often nicknamed the "redemptive-historical" model.

The Scarlet Thread

All faithful Christians acknowledge the importance of redemption, and many hold history in high esteem as well. As the Apostles' Creed says, Christ was "crucified *under Pontius Pilate.*" But the redemptive-historical approach says more than this. All of Scripture is about Christ, advocates of this view insist, even when he is not center stage at every point. Even when he is in the shadows, the plot that unfolds continues to congeal around him. And in every scene, the story behind the story is God's victory over Satan's attempts to thwart God's just and gracious designs. Remarkably, the religious leaders of Jesus' day could see the Scriptures almost entirely as a rule book. Looking for something other than the plot and its central figure, the Pharisees missed the entire point of the book they revered: "But you do not have his word abiding in you, because whom he sent, him you do not believe. You search the Scriptures, for in them you think you have eternal life; and these are they which testify of me. But you are not willing to come to me that you may have life" (John 5:38–40 NKJV). Scripture, Peter adds, is unified by this redemptive-historical plot:

> Of this salvation the prophets have inquired and searched diligently, who prophesied of the grace that would come to you, searching what, or what manner of time, the Spirit of Christ who was in them was indicating when he testified beforehand the sufferings of Christ and the glories that would follow. To them it was revealed that, not to themselves, but to us they were ministering the things which now have been reported to you through those who have preached the gospel to you by the Holy Spirit sent from heaven— things which angels desire to look into.

> 1 Peter 1:10–12 NKJV

Notice here that the Holy Spirit who breathed these Old Testament writings is, even before the incarnation of our Lord, called "the Spirit of Christ." The Spirit was witnessing to Christ even when he inspired the writings of Moses and the prophets. Even when they did not know clearly that this was what they were doing in every instance, the heavenly author did.[1]

The Central Character

Jesus Christ is the sum and substance of all of Scripture: "For all the promises of God in [Christ] are Yes, and in him Amen" (2 Cor. 1:20 NKJV). If anyone is qualified to define the purpose of preaching, it is Jesus and his apostles, and they appear to take it for granted that Scripture is not about some other plot that individuals and societies construct. It is about "the sufferings of Christ and the glories that would follow." Once we understand how everything points to Christ, we will be ready to respond to preaching as the disciples did on the Emmaus road: "Were not our hearts burning within us while he talked with us on the road and opened the Scriptures to us?" (Luke 24:32). For the next forty days, Jesus schooled his apostles in the proper interpretation of the Old Testament, with himself at the center. Even Satan reads the Bible redemptive-historically, although he does not encourage us to follow him in this approach. Tempting Jesus with instant gratification, the devil knew that Jesus was fasting in the wilderness for forty days as a recapitulation of Israel's forty years of temptation in the wilderness. He even quoted Old Testament prophecies, recognizing that Christ was their fulfillment (Matt. 4:1–11). We learn from these passages that the Bible is not an end in itself but a means to the end of knowing Christ and being found in him as living members of his body.

But isn't it a bit simplistic to say that all of Scripture is about Christ? Does that mean we have to force him into every text, even if it's not obvious? Those are good questions, because we do not want to suggest that every passage equally or explicitly speaks of Christ's person and work. Think of the relationship of Christ and Scripture to that between the box top of a jigsaw puzzle and its pieces. Let's say that it is a forest scene. In putting a puzzle together, we have to guard against two extremes: One is the tendency to miss the forest for the trees—to be so narrowly focused on this or that piece that we have no idea what is supposed to bring unity to these fragments. The other danger (especially familiar to those of us who are impatient) is to miss the trees for the forest—to be so generally focused on Christ (having seen the box top) that pieces of the puzzle are forced to reveal Christ more directly and explicitly than is actually the case in a particular passage. As the whole puzzle is unified by one scene without doing violence to the diverse puzzle pieces, Scripture is unified around the person and work of Jesus Christ without losing the enormous diversity in the biblical text.

How the New Testament Preaches the Old

Look at the examples of how New Testament writers interpret and preach the Old Testament. Relating the story of the flight of Mary, Joseph, and Jesus to Egypt during Herod's scourge, Matthew writes, "And so was fulfilled what the Lord had said through the prophet: 'Out of Egypt I called my son'" (2:15). While a Jewish person might, quite understandably, balk, having interpreted this passage, Hosea 11:1, as referring to the nation of Israel returning from captivity, the evangelist announces the true Israel, Jesus Christ, as God's Son and the referent of the prophecy. Similarly, Paul confidently asserts that the true rock that followed Israel in the wilderness, giving the water of life, was none other than Jesus Christ (1 Cor. 10:4). Hebrews is perhaps the greatest example of this exegesis, in which the typological significance of Old Testament shadows is relentlessly mined for its richness in pointing to Christ and his heavenly reign in the Jerusalem that is above as our prophet, priest, and king. This exegetical method forms the central nervous system of the entire New Testament, whether the Gospels or the Epistles. It is what makes sense out of the otherwise closed Book of Revelation. In fact, it is the Lamb alone who can break the seals of history and open the scroll because he is its Alpha and Omega (Rev. 5:1–14). If this is how the Bible interprets itself, we surely are in no position to quarrel with a redemptive-historical approach to exegesis.

The sermons in the Book of Acts reflect this way of preaching the Scriptures: Christ is proclaimed from the Old Testament. The first Christian sermons, therefore, do not proclaim Moses as an exemplary Christian leader, nor is the purpose to set forth the example of Joshua's courage and guiding principles of leadership or David's heart for the Lord. Nor is Gideon's fleece a parable of seeking the Lord's will for our lives. Rather than being a textbook for determining the age of the earth, Genesis is ultimately directed at God's lordship and sets the stage for the drama of redemption. Instead of being an almanac of end-times predictions, Revelation is thoroughly centered on Christ and his triumph over sin and death on behalf of his people. Scripture is about Jesus Christ, from beginning to end, God's first word at creation and God's last word at the consummation. "I am the Alpha and the Omega, the Beginning and the End," Jesus says (Rev. 1:8 NKJV).

This means, of course, that even if one appeals to scores of verses from Daniel and Revelation, that person is not proclaiming Scripture if the "box top" is a picture of someone or something other than our Savior. If Scripture becomes a source for practical quotations or for speculations, then the preaching that emerges will not be the preaching of Scripture but the exploitation of Scripture for one's own purposes.

Many people will say that they simply read or preach "whatever is there in the text." A pastor told me once, "I just preach the Word. If I'm in Galatians, I sound like an antinomian, but if I'm in the Sermon on the Mount, I sound like a legalist." The unspoken assumption here is that some of us at least come to Scripture without looking for anything in particular. Every passage is a collection of puzzle pieces, often without any recourse to the box top. If this pastor had the checks and balances of a good systematic theology and an eye for the unifying plot, he would not have confused his hearers, who could hear antinomianism and legalism from the same minister. This same unwitting assumption of the Bible's disunity is behind the recourse one sometimes hears among

Christians debating a particular point of theology. "Well, you have your verses and I have mine," one says. But if God is the ultimate author of Scripture, do we really want to say that the Bible is inconsistent or even contradictory?

We come without any prejudices, many people assume, without having been raised in a particular ecclesiastical background and without having any experiences or instruction. We come merely as objective, neutral observers. But, of course, this is impossible. Nobody can erase his or her identity. Our background assumptions may be right or wrong, but nobody comes to a verse without a pre-understanding of what he or she expects to find. That is why we are (hopefully!) *surprised* from time to time by Scripture. We are not neutral but sinful—and so our tendency is to "suppress the truth in unrighteousness" (Rom. 1:18). But we are also created in God's image and, as believers, are being remade in that image. We bring a lot of baggage to the study of Scripture, some good, some bad, and instead of pretending to rid ourselves of these prejudices, we need to bring them out into the open. Only then can we analyze our thoughts. Some of those biases, we will conclude, arise naturally from the text. For instance, we do not come to passages about rewards for good works and conclude that salvation is by our own efforts. But why not? It is because we have learned from so many other passages—indeed, the whole warp and woof of Scripture—that salvation is by grace alone, through faith alone, because of Christ alone. So we cannot get out of this dialectical (back-and-forth) movement between the parts and the whole. Scripture interprets itself precisely by means of this movement back and forth, just as the puzzle pieces and the box top constantly interpret each other.

Other prejudices, however, are sinful, as when leading pastors and theologians vigorously defended American slavery in the nineteenth century. Texts became pretexts for saying the very opposite of what the Bible actually teaches. That happens in a variety of ways in our own lives, and we should beware of it. Those who have had trouble accepting a difficult biblical doctrine will often reply, "I guess I've never looked at it that way before. It's just not part of my background." Nobody approaches Scripture as a clean slate—and that's fine, as long as we seek to "take captive every thought to make it obedient to Christ" (2 Cor. 10:5). We cannot even *have* a new thought apart from the language that we have learned in our distinct communities. Prejudices are necessary, but we have to be careful to critique them in the light of scriptural prejudices.

We come to every passage knowing a lot of other passages, and this naturally predisposes our reading of each text. Jesus Christ, then, is the interpretive key to Scripture, the grand prejudice that we bring with us to every passage simply because all of Scripture testifies to him as this plot's central character. It is a faithful prejudice because it is cultivated in us by Scripture itself. And it is as true of the Old Testament as the New. Many of us were raised with a certain degree of ambiguity as to the purpose and usefulness of the Old Testament, but starting with Matthew is like walking into the middle of a movie. In fact, Matthew's Gospel begins with the line, "The book of the genealogy of Jesus Christ, the Son of David, the Son of Abraham," and then lists the most prominent Old Testament figures in his line of descent.

The person of Jesus does not swallow Scripture whole, and each part must have its own special place in the larger scene. The Old Testament cannot really be understood apart from Jesus Christ, it is true, but neither can Jesus Christ be truly understood apart from the history of Israel. Sometimes Jesus stands in the shadows of the stage; at other times, he is front and center; at still other times, he is in the audience. But like Shakespeare's *Macbeth,* in which the central player is never lost from the plot even when he does not appear directly in a scene, the drama of Scripture is Jesus' story at all times. It is his plot that opens Genesis and closes Revelation, climaxing in his own incarnation, atonement, resurrection, and return in glory.

Redemptive-Historical Interpretation

All of these points coalesce around what is often called the "redemptive-historical" approach to interpretation. First, it is "redemptive" because it recognizes this plot as concerned chiefly with reconciling sinners to God and forming out of that reconciliation a community of faith and obedience. It is called "historical" because it concentrates on God's saving action in this world. There was a creation, a fall, a flood, an exodus, a nation, a cross and resurrection, a Pentecost, and there will be a return of our faithful Savior in human history. Instead of seeing the Bible as a collection of timeless truths and ethical principles, this approach is sensitive to the unfolding plot of redemption in genuinely historical events that end finally in the consummation of all things in Christ. The history of redemption is seen as an organic growth with real change within continuity.[2]

The contrast between a "timeless principle" and a redemptive-historical approach, especially in relation to worship, is easily discerned by interpreting John 4. This familiar text reads:

Jesus said to [the Samaritan woman], "Woman, believe me, the hour is coming when you will neither on this mountain, nor in Jerusalem, worship the Father. You worship what you do not know; we know what we worship, for salvation is of the Jews. But the hour is coming, and now is, when the true worshipers will worship the Father in Spirit and truth; for the Father is seeking such to worship him."

verses 21–23 NKJV

Interpreting it as setting forth a timeless principle, one might say that its point is this: "It's about the heart, not about the location." But the redemptive-historical approach would interpret it differently. What Jesus is announcing is a historical transition. He does not offer a general statement about genuine worship being a matter of the heart rather than a place. In fact, he actually endorses the temple in Jerusalem. That has been the right place to worship, not here in Samaria. Salvation comes from the Jews—in other words, through the historical line of Abraham, Judah, and David until it reaches the Messiah. But now something new has happened. It is a new day. God's kingdom is no longer identified with an earthly Jerusalem but is even now coming down out of heaven where the King is present among us. He is the temple, as we have already observed.

Edmund Clowney examines the diverse approaches to Scripture, using the exodus event as an example. He writes, "To preach the exodus event as an example of political liberation obviously does not do justice to the framework of God's covenantal promise by which He delivers Israel." Nor does allegorizing—that is, taking the exodus as a symbol "for illustrating any significance that the preacher chooses to find in them."

> The preacher can then read the account of Moses' sign and hold forth on rods that become snakes to warn against the misuse of authority, or to describe virtues becoming vices. His imagination is free of any constraint of Scripture. A less blatant failure in scriptural interpretation is moralizing. . . . The moralizing preacher does not arbitrarily seize on any element in the text that catches his fancy. He does take account of the meaning of the text in its original setting. He interprets for his hearers the significance that this truth has for them in their own lives and experience. But he completely fails to show how this truth comes to its full meaning in Christ, and only in Christ.[3]

Moralistic preaching may be the dominant approach today. It is employed by liberals and conservatives alike. For liberals, the goal may be to get the people to volunteer for the soup kitchen, while for conservatives it may be simply to get them to improve their personal piety. It isn't that the goals are bad but that they are reached by way of improper biblical interpretation. Explaining true religion as James does (1:27) directly supports assistance to the homeless and needy, and attention to the "fruit of the Spirit" is biblically grounded (Galatians 5). But even these ethical passages must be interpreted in the light of God's saving plan in Christ, as those very passages indicate. The "Goliaths" of our lives may be as different as the "five smooth stones" that we use to defeat them. But the tie that binds us is that we read (and too often preach) the Bible today as if it were a general collection of common sense and moral wisdom—a variation on *Aesop's Fables,* complete with a moral to the story. Whether using the Bible or William Bennett's *Book of Virtues,* the sermon is the same either way, and one may gain the impression that the minister was going to say whatever he came to say quite independently of the text. In this way, Scripture is called upon to substantiate or illustrate worldly wisdom rather than to call it into question and substitute divine truth.

The goal of so much preaching in both liberal and conservative churches is to make good people a bit better (or at least to feel a bit better), instead of proclaiming from the biblical text the saving acts of God. I tell seminary students to ask themselves after completing a sermon, "Now would it have been necessary for God to have given us the Bible for that sermon?" Methodist minister William Willimon gave me a better question: "Would it have been necessary for Jesus Christ to have died in order for this to be true?"[4] If our preaching stumbles over the cross—the bloodied body of the Lamb of God crucified for our sins and punished for our transgressions—then its character as Christian proclamation is already compromised. As our Savior experienced so deeply in his own experience, there is no getting around the cross, splinters and all.

Redemptive-historical preaching aims at discerning God's nature in terms of God's action. God reveals who he is not chiefly by propositions but by reported action. "God is known through his works" is a long-standing dictum in theology. It also emphasizes the genuine change that occurs in the history of redemption. The Jewish theocracy is a type of the kingdom that will come when the Messiah arrives, not a timeless blueprint for establishing a Christian America. Having passed from the tutelage of Moses into the household of Christ, the types and shadows of the Old Testament civil legislation are no more in force for us than the ceremonial laws. Throughout both sets of legislation, everything was pointing to Christ, not indicating a timeless arrangement that every nation may emulate. Therefore, we can no longer appeal to 2 Chronicles 7:14 for national renewal: "If my people, who are called by my name, will humble themselves and pray and seek my face and turn from their wicked ways, then I will hear from heaven and will forgive their sin and will heal their land." This verse's historical context is discarded by many interpreters today in favor of a universal and timeless principle of reciprocity, as if any nation could invoke the terms of that sacred treaty that God made with Israel.

Similarly, the Book of Acts reports the ministry of the apostles (the "extraordinary ministry"), not timeless principles for our ministry today (the "ordinary ministry"). Pentecost was a once-and-for-all event, unrepeatable in its essence, and in that event the Holy Spirit equipped his apostles to be witnesses to Jesus Christ. That anointing that rested on them also rests on all believers, although only some are called as ministers. These events are not in the text merely to illustrate general truths or to trigger observations about life, church growth, ministry, evangelism, and community. Rather, they are there to be taken seriously as events that, in their own particular way, contributed another significant piece of the redemptive-historical puzzle. Perhaps here the puzzle analogy itself breaks down, given its static imagery. It might be better to say that each event actually *advances* a further stage—real change within continuity. Each event is part of the new thing that God is doing.

Suggestions for Christ-Centered Reading and Preaching

We will conclude with five practical suggestions. *First, in the reading of Scripture, whether privately or in public worship, one might consider including an Old Testament and a New Testament reading, the former selection related to the latter as promise to its fulfillment.* We begin to think in terms of this pattern by hearing the connections. Often one can find help in this area by consulting a lectionary, a book that lists the Old Testament, Epistle, and Gospel readings for each Lord's Day. Many mainline and a few evangelical denominations employ a lectionary in their worship service, and they can be easily ordered from denominational publishing houses. Some will be better than others, of course. Some preach one of the lectionary passages (or both), while others comment on the relationship of the readings but use a different text for their sermon. But even without a lectionary, when we know what we're looking for, we can find Old Testament passages for our New Testament sermons and vice versa.

Second, you might ask yourself, What's the stage of redemptive history at which we find ourselves in this passage? If this question were asked each time, it could clear up the tendency to convert a significant event in the past into an unhistorical example or symbol for us today. One might be less inclined to apply the Old Testament theocracy to our contemporary situation, or to appeal to temple worship in support of directives for new covenant worship, or to see the Book of Acts as a handbook for ministry in the post-apostolic era.

Third, you might ask yourself, How do I find myself in Christ (and therefore with his church) in this story? Instead of trying to find room for God in myself, God makes room for us in his drama. His is much grander, more interesting, far thicker in his descriptive power and far richer in its resolution than can be found in the secular narratives that surround us.

Fourth, read and hear the Bible with the church. Creeds, confessions, a good systematic theology can all help us to see the limitations of our own narrow range of ideas, presuppositions, experiences, and longings. We must rid ourselves of the notion that it matters little what others have said in their reading of Scripture through the ages, since we are just reading the Bible. So, too, of course, were those others who have gone before us. The choice is not between following "mere men" and Scripture directly; it's a choice between interpreting Scripture with the larger church rather than thinking of ourselves as omnicompetent. It is a sign of humility when we are able to conclude that we, like the Ethiopian eunuch, are hampered by our own blind spots. "So Philip ran to him [the Ethiopian], and heard him reading the prophet Isaiah, and said, 'Do you understand what you are reading?' And he said, 'How can I, unless someone guides me?' And he asked Philip to come up and sit with him. . . . Then Philip opened his mouth, and beginning at this Scripture [Isa. 53:7–8], preached Jesus to him" (Acts 8:30–31, 35 NKJV). Instead of pretending to start from scratch, join the conversation already in progress since Abraham, Isaac, and Jacob.

Fifth and finally, read and hear prayerfully. We will take a closer look at this one near the end of the book. The Holy Spirit, who inspired Scripture, illumines believers so that they may understand its significance. Interpretation is never simply an intellectual exercise; rather, it involves the imagination, the heart, and the will. In every act of interpretation, we are entirely dependent on the Spirit, and, as our Savior promised, "He will testify about me" (John 15:26).

Part 2

Signs and Seals
of the Covenant:
The Ministry of Baptism
and the Lord's Supper

SIX

Signed, Sealed, and Delivered

If one were to ask you to list the top two instruments of spiritual growth in your life, what would you answer? Most of us would probably list things such as a daily quiet time, personal Bible study, participation in an accountability or prayer group, personal evangelism, or similar useful activities. Additionally, there is always, it seems, some new fad for Christian growth, a "key" to unlock spiritual renewal. Try this "secret" formula, pray this newly discovered prayer, imitate that successful church model. In evangelical circles, "spirituality" or "piety" is most often thought of in quite personal, individualistic terms—as something that one engages in for the purpose of attaining one's spiritual goals. Our relationship with God is most often conceived in one-on-one terms. Consequently, the corporate aspect—especially the church—is secondary. At least for many of us, the preached Word and the sacraments of baptism and the Lord's Supper would probably not make the short list for the top instruments of spiritual growth, either for individuals or churches.

While the Protestant Reformation cleared away the superstition surrounding the sacraments, it nevertheless recognized the place given by Scripture to baptism and the Lord's Supper, which, alongside the Word, deliver the gospel to sinners. The successors of the Reformers concurred: "The visible church is a fellowship of people called to the state of grace by Word and sacrament," said Johannes Wollebius (1586–1629).[1] In the twentieth century, Louis Berkhof summarized this position when he wrote that the church "is not instrumental in communicating grace, except by means of the Word and of the sacraments."[2] All of the Reformers and their successors believed that the two indelible marks of the true church were the rightly preached Word and the rightly administered sacraments.

However, the eighteenth century saw the rise of a movement known as pietism, partly in reaction to what many regarded as a stale, dead orthodoxy then prevalent in the state churches. This movement, identified with such pioneers as Jacob Spener and August Francke, and later leaders such as Count Zinzendorf and John Wesley, began as a "church within the church." While unwilling to separate from their established churches, pietists founded "conventicles"—what we today would call small groups—where they thought the real growth took place. Religion increasingly became an affair of the heart rather than the mind, of self-directed and inward piety rather than an outwardly directed piety, and individualistic rather than corporate. Suspicious of outward forms, pietism eventually evolved into its own distinct denominations. As pietism coalesced into revivalism in America especially, sectarian groups sprouted up across the landscape, each promising a better, more direct way to God than that afforded by the traditional churches around them. Eschewing creeds, confessions, catechisms, an educated ministry, and liturgy, many merely ended up setting up their own versions of these—and their own sacraments (the "altar call," for instance)—in their place. New anti-denominational denominations tore sections of the membership from parent bodies and populated the landscape with ever new eccentricities.

It is not surprising, then, that our own period is filled with examples of this tradition of American sectarianism, where even the Scriptures do not have to be followed when there is a practical argument to be made. One of the most extreme examples I've run across is in an article titled "Supper for One," in which the writer advocates supplementing private devotions with a private communion service with water or juice and crackers. "Communion helped me focus blurry thoughts in the morning," she said.

Today, the triumph of pietism and revivalism seems to have drowned out the cry of those who, throughout this period, have warned churches to abandon their new means of grace in favor of those established by God in his Word. But evangelicals have tended to be suspicious of even the term *sacrament*, often regarding it as a vestige of Roman Catholicism. Like raised Lazarus still bound in his grave clothes, the churches of the Reformation were alive but still bound to the traditions of men, many thought. God works directly, without means, or perhaps through practically any means, according to the prevalent assumptions of our day. The more spectacular and extraordinary the means, the better to grab people's attention.

So it would seem that anyone who wants to argue for the classic Reformational view of the sacraments and their importance in the Christian life has an uphill battle. Who wants to submit to the ordinary means of grace when there are so many extraordinary means being advertised? The real question, however, is what the Scriptures teach on this matter, and that is the question we will seek to answer in the next two chapters. We will begin with a discussion of baptism and then approach the equally controversial but remarkably practical subject of the Lord's Supper.

Baptism and the Bible

Ordinarily, one should begin such discussions with definitions. "What is a sacrament?" might have been a good place to start. However, I would prefer to define both baptism and the Lord's Supper not by a general definition up front (although there's nothing wrong with that) but by first working our way through the most important biblical passages. A definition will emerge as we do this, but first we must pay attention to the unfolding drama.

Throughout the Old Testament, God not only promised the covenant of grace in word but visually signified and sealed it through dramatic rituals: circumcision and Passover. In instituting circumcision, God told Abram:

> And I will establish my covenant between me and you and your descendents after you in their generations, for an everlasting covenant, to be God to you and your descendents after you. . . . This is my covenant which you shall keep, between me and you and your descendents after you: Every male child among you shall be circumcised; and you shall be circumcised in the flesh of your foreskins, and it shall be a sign of the covenant between me and you. . . . And the uncircumcised male child, who is not circumcised in the flesh of his foreskin, that person shall be cut off from his people; he has broken my covenant.
>
> Genesis 17:7, 10–11, 14 NKJV

Throughout this study we have seen the weight that the Bible gives to the covenant as the structure for this plot. Here, the ritual of circumcision is directly tied to that plot as "a sign of the covenant between me and you" (v. 11). In fact, the sign (circumcision) is so tied to the thing signified (salvation) that the ritual itself is called "the covenant" (v. 10).

So the first thing that Scripture teaches about sacraments is that they are signs of the covenant of grace. Promises are heard, while signs are seen. Thus far we have emphasized the verbal nature of God's communication: While the gods of the nations are idols that may be seen and touched, Yahweh is present among his people chiefly through the proclamation of his Word. However, God has always attended his verbal promise with visual confirmation. The rainbow is an "everlasting sign" of God's faithfulness to the earth in his common grace (Gen. 9:8–17), just as the visible arrival of the Messiah will be "an everlasting sign that shall not be cut off" (Isa. 55:13 NKJV). The people in Jesus' day, especially the religious leaders, demanded a sign (Matt. 12:38) but were denied one because of their unbelief (v. 39). Signs in the heavens are used figuratively by Jesus as portents of his second coming (Matthew 24), and they appear in Revelation 12:1. Signs accompanied Jesus' preaching, confirming that he was the one sent from God, but Jesus is repeatedly frustrated with the people following him because they see his miracles not as signs pointing to him and to his message but rather as ends in themselves (John 6:26–27).

A sign, then, at the very minimum, is a testimony on the part of the one who promises something that he will fulfill it. It is more than a wedding ring, which is more of a symbol than a sign, in that a sign not only points to the thing signified but is somehow bound together with it, so that—as we have seen in Genesis 17—circumcision can be called "the covenant." In literature, this is called a synecdoche. As the *Oxford Desk Dictionary* defines it, a synecdoche is a "figure of speech in which a part is made to represent the whole or vice versa (e.g., new faces at the meeting)."[3] In this example, "new faces" means "new people," but the face is taken for the whole person. Similarly, the sign of circumcision is so linked to and representative of the covenant of grace that God can actually call *it* the covenant, just as he refers to the ark of the covenant, the tabernacle, and the temple as if they were he himself. Only when Jesus Christ comes is the sign (Jesus the living temple) fully the thing signified (God in flesh). Apart from the person of Christ, signs both are and are not the thing signified.

No one is to worship the sign. In Numbers 21, after God sent venomous snakes to strike many of the complacent Israelites, the people confessed their sin, and God mercifully provided for them by commanding Moses, "Make a fiery serpent, and set it on a pole; and it shall be that everyone who is bitten, when he looks at it, shall live" (v. 8 NKJV). Here the sign is itself powerless, but because of God's promise, those who look to it—and only to it—are rescued. Through the sign they look in faith to the thing signified and place their trust in the God who promises salvation. But much later in Israel's history, this historical artifact became an object of worship. Part of King Hezekiah's high approval rating in God's sight was that "he removed the high places and broke the sacred pillars, cut down the wooden image and *broke in pieces the bronze serpent that Moses had made;* for until those days the children of Israel burned incense to it, and called it Nehushtan" (2 Kings 18:4 NKJV). When the sign becomes the object of worship, it ceases to function as a sacrament and instead becomes an idol. Instead of being a means of grace, it becomes a means of judgment. (This is true of all signs except for Christ, who, like the bronze serpent, was lifted up so that all who look to him alone may be saved. In him, the sign and the thing signified become indistinguishable.)

Signs live in this limbo of the synecdoche, between symbols and the reality signified. They are not the reality, but they are also not divorced from it—mere symbols. Circumcision, then, both is and is not the covenant of grace. The apostle Paul makes the point that Abraham was justified by grace through faith before he was circumcised, so the covenant must be more than circumcision. And yet, they are so intimately and inextricably linked that God could say that those who do not circumcise their children under the old covenant are cut off from the people of God. Through signs, God not only testifies to us by word but by deed, not only through the ear but through the eye. What we behold is not a mere symbol, nor is it the reality itself "face to face." Rather, we look through the sign by faith to "see through a glass darkly," beholding our salvation that awaits us. The word promises, while the sign confirms.

But Scripture indicates that a sacrament is not only a sign; it is something more. Of Abraham, the apostle writes, "And he received the *sign* of circumcision, a *seal* of the righteousness that he had by faith" (Rom. 4:11, emphasis added). In the context of ancient treaties, a seal would have been similar to the wax imprint that a European monarch would have made on a state document. Without the seal, how could a rival be confident that the cease-fire was permanent and that hostilities had truly ended and an alliance had been firmly established? Perhaps the document is full of encouraging promises, but they fall flat when one is not certain that they are (1) the promises of one who has the authority to make them and (2) promises that are in fact made *to the recipient* of the treaty. The treaty-making king may have written the document or approved it, but it is not in force—it is not binding or official—if there is no seal.

Circumcision was not called a seal without warrant and full awareness of its meaning in this context. It brought the covenant partner into a relationship with the divine king that held forth curse and blessing— the former for breaking the covenant and the latter for keeping it. In the historical prologue to this institution of circumcision, however, God himself has taken upon his own head the responsibilities for the covenant's success (Genesis 15). In Abraham's vision in Genesis 15, God walked alone through the severed halves of various animals—a typical ancient Near Eastern treaty-making rite. Here he was calling down upon himself the same terrible fate if he should violate the treaty. So identified were these rituals of cutting animals in half that the verb *karat* ("to cut") often appears before the noun *berit* ("covenant"). As we saw earlier, ancient Near Eastern treaties spoke not of making covenants but of cutting covenants. The shedding of blood was that essential to it.

Seen in this light, circumcision is a radical example of this practice of "cutting a covenant." Here, not merely a sacrificial substitute but the believer and his male infants were to be cut. But this would not be a shedding of blood that would ultimately end their life; it would merely cut away the foreskin, which symbolized uncleanness. It was not for hygienic reasons that this was done but for the purpose of indicating that sin is inherited from Adam from the very moment of conception and that this sin must be "cut away" from the body if the person is not to be "cut off" (Gen. 17:14). To refuse this external rite was, by inference, to refuse the covenant and therefore God himself. It was to be cut off from the land of the living, to be dead in sin and a stranger to God's promises, storing up wrath for the last day.

But, as Meredith Kline demonstrates, circumcision was also consecration. In his first cutting (circumcision), Isaac was consecrated to God, but in the second cutting ordeal, where God commanded Abraham to take up the knife again, Isaac was being offered up *in his entirety* to God (Genesis 22). What a strange command and a source of speculation through the ages. But Kline explains:

> Read together in the light of fulfillment, the three cutting rituals of Genesis 15, 17, and 22 proclaim the mystery of a divine circumcision—the circumcision of God in the crucifixion of his only-begotten. Paul called it "the circumcision of Christ" (Col. 3:11). The circumcision of the infant Jesus in obedience to Genesis 17, that partial and symbolic cutting off, corresponded to the ritual of Genesis 15 as a passing of one who was divine under the curse threat of the covenant oath. That was the moment, prophetically chosen, to name him "Jesus." But it was the circumcision of Christ in crucifixion that answered to the burnt-offering of Genesis 22 as a perfecting of circumcision, a "putting off" not merely of a token part but "of the [whole] body of the flesh" (Col. 2:11 ARV), not simply a symbolic oath-cursing but a cutting off of "the body of his flesh through death" (Col. 1:22) in accursed darkness and dereliction.[4]

So the Servant was "cut off from the land of the living; for the transgressions of my people he was stricken" (Isa. 53:8 NKJV). The curses of the covenant have been executed, but on the head of a substitute, the same God who walked through the severed halves in Genesis 15. And just as this greater Son of Abraham was "cut off" only to be raised to life (foreshadowed in Isaac's being received back by Abraham), so too his people are "buried with him through baptism into death in order that, just as Christ was raised from the dead through the glory of the Father, we too may live a new life" (Rom. 6:4).

In baptism, then, the new covenant finds a fuller sign and seal for a fuller reality. Not only is a part of the body consecrated to God, but the whole person is baptized into Christ's death, burial, and resurrection: "For if we have been united together in the likeness of his death, certainly we also shall be in the likeness of his resurrection, knowing this, that our old man was crucified with him, that the body of sin might be done away with, that we should no longer be slaves of sin. . . . Now if we died with Christ, we believe that we shall also live with him, knowing that Christ, having been raised from the dead, dies no more. Death no longer has dominion over him" (Rom. 6:5–6, 8–9 NKJV). Those who are identified with Christ in baptism, then, are those over whom sin, death, and the curses of the law no longer reign. Jesus says, "Whoever tries to keep his life will lose it, and whoever loses his life will preserve it" (Luke 17:33). The bath of baptism is, like the offering of Isaac, the giving up of the whole person to being "cut off," but, also like Abraham's offering of Isaac, in it we are actually received back because a ram has been caught in the thicket. "God will provide," Abraham told his son, and so God did.

In Colossians, Paul expands on the sort of treatment he gave in Romans:

> In him [Christ] you were also circumcised with the circumcision made without hands, by putting off the body of the sins of the flesh, by the circumcision of Christ, buried with him in baptism, in which you also were raised with him through faith in the working of God, who raised him from the dead. And you, being dead in your trespasses and the uncircumcision of your flesh, he has made alive together with him, having forgiven you all trespasses, having wiped out the handwriting of requirements that was against us, which was contrary to us. And he has taken it out of the way, having nailed it to the cross.
>
> 2:11–14 NKJV

Notice the explicit parallel that Paul makes between circumcision and baptism. Jesus Christ was the Son of Abraham who was fully offered up to God as a sacrifice. Not only his foreskin but his whole body was cut off from God and his people, but he was raised to life, leaving our offenses in the grave. Our circumcision, then, is not a cutting away of the foreskin but being "buried with him in baptism." We are wholly consecrated to God because we are baptized into the faithful Son. This should give us a deeper sense of baptism, then, and of the greater reality of which it is both a sign and seal.

It is with this background that we can make more sense of the Gospels, where it is largely assumed that we know its meaning. We begin on the banks of the Jordan, where that strange character John the Baptist is gaining a wide following. We read in Scripture:

> "Behold, I send my messenger, and he will prepare the way before me. And the Lord, whom you seek, will suddenly come to his temple, even the messenger of the covenant, in whom you delight. Behold, he is coming," says the LORD of hosts. "But who can endure the day of his coming? And who can stand when he appears? For he is like a refiner's fire and like fuller's soap. He will sit as a refiner and purifier of silver; he will purify the sons of Levi, and purge them as gold and silver, that they may offer to the LORD an offering in righteousness."

This passage is not from Matthew's Gospel but from Malachi (3:1–3 NKJV)—the last biblical prophet until John the Baptist. Like Isaiah (40:3), Malachi prophesies a forerunner of the Messiah and then the Messiah himself. John the Baptist is not only the "forerunner" in view but stands in their prophetic line as prosecutors of God's covenant curses. Defending the covenant and sharply rebuking its violators, John the Baptist prepares a people for Jesus as the shadows of the law prepare the way for the reality of the gospel and the old covenant prepares to give way to the new (John 1:17). John stands in the river, baptizing for repentance, answering the people's questions about his identity ("Are you the promised prophet?") by extending one last prophetic finger toward the Coming One. In fact, it is no longer a prophetic finger, since the reality now stands before him:

> Now those who were sent were from the Pharisees. And they asked him, saying, "Why then do you baptize if you are not the Christ, nor Elijah, nor the Prophet?" John answered them, saying, "I baptize with water, but there stands One among you whom you do not know. It is he who, coming after me, is preferred before me, whose sandal strap I am not worthy to loose." . . . The next day John saw Jesus coming toward him, and said, "Behold! The Lamb of God who takes away the sin of the world! . . . I did not know him, but he who sent me to baptize with water said to me, 'Upon whom you see the Spirit descending, and remaining on him, this is he who baptizes with the Holy Spirit.'"
>
> John 1:24–27, 29, 33 NKJV

John baptized in water, preparing a people for the Messiah, but it was the Messiah himself whose baptism would not only anticipate the outpouring of the Spirit but inaugurate that outpouring. But always this baptism is overshadowed by the baptism that he himself will have to undergo (Matt. 20:22; Luke 12:50) in order for the baptism that he gives to be effective, and this is already indicated here, with the Baptist's announcement, "Behold! The Lamb of God who takes away the sin of the world!" The ram caught in the thicket, as a substitute for Isaac, appears now not as shadow but as reality.

It is in John 3 where Jesus tells the sympathetic Pharisee, Nicodemus, "Most assuredly, I say to you, unless one is born of water and the Spirit, he cannot enter the kingdom of God" (v. 5 NKJV). While we recognize a distinction, there is no separation of water baptism (the sign) and the baptism of the Spirit (the thing signified), for they are regarded already as united. Christian baptism will not differ from John's in form—both are by water. But they do differ in that John's baptism is *toward* the reality of Jesus and the kingdom, while Jesus, or rather, his disciples, baptize people *into* the reality itself. The one who baptizes with fire (judgment) and the Spirit (salvation) has arrived.

After Jesus does go through his own circumcision through crucifixion and is raised to life, he is bold to announce with divine authority, "Go into all the world and preach the gospel to every creature. He who believes and is baptized will be saved; but he who does not believe will be condemned" (Mark 16:15–16 NKJV). Here is the language again of the covenant stipulations: Those who believe and are baptized into Christ will escape the judgment. On that last day, all will be consecrated to God, as he created humanity to be, but like the Israelites in the exodus, some will go through the watery grave unharmed because they are in Christ, while the rest will be consumed in judgment just as Pharaoh and his army. On that day there will be no rebels but only those who either have a substitute or must themselves be offered up to God unto death. Similarly, Matthew records the Great Commission: "All authority has been given to me in heaven and on earth. Go therefore and make disciples of all the nations, baptizing them in the name of the Father and of the Son and of the Holy Spirit, teaching them to observe all things that I have commanded you; and lo, I am with you always, even to the end of the age" (Matt. 28:18–20 NKJV).

At Pentecost, the Spirit was poured out on all flesh—that is, young and old, male and female, rich and poor—as Peter proclaimed in the first Pentecost sermon (Acts 2:16–21). The Spirit is poured out to make the disciples witnesses to Christ, and Peter does just that: He preaches Christ as the fulfillment of the Old Testament. And what is the application part of Peter's sermon? "Now when they heard this, [the people] were cut to the heart, and said to Peter and the rest of the apostles, 'Men and brethren, what shall we do?' Then Peter said to them, 'Repent, and let every one of you be baptized in the name of Jesus Christ for the remission of sins; and you shall receive the gift of the Holy Spirit. For the promise is to you and to your children, and to all who are afar off, as many as the Lord our God will call'" (vv. 37–39 NKJV). In his first epistle, Peter tells us that Noah and the flood episode served as a type, "in which a few, that is, eight souls, were saved through water." "There is also," Peter adds, "an antitype which now saves us, namely baptism (not the removal of filth of the flesh, but the answer of a good conscience toward God), through the resurrection of Jesus Christ, who has gone into heaven and is at the right hand of God, angels and authorities and powers having been made subject to him" (1 Peter 3:21–22 NKJV).

Although it is called a bath or washing, its purpose is to wash our conscience even as the outward washing both signifies and seals. Christ so loved his church, says Paul, that he "gave himself for it, that he might sanctify and cleanse it with the washing of water by the word" (Eph. 5:25–26 NKJV). John writes:

> This is he who came by water and blood—Jesus Christ; not only by water, but by water and blood. And it is the Spirit who bears witness, because the Spirit is truth. For there are three that bear witness in heaven: the Father, the Word, and the Holy Spirit; and these three are one. And there are three that bear witness on earth: the Spirit, the water, and the blood; and these three agree as one.
>
> 1 John 5:6–8 NKJV

Notice the courtroom language here: The Spirit, the water, and the blood agreeing (as more than one witness was required in a legal case) that we are indeed no longer under judgment but are safe in Christ.

John's statement here is as profound as it is concise. While several interpretations are available, it would seem that the background of the covenant and its circumcision rite directs us to one in particular. Not only was Jesus born of water and consecrated to the Lord in circumcision on the eighth day (like Isaac), but he was also offered up on the cross. Water and blood flowed from his pierced side, certifying his death. Similarly, then, God has provided an apt sign and seal for the new covenant. Jesus "came by water and blood" and so must we. But we undergo our consecration to God by being baptized into Christ: The water and the blood belong together, just as the work of the Spirit and the Son are integrally related. We need witnesses—seals—to confirm our salvation in heaven, and we need witnesses to confirm our salvation here below, in our own experience. As with the rainbow, God looks at his covenant children with favor because they are in Christ. Whenever God's just anger is aroused at sin in this age, he remembers the rainbow. Similarly, whenever we arouse God's displeasure, he looks at the sign and seal. Luther was fond of saying that whenever the devil either tempted him to sin or filled him with fear of damnation he would cry out, "Away with you, for I am baptized!" The Trinity—Father, Son, and Holy Spirit—testifies to the "unchangeable oath" that they made to each other before the world was created for the salvation of those whom God had chosen.

But we were not involved in that eternal pact, so how could we obtain assurance and certification that we belong to God? Condescending once more, God provides not only heavenly witnesses (the Trinity) but earthly ones: "the Spirit, the water, and the blood." The Holy Spirit assures us of our salvation, but he does so through tangible means: the water and the blood. I understand this to be a reference first of all both to Jesus' new covenant consecration (baptized by John in the Jordan) and to his sacrificial death that turned aside God's wrath toward us. Second, it refers to baptism (the Spirit and water) and the Lord's Supper (the Spirit and blood), the signs and seals of the covenant of grace.

It is important for us to see that the ritual act of applying the sign and seal is not itself a work that we do to secure our destiny. Many evangelicals have a problem with sacraments precisely because they regard them chiefly as human works, but Scripture presents them as *God's* testimony to *his* work. For instance, Paul reminds us that we have been reconciled to God "not by works of righteousness which we have done, but according to his mercy he saved us, through the washing of regeneration and renewing of the Holy Spirit, whom he poured out on us abundantly through Jesus Christ our Savior, that having been justified by his grace we should become heirs according to the hope of eternal life" (Titus 3:5–7 NKJV). As with circumcision, where the sign and seal so participate in the reality that it can actually be called the covenant, such clear statements imply a synecdoche with respect to baptism. It would be arbitrary of us to regard the "washing of regeneration and renewing of the Holy Spirit" as something distinct from baptism. The same would be true of those passages in which we read commands to "be baptized, and wash away your sins, calling on the name of the Lord" (Acts 22:16 NKJV); "let every one of you be baptized in the name of Jesus Christ for the remission of sins; and you shall receive the gift of the Holy Spirit" (Acts 2:38 NKJV).

We must beware of spiritualizing or allegorizing such passages, as if what is really meant is a spiritual, inward baptism as opposed to a physical, outward baptism. When Paul says that "as many of you as were baptized into Christ have put on Christ" (Gal. 3:27 NKJV), he has all three ingredients of baptism in mind: the Spirit, the Word, and the water. We may assert that the Word brought us to saving faith, and yet we recognize that there is no amount of gospel preaching that could give us faith apart from the activity of the Spirit. In exactly the same way, Scripture refers to water baptism as the laver of regeneration and forgiveness because the sign does truly participate in the thing signified. Just as circumcision could be called "the covenant," baptism is called "the washing of regeneration."

At the same time, it would be wrong to regard the inward and outward washing as *identical,* as Paul's running polemic against the circumcision party reveals. Abraham was justified before he was circumcised, when he believed (Rom. 4:9–12), although the succeeding generations of males were circumcised on the eighth day. Apart from the Spirit's effectual working, an external cutting cannot by itself save any more than the external preaching of the gospel can. The same is true of baptism. While we must never separate the external and internal actions, we must recognize that this gift that God gives his people in the covenant must be *received.*

To reject the covenant of grace is to become not merely an unbeliever but one "who has trampled the Son of God underfoot, counted the blood of the covenant *by which he was sanctified* a common thing, and insulted the Spirit of grace" (Heb. 10:29 NKJV, emphasis added). It is the same as spurning the seal of the king attached to a royal pardon. Through their baptismal participation in the covenant, even the unregenerate are in a sense sanctified—set apart as belonging to God's people—and this fact is precisely what the writer uses as the basis for warning the latter against unbelief. The writer to the Hebrews warns covenant heirs in the new covenant not to imitate the faithless generation in the wilderness whom God barred from entering his rest: "Therefore, since a promise remains of entering his rest, let us fear lest any of you seem to have come short of it. For indeed the gospel was preached to us as well as to them; but the word which they heard did not profit them, not being mixed with faith in those who heard it" (Heb. 4:1–2 NKJV).

The sacraments have precisely the same ministry as the Word. As the Westminster Larger Catechism puts it, "The sacraments become effectual means of salvation, not by any power in themselves or any virtue derived from the piety or intention of him by whom they are administered; but only by the working of the Holy Ghost, and the blessing of Christ by whom they are instituted" (L.C., Q. 161).

Practical Questions

Obvious practical questions arise after such a treatment. First, we naturally wonder whether everybody who is baptized is thus saved. While many Christians do believe that this is the case, it seems to be a difficult position to sustain in the light of Scripture. The circle of the covenant is larger than the circle of election. Paul expressed this point to those who thought they were elect even apart from faith in Christ: "But it is not that the word of God has taken no effect. For they are not all Israel who are of Israel, nor are they all children because they are the seed of Abraham. . . . That is, those who are the children of the flesh, these are not the children of God; but the children of the promise are counted as the seed" (Rom. 9:6–8 NKJV). The preaching of the Word is still effective, even if it hardens a person who resists it (Isa. 55:11). Similarly, baptism remains a sign and seal of the covenant of grace—even if that very baptism and covenant are spurned. For these dead branches that are broken off of the Tree of Life, the bath of regeneration is made a bath of judgment, and the curses for violating God's law are now reserved for the one who has rejected his or her Substitute. Baptism into Christ, the mediator of the covenant of grace, confers eternal life, even if its efficacy is not tied to the moment that it is administered. Like a seed that sends up its shoots, some covenant children may actually be regenerated later in life, and with most, that moment is impossible to discern. But as we have seen, there is no assurance of salvation—for those baptized under the new covenant any more than those circumcised under the old—apart from faith in Jesus Christ.

A second practical question has to do with the opposition that many evangelicals see between external rites and internal realities. On one level, we have seen, it is often feared that tying baptism so closely to salvation is a denial of salvation by grace alone. On another level, the worry is that this can lead only to a dead formalism. Let's briefly tackle both concerns as we try to answer this question. First, level one. Both sacraments (baptism and the Lord's Supper) contain two parts: the sign and the thing signified. We have seen how the New Testament refers to baptism as conferring regeneration and forgiveness. However, water cannot of itself accomplish anything redemptive. (Otherwise, we would simply spray it indiscriminately in public places.) Rather, through the sign one receives the thing signified. To put it more clearly, one who has been baptized may nevertheless fall short of faith because he or she has placed confidence in the sign as an end in itself. This is what Paul and the writer to the Hebrews especially labor to make plain to Jewish Christians: You who have received the sign beware lest you fall short of trusting in Christ and all his benefits (the thing signified).

The sacraments, like the preached Word, are not opposed to grace but are in fact the very means of grace. Most of us would consider it odd to suggest that if faith comes by hearing the preached gospel, we are therefore saved by a human work. Why would that sound odd? Because we do not believe that preaching is a meritorious human work but that it is God's work through the words of an earthly ambassador. Exactly the same response pertains with respect to the sacraments: Baptism does not confer any additional degree of salvation or blessing than that which is conferred through the preached gospel. In both, the substance is the same: Christ and all his benefits. What could proclaim God's grace more fully than witnessing his promise to be a father to us and to our children as we bring our offspring to the Lord for baptism?

And this brings us to a third practical question: What about babies? Given the continuity that we have observed through this covenantal plot running from Abraham to his seed "in the fullness of time," inclusion of the believers' children is taken for granted when we arrive at the New Testament. God works with generations, not simply with individuals. So when we hear Peter's invitation, "The promise is for you and your children . . . ," or read about household baptisms in Acts, something is taken for granted that we too often do not assume. Sometimes our American individualism gets in the way of understanding this covenantal paradigm we see in Scripture. Circumcision differed from baptism only in the earthly sign, not in the thing signified. In both, what is offered and in fact given by the Spirit is exactly the same: Christ and all his benefits, however indistinctly our brothers and sisters might have understood that in the old covenant in comparison to the new. Let me summarize what I regard as the most compelling arguments for infant baptism:

1. God has brought us into a covenant of grace, and although not all members of this covenant will persevere (i.e., they are not elect and have not been regenerated), they enjoy special privileges of belonging to the covenant people. This was true of Israel, and the New Testament simply applies this to the New Testament church as well (Deut. 4:20; 28:9; Isa. 10:22; Hosea 2:23; Rom. 9:24–28; Gal. 6:16; Heb. 4:1–11; 6:4–12; 1 Peter 2:9–10).

2. Even though bringing someone under the protection of God's covenantal faithfulness does not guarantee that that person possesses true, persevering faith (Heb. 4:1–11), that does not mean it is unimportant as to whether children of believers are given the seal of the covenant.

3. Children were included in the covenant of grace in the Old Testament through the sacrament of circumcision, and in the new covenant (called the "better covenant"), God has not changed in his good intentions toward our children (Acts 2:38). Circumcision has been replaced by baptism (Col. 2:11). Therefore, our children must receive God's sign and seal of covenant ownership.

4. The children of unbelievers are unholy, but the children of believers are set apart unto God. This is a distinction not only of the Old Testament (see the Passover, Exod. 12:42–51; also the distinction between the "house of the wicked" and the "house of the righteous," especially in the psalms) but is continued in the New, where a believer's children are regarded as holy (1 Cor. 10:2). How are they marked or distinguished from unbelievers, then? By the sign and seal of the covenant.

5. Household baptisms are common in the New Testament reports of such events. Surely at least some of them included infants. If so, this would have been perfectly consistent with the Jewish understanding of the Abrahamic covenant (above, #4).

6. There is an unbroken record in church history supporting the practice of infant baptism, beginning with the earliest generations. There would surely have been a major controversy if the immediate successors of the apostles departed from apostolic practice on such a vital point. However, no such record exists.

7. If baptism were a testimony of the believer's faithfulness to the covenant, it would not be capable of being applied to those who have no faithfulness to offer. However, baptism is the work of God, not of human beings. It is not chiefly a sign of the believer's commitment to God (although it certainly entails that) but of God's commitment to call out a people for himself. Because salvation is by grace alone, God acts in salvation prior to any human choice or action (Rom. 9:12–16). Infant baptism is an extraordinary divine testimony to his prevenient grace. Consequently, it obligates those who are baptized to remain faithful to the covenant but does not make their faithfulness a prerequisite of their inclusion.

8. The reason there are so many examples in the New Testament of baptism only upon profession of faith is that the first generation is in view. As with Abraham's circumcision, an adult trusts in God's promise and is justified—and only afterward is baptized. But also like Abraham, we present our household to receive the sign and seal. No orthodox Christian body would accept the practice of baptizing *adults* without a profession of faith.

So we already come to the New Testament expecting God to work with families across generations. New Testament believers, after all, belong to the covenant of grace that God made with Abraham: "For the promise that he would be the heir of the world was not to Abraham or to his seed through the law, but through the righteousness of faith" (Rom. 4:13 NKJV). Paul elaborates: "And this I say, that the law, which was four hundred and thirty years later [than the covenant with Abraham], cannot annul the covenant that was confirmed before by God in Christ, that it should make the promise of no effect. . . . And if you are Christ's, then you are Abraham's seed, and heirs according to the promise" (Gal. 3:17, 29 NKJV).

Many people reject infant baptism because they do not believe that it is clearly commanded in the New Testament. However, this is to ignore the first half of the movie! It is to miss the point that we are children of Abraham in the same covenant of grace. It would seem, therefore, that one should believe in applying the sign and seal of the covenant to our children unless there is an obvious New Testament passage forbidding it. The only thing that has changed from Old Testament promise to New Testament fulfillment is the external sign and its extension, on the basis of prophetic fulfillment (Joel 2:28; Gal. 3:28), to females.

When we do arrive at the New Testament, we not only discover that there are no passages announcing that the children are excluded from the covenant, but we find the contrary. Adult converts are to "be baptized in the name of Jesus Christ for the remission of sins," thereby receiving "the gift of the Holy Spirit." But the very next sentence reads, "For the promise is to you and to your children" (Acts 2:38–39 NKJV). After "the Lord opened [Lydia's] heart to heed the things spoken by Paul," "she and her household were baptized" (Acts 16:14–15 NKJV). Later in the same chapter, the Philippian jailer embraces the gospel. "Sirs, what must I do to be saved?" he asks Paul and Silas. They answer, "'Believe on the Lord Jesus Christ, and you will be saved, you and your household.' . . . And immediately he and all his family were baptized" (vv. 30–31, 33 NKJV). Here is the pattern of Abraham and Isaac: The first generation of believers embraces the covenant in adulthood, after trusting the promise, while the following generations are presented for the initiation rite in their infancy.

Given the continuity of the covenant of grace in both testaments, we are not surprised to learn that when the head of the household became a believer, the children were given the mark of divine ownership. Notice how far Paul takes this in his counsel to a Christian wife of an unbelieving spouse: "For the unbelieving husband is sanctified by the wife, and the unbelieving wife is sanctified by the husband; otherwise your children would be unclean, but now they are holy" (1 Cor. 7:14 NKJV). When recognized in the light of the earlier scenes (viz., the avenging angel's "passing over" the homes of the Israelites in Egypt wherever the blood appeared on the doorpost), this fits perfectly. Paul is saying that the presence of even one believing parent is "blood on the doorpost." If believers are incorporated into Christ and his visible body along with their children, then they ought to receive God's sign and seal.

Water Is (or Should Be) Thicker than Blood

The question, Are you baptized? should be more definitive for our fellowship than whether one belongs to our ethnic, national, socioeconomic, political, or even denominational group. Sadly, the very bath that unites the visible body of Christ is the occasion for some of the sharpest divisions. It is not because Scripture is unclear or contradictory; nor is it that Scripture shows relatively little interest in this question. Rather, it is because of our own sin—both in the way we often communicate our position or because our prejudices against looking at things differently than we previously had keep us from struggling with and being overcome by God's own Word. Regardless of how one sizes up the arguments I have listed here, one hopes for a day when such topics are no longer regarded as off limits for general Christian conversation and debate but are discussed vigorously by those on various sides who share at least one point in common on the subject: It is taken seriously by Scripture and should therefore be taken seriously by us.

SEVEN

A Table in the Wilderness

"Can God spread a table in the wilderness?" the complacent generation asked, even after God had, with a mighty hand, delivered Israel from Egyptian oppression (Ps. 78:19 NRSV). In fact, the psalmist, in recounting Israel's faithlessness and God's faithfulness, includes this episode: "But they sinned even more against him by rebelling against the Most High in the wilderness. And they tested God in their heart by asking for the food of their fancy. Yes, they spoke against God: They said, 'Can God prepare a table in the wilderness? Behold, he struck the rock, so that the waters gushed out, and the streams overflowed. Can he give bread also? Can he provide meat for his people?'" (Ps. 78:17–20 NKJV).

We cannot help but see our own lives mirrored in the lives of those who had experienced firsthand God's deliverance and yet longed for Egypt, the land of their captivity. Here we have the first mention of God's covenant people as a "mixed multitude." It is not a pure church filled only with the truly regenerate but a field in which wheat and weeds grow up together. "Now the mixed multitude who were among them yielded to intense craving; so the children of Israel also wept again and said: 'Who will give us meat to eat? We remember the fish which we ate freely in Egypt, the cucumbers, the melons, the leeks, the onions, and the garlic; but now our whole being is dried up; there is nothing at all except this manna before our eyes!'" (Num. 11:4–6 NKJV). The psalmist's version of this scene contains a couple items of note in the light of our topic. First, "they tested God in their heart by asking for [a closer translation, 'demanding'] the food of their fancy."

Like undisciplined children, the redeemed Israelites demanded that every felt need be satisfied. There are hints here of Adam and Eve: "When the woman saw that the fruit of the tree was good for food and pleasing to the eye, and also desirable for gaining wisdom, she took some and ate it" (Gen. 3:6). Like Adam and Eve, Israel questioned God's provision and goodness. Either he was not good enough to desire the best for them or he was not powerful enough to get the job done, they reasoned. Promises, promises. What they wanted was not a good promise but a good meal. All they knew was that their cravings were not being satisfied. They missed Egypt. There is no sense here that God had liberated them from a horrible slavery and that they belonged to him now as his people. Imagine that: After God rescues his chosen people and seeks eagerly to make his dwelling among them, this is the thanks he receives!

Still, it is a mirror of our own lives as God's people today. We too are a "mixed multitude," consisting of genuine believers and unbelievers, but even we who believe are double-minded, finding ourselves longing for the very world out of which God has rescued us. Our pilgrimage to the City of God is often so dry, dusty, and difficult while we pass the nations on highways of apparent plenty that we long for the immediate satisfaction of short-term goals. "Yes, they spoke against God: They said, 'Can God prepare a table in the wilderness? Behold, he struck the rock, so that the waters gushed out, and the streams overflowed. Can he give bread also? Can he provide meat for his people?'" (Ps. 78:19–20 NKJV).

It has been announced to us the reality to which this sign in the wilderness pointed: the Rock who was struck for us in the wilderness, so that the living water would cleanse and sustain us. Paul draws this parallel: "Moreover, brethren, I do not want you to be unaware that all our fathers were under the cloud, all passed through the sea, all were baptized into Moses in the cloud and in the sea, all ate the same spiritual food, and all drank the same spiritual drink. For they drank of that spiritual Rock that followed them, and that Rock was Christ" (1 Cor. 10:1–4 NKJV). As water and blood poured from his side, so too he has instituted baptism and the Lord's Supper for sustaining us. God *can* prepare a table in the wilderness, and he *has*. The problem is that we, like the first-century Corinthians and the rebellious generation in the wilderness to whom he compares them, have our own shopping list. If God will only do this or if he will only show himself in that area or decision of my life, solve this problem or keep that terrible likelihood from coming to pass, we will continue to claim him. But what happens when our lives unravel? Do we not respond just as the psalmist and Paul indicate? We have been baptized into Christ. "Behold, he struck the rock, so that the waters gushed out, and the streams overflowed," the Israelites recalled. "Can he give bread also?" He says he is present, but we demand a sign.

What is so remarkable is that God not only continually spares his rebellious, complacent people but that he actually condescends to meet their request. He did provide bread in addition to the water, and he does provide not only onetime baptism but the perpetual use of the Lord's

Supper to sustain us on our journey to the Promised Land. "You prepare a table before me in the presence of my enemies; you anoint my
head with oil; my cup runs over. Surely goodness and mercy shall follow me all the days of my life; and I will dwell in the house of the Lord
forever" (Ps. 23:5–6 NKJV). Thus far we have seen not only the internal
symmetry between the Old and New Testament administrations of the
one covenant of grace; we have also recognized how the New Testament
itself draws the parallel between circumcision and baptism. The same
is true of Passover and the Lord's Supper: "For indeed Christ, our
Passover, was sacrificed for us. Therefore let us keep the feast" (1 Cor.
5:7–8 NKJV). That feast is kept in the new covenant, as Paul makes clear
later in his epistle, by the sacrament of Holy Communion.

But this parallel will not strike home unless we have some reminder
of what we are dealing with in the Passover meal of the Old Testament.

Institution of Passover

In response to Pharaoh's refusal to let God's people go, God sent
plagues—each answering to one of the chief gods of the Egyptian pan-
theon. After claiming victory over Egypt's idols, God again came to
Pharaoh through Moses, and Pharaoh still refused to submit to the terms
of a truce. So just as Pharaoh had claimed God's firstborn, Israel, God
announced his plans to claim Egypt's firstborn in every house, from
Pharaoh's firstborn to the firstborn of the animals. This would be a tac-
tical strike of massive proportions, since the firstborn in a family was
the heir of the entire household.

That night, God instituted the Passover:

> Now the Lord spoke to Moses and Aaron in the land of Egypt, saying,
> "This month shall be your beginning of months; it shall be the first month
> of the year to you. Speak to all the congregation of Israel, saying: 'On the
> tenth day of this month every man shall take for himself a lamb, accord-
> ing to the house of his father, a lamb for a household. . . . Your lamb shall
> be without blemish, a male of the first year. . . . Then the whole assembly
> of the congregation of Israel shall kill it at twilight. And they shall take
> some of the blood and put it on the two doorposts and on the lintel of the
> houses where they eat it. Then they shall eat the flesh on that night; roasted
> in fire, with unleavened bread and with bitter herbs they shall eat it. . . .
> And thus you shall eat it: with a belt on your waist, your sandals on your
> feet, and your staff in your hand. So you shall eat it in haste. This is the
> Lord's Passover.'"

Exodus 12:1–3, 5–8, 11 NKJV

On the night of the judgment event itself God instituted a rite for future generations, so that they could participate together with their fathers and mothers in this redemptive event. Just as God told them, by morning the firstborn of Egypt were dead, but those Israelites (and perhaps some believing Egyptians) who had placed the blood on their doorposts were delivered.

It is important to notice that the rite of Passover was instituted on the very night that Egypt's firstborns were delivered up to judgment. God did not institute a ritual for imitating or celebrating the cycle of nature, nor did he institute a memorial to a great idea or universal moral principle. It is a rite of commemoration of and participation in a redemptive-historical event that God brought about in the concrete existence of a particular people. Furthermore, it is not an event that grows up over time, like the legend of Santa Claus from the philanthropic exploits of St. Nicholas. The sacrament is instituted on the same night as the event. Passover is the oldest and most important festival in the Hebrew calendar, as it fell on the night that the firstborns were claimed and it anticipated the most significant event in Old Testament history: the exodus from Egypt.

Institution of the Lord's Supper

The parallels of Passover and the Last Supper are fairly obvious. In fact, Paul writes, "Therefore purge out the old leaven, that you may be a new lump, since you truly are unleavened. For indeed Christ, our Passover, was sacrificed for us. Therefore let us keep the feast" (1 Cor. 5:7–8 NKJV). On the first day of the Feast of Unleavened Bread, we read that "the disciples came to Jesus, saying to him, 'Where do you want us to prepare for you to eat the Passover?'" (Matt. 26:17 NKJV). Jesus directed them to a certain man's house, noting that "my time is at hand" (v. 18). The institution of the Supper follows:

> And as they were eating, Jesus took bread, blessed it and broke it, and gave it to the disciples and said, "Take, eat; this is my body." Then he took the cup, and gave thanks, and gave it to them, saying, "Drink from it, all of you. For this is my blood of the new covenant, which is shed for many for the remission of sins. But I say to you, I will not drink of this fruit of the vine from now on until that day when I drink it new with you in my Father's kingdom."
>
> verses 26–29 NKJV

Like Passover, the event and the institution of this sacramental rite occur on the same night. Paul notes this: "that the Lord Jesus on the same night in which he was betrayed" instituted the supper (1 Cor. 11:23 NKJV). When the Israelites ate the unblemished, firstborn, male lamb with wine and unleavened bread, they were not only celebrating God's act that night of delivering their firstborn children, but they were having held out to them the greater substitution to come. Instead of sacrificing a lamb, putting its blood on the doorposts, and then eating the flesh inside the house, God himself would offer up his own Son as the firstborn lamb.

Luke's Gospel illuminates Matthew's account:

> When the hour had come, [Jesus] sat down, and the twelve apostles with him. Then he said to them, "With fervent desire I have desired to eat this Passover with you before I suffer; for I say to you, I will no longer eat of it until it is fulfilled in the kingdom of God." Then he took the cup, and gave thanks, and said, "Take this and divide it among yourselves; for I say to you, I will not drink of the fruit of the vine until the kingdom of God comes." And he took bread, gave thanks and broke it, and gave it to them, saying, "This is my body which is given for you; do this in remembrance of me." Likewise he also took the cup after supper, saying, "This cup is the new covenant in my blood, which is shed for you. But behold, the hand of my betrayer is with me on the table."
>
> 22:14–21 NKJV

There is a definite divine strategy for instituting the supper on this night, "when the hour had come"—the hour of the firstborn, spotless Lamb being delivered over to the judgment in the place of sinners. Although the disciples were miles away from recognizing what was about to happen, even though Jesus had been talking about the crucifixion to come in Jerusalem, Jesus loved his disciples and clung to them this night as he knew that this would be the last night he would spend in their company. It is precisely this communion that the Supper would both continue and anticipate in its full expression, the marriage supper of the Lamb. "For as often as you eat this bread and drink this cup, you proclaim the Lord's death till he comes," Paul writes (1 Cor. 11:26 NKJV).

In all of these accounts, the words of institution are the same: Jesus takes the bread, breaks and distributes it to them with the words, "This is my body which is given for you," and then he does the same with the wine: "This cup is the new covenant in my blood, which is shed for you." Here we meet up again with that precocious term *synecdoche*. You will recall that this is what happens when one refers to the part as if it were the whole. Circumcision is called "the covenant," the Passover meal is called "the Lord's Passover" (literally, "passing over"), just as baptism is called "regeneration" and "the forgiveness of sins." The signs and seals of the covenant so participate in the reality of the covenant itself that they are expressed as if they were the reality. Here too, then, Jesus calls the bread his body, and the wine he calls his "blood of the new covenant," or "the new covenant in my blood."

All of this raises the question, then, as to the meaning of "this is my body" and "this is my blood." Do the bread and the wine actually become the body and blood of Christ? Or are they merely symbols of his body and blood? Or is there a different explanation of these words?

The Nature of the Supper

At the outset, it is important to state my prejudices up front, since nobody comes to the Bible with a clean slate but rather interprets it in the light of the teachers that one has had over the years. That is why there is a Roman Catholic view of the Supper, a Lutheran view, a memorialist view, and a Reformed view. I am convinced that the Reformed view makes the most sense of the biblical material, but I am always open to being challenged by my brothers and sisters in other traditions. My interpretation of the following passages, then, will be a characteristically Reformed one. "Buyers, beware!"

According to the Roman Catholic view, the words "this is my body," "this is my blood" mean, literally, that this bread, after it has been consecrated by a priest, is no longer bread but the true, physical body of Jesus Christ. In his ordination, the priest is given the power to make this transformation in the elements. Here a distinction is made, ever since Thomas Aquinas, between "substance" and "accidents," according to which one may say, "I know that it looks like bread, tastes like bread, feels like bread (i.e., has the 'accidents' of bread), but in substance it is the very body of Christ." While there are a number of variants on this view in contemporary Roman Catholicism, this is the one that still receives official support as dogma.

On the other end of the spectrum of the debate have been the Anabaptists, who regard baptism and the Supper as a pledge of the believer's enlisting among the faithful. It is a pledge of the believer's commitment rather than a pledge of divine acceptance. Just a slightly less radical view is expressed by Ulrich Zwingli, the sixteenth-century reformer of Zurich, who was able to reach agreement with Luther on every doctrinal point except the nature of the Supper. Zwingli held that the words "this is my body," "this is my blood" meant, "this represents my body," "this represents my blood." The bread and the wine, like a wedding ring, represent but do not in any way confer or participate in the body and blood of Christ. In Communion, then, we are not receiving Jesus Christ in any way that is different from our ordinary exercise of faith. It is all spiritual: a memorial of Jesus' sacrifice. The Communion service, then, offers an opportunity for believers to reaffirm their loyalty to God and his people.

Between these positions lie the Lutheran and Reformed (Calvinistic) interpretations, and their differences continue to divide classic, confessional bodies, despite attempts at reconciliation over the centuries. Although it is impossible to do justice to each position here, we might summarize these two briefly. Lutherans insist that their position takes the words of institution seriously: Jesus is physically present at every altar where the words of institution are invoked. Both believers and unbelievers receive the body and blood of Christ in, with, and under the bread and wine. Their concern here is to guard the objectivity of the sacrament: The physical body and blood of Christ are truly received by believer and unbeliever alike, since Jesus is physically present at the altar.

The Reformed insist that they are no less concerned about taking the words of the institution seriously. "This is my body," "this is my blood" cannot be explained away. However, they must be interpreted according to ordinary rules of language and the teaching of Scripture in other places. Thus, the Reformed understand the words of institution to be examples again of a synecdoche, which, as we have seen, is common when it comes to sacraments. In every sacrament there are two things: a sign and a thing signified.

In baptism, then, there is water (sign) and regeneration (the thing signified). Similarly, in Communion, there are bread and wine (signs) and Christ and all of his benefits (the thing signified). This is called a "sacramental union," in which the sign and the thing signified are so related that one may speak of baptism as regeneration without simply identifying the former with the latter, and one may speak of the Supper as feeding upon Christ according to both natures, God and man, even though the bread and the wine are not and do not contain the physical body and blood of Christ. Jesus Christ bodily ascended and will return to earth one day. This truth disallows the view that he is bodily present *on earth* until that time. Otherwise, what does it mean to say that our Savior is even now fully human, with a body like ours?

Instead, the Holy Spirit—who plays a prominent role especially in Paul's explanation of the sacraments—overcomes the distance between us and the risen Savior, making that sacramental union effective. Because of his mysterious working, believers truly receive the same body that was born of Mary and the same blood that was poured out on Calvary. The Reformed emphasize the mystery at this point. We simply do not know how this happens, but Scripture affirms that it does. Though reigning at God's right hand, the true and natural body of Christ and all his benefits are given to us as the empty mouth of faith receives the thing signified just as the empty mouth of flesh receives the bread and the wine.

This is not to suggest that the Holy Spirit plays a minor role in non-Reformed understandings. Rather, this role is especially accented in the Reformed understanding as the way in which Scripture explains how the physical body of Christ can be spatially absent "till he comes again" (1 Cor. 11:26) and yet believers are said to truly feed on his crucified body and shed blood through Holy Communion (1 Cor. 10:16).

Even more fully than those who ate the Passover lamb, feeding on the substitute whose death was their life, those who receive the Supper in faith do not just receive the bread and the wine; in receiving them they feed on Christ in heaven by faith. The thing signified (Christ and all his benefits) is not present either in the place of bread and wine (Roman Catholic), or in, with, and under the bread and wine (Lutheran), or merely symbolically (memorialist). It is present in the sacrament inasmuch as the Holy Spirit is able to unite us to Christ in heaven. It is therefore not a mere memorial or a pledge of our fidelity but is first and foremost a means of grace and a pledge of God's faithfulness. But just as the unbelieving generation in the wilderness received circumcision and Passover but were barred from entering God's rest because of unbelief, only believers receive that which is promised (the thing signified) in the sacrament.

The Benefits of the Supper

The New Testament in various texts clearly outlines the benefits of receiving the Supper in faith, but the lodestar is found in Paul's epistles, especially in 1 Corinthians. First, the redemption of Israel in the Red Sea crossing through identification with Moses is correlated with New Testament baptism through identification with Christ. Even under Moses, the ultimate identification was already with Christ: "All ate the same spiritual food, and all drank the same spiritual drink. For they drank of that spiritual Rock that followed them, and that Rock was Christ" (1 Cor. 10:3–4 NKJV). These fathers in the wilderness were given an anchor for God's promised future. "But with most of them God was not well pleased, for their bodies were scattered in the wilderness" (v. 5

NKJV). They failed to look beyond the sign (a miraculous supply of water) to receive Christ himself. Like the preached gospel and baptism, the Supper remains the Supper whether anyone believes, and yet the reality is not received apart from faith.

When received in faith, the Supper's benefits are, in substance, the same as those communicated through preaching and baptism: Christ and all his benefits. The person and work of Christ are received and enjoyed.

A likely response to this might be, "Why do I need to receive Christ and all his benefits again and again? I accepted Christ once and that's sufficient." One might further wonder, "What if a believer doesn't take the Supper on a given occasion. Is that person somehow less forgiven, less united to Christ?" These are great questions. But comparing the Supper to the preached Word is helpful here, as it was in considering baptism. I have never heard anyone say, "Because I accepted Christ years ago, I have no need of hearing the gospel in a sermon." Saints and sinners at the same time, our faith is never so strong that it can stand without the supports God has given it. One can never reach a point in the Christian life where the gospel is sufficiently understood and embraced that the preaching of God's good news is no longer required. Faith is not just a matter of having all our facts right but of being inwardly persuaded of their truth as the Holy Spirit witnesses to his Word. Even if we could amass sufficient information, our faith would be weak apart from God's constantly persuasive rhetoric. Precisely the same is true of the Supper. Although baptism is a sign and a seal never to be repeated, the Supper is often repeated because it conveys the same gospel. If baptism is a means of initiating grace, the Supper is a means of persevering grace—not because it gives us an additional ingredient or a power not present in preaching or baptism but because it is a perpetual ratification of God's peace treaty with his people. Faith is created by the preached gospel and confirmed and strengthened by the sacraments. God works supernaturally through natural, created things.

The church of Corinth was renowned for its vices, chief among them sectarian strife, sexual immorality, disorder in worship, and selfishness. "Therefore when you come together in one place, it is not to eat the Lord's Supper" but to have a party. It was "each man for himself," and all of this threatened the unity and community of Christ's body there. So Paul repeats the Lord's institution of the Supper and calls the people to examine themselves. He writes, "Therefore whoever eats this bread or drinks this cup of the Lord in an unworthy manner will be guilty of the body and blood of the Lord. . . . For he who eats and drinks in an unworthy manner eats and drinks judgment to himself, not discerning the Lord's body" (1 Cor. 11:27, 29 NKJV). Notice the integral union of the sign and the thing signified: To sin against the bread and cup is to sin against the body and the blood. In order for that statement to hold up syntactically, one cannot simply dissolve the sign into the thing signified (as in the Roman Catholic view), for they are clearly distinct in Paul's mind: The bread and wine are one thing, the body and blood are something else. Nevertheless, they are not separated (as in the memorialist view) but are bound by Word and Spirit, so that the physical eating of the bread and wine in an unworthy manner constitutes the eating and drinking of God's wrath for "not discerning the Lord's body" (v. 29). Some even died because of their wickedness at the Lord's Table.

Some have used Paul's exhortation to self-examination in a manner that actually undermines the very point of the sacrament, as if Communion were a reward rather than a means of grace. The context of these verses makes abundantly clear how important it was that the Corinthians not come to the Supper with so little respect for the sign or that which is signified. Here is a sacrament, says Paul, that testifies to and in fact confirms and strengthens the unity of Christ's body, and the church is riddled with division and strife. Here is a sacrament that signifies and seals the believer's union with Christ, that gives the body and blood of Christ, and yet they are uniting their bodies to prostitutes and adulterers. Spiritual adultery is also in view: How can one enjoy communion with Christ and participate in pagan rituals? "Therefore, my beloved, flee from idolatry. I speak as to wise men; judge for yourselves what I say. The cup of blessing which we bless, is it not the communion of the blood of Christ? The bread which we break, is it not the communion of the body of Christ? For we, being many, are one bread and one body; for we all partake of that one bread" (1 Cor. 10:14–17 NKJV).

The word here for "communion" is *koinonia*, which can also be translated "fellowship" or, better yet, "participation." It is the perfect word for this "sacramental union" of the sign and the thing signified. In receiving Holy Communion, believers share in Christ's true body and blood and also share together in his covenantal body, the church. We cannot identify with Christ apart from our identification with his church, nor can we truly receive the benefits of this sacrament apart from personal faith in Christ. The communion occurs through the ministration of the church, but it derives its efficacy only through the powerful working of the Holy Spirit.

In this covenant assembly, where God takes the judgment seat, believers are not only acquitted and justified because of Christ; they are also assured that God has done this *for them* in particular through the internal witness of the Spirit (Rom. 8:16–17; Heb. 10:15), baptism ("the water"), and the Lord's Supper ("the blood"). There is a triple seal of the King on the treaty of our redemption. So one benefit of the sacraments in general and Communion in particular is that we can respond to the accusations of Satan, and our own consciences, with the royal pledge: "I have been sealed with the Holy Spirit as a deposit on my future redemption" (Eph. 1:13–14; 4:30, author's translation); sealed in baptism and regularly confirmed through the communion of Christ's body and blood.

Ultimately, the Supper is not merely a benefit to us as individuals but to us as members of Christ and therefore of each other. The sacraments are integral to the unity of Christ's body, says Paul: "For as the body is one and has many members, but all the members of that one body, being many, are one body, so also is Christ. For by one Spirit we were all baptized into one body—whether Jews or Greeks, whether slaves or free— and have all been made to drink into one Spirit" (1 Cor. 12:12–13 NKJV). At a time when we seek so many alternatives to Christian unity, recovery of frequent Communion and an understanding of its significance could once again strengthen the brittle walls of our earthly fellowship.

Taking Advantage of God's Provision

As with baptism, the Lord's Supper has fallen on some hard times in contemporary Christian circles. On one hand, it is attended with an idolatrous veneration of the signs as the very embodiment of God; on the other, a vague sentimentality reigns. In our day, there is a frantic search for the sacred, for a touch from God, for experience of the transcendent. In this chapter, we have argued that when the table is set in the wilderness, along with the preaching of the gospel, we are witnesses to and recipients of the genuine "signs and wonders" ministry. "I would rather adore the mystery than explain it," Calvin wisely concluded.[1]

We do know this, however: In this covenant, through the ministry of Word and sacrament, we have been "once enlightened [the early term for baptism], and have tasted the heavenly gift, and have become partakers of the Holy Spirit, and have tasted the good word of God and the powers of the age to come" (Heb. 6:4–5 NKJV). In this inner sanctuary of the Triune God, the three witnesses above and the three witnesses below agree in confirming our share in the inheritance of Christ. In our day, when people are longing for some sign from God, some sense of his presence, some token of his having accepted them despite the weakness of their faith and obedience, how can we withhold this divine testimony from believing and repentant sinners? Here, at this table, the holy One whose mere voice sent terror into Israel's bones clothes himself in humility, as he did two thousand years ago. Here we worship at the heavenly

Zion, not at the earthly Sinai that burned with fire. Then, as now, the unclothed God of majesty and power would have sent us running from God's presence, but he has become flesh of our flesh. And even now, he gives his body as the Bread of Life. Like the recently liberated Israelites, we too find ourselves asking, sometimes cynically, "Can God spread a table in this wilderness?" That was the question that the Jews asked Jesus, as they demanded the food they craved:

> They said to him, "What sign will you perform then, that we may see it and believe you? What work will you do? Our fathers ate the manna in the desert; as it is written, 'He gave them bread from heaven to eat.'" Then Jesus said to them, "Most assuredly, I say to you, Moses did not give you the bread from heaven, but my Father gives you the true bread from heaven. For the bread of God is he who comes down from heaven and gives life to the world. . . . I am the bread of life. He who comes to me shall never hunger, and he who believes in me shall never thirst. . . . If anyone eats of this bread, he will live forever; and the bread that I shall give is my flesh, which I shall give for the life of the world. . . . Your fathers ate the manna in the wilderness, and are dead. This is the bread which comes down from heaven, that one may eat of it and not die. . . . Most assuredly, I say to you, unless you eat the flesh of the Son of Man and drink his blood, you have no life in you. Whoever eats my flesh and drinks my blood has eternal life, and I will raise him up at the last day. For my flesh is food indeed, and my blood is drink indeed."
>
> John 6:30–33, 35, 51, 49–50, 53–55 NKJV

Entering the heavenly Holy of Holies through the torn curtain of Jesus' body, we behold the New Eden's Tree of Life, Noah's rainbow, the divine flame walking alone between the sacrifice's severed halves, Abraham's circumcision, the blood on the doorpost, the true Israel's pillar of cloud by day and fire by night, the water and blood flowing from the Messiah's side! Maybe the good news is for others but not for me, we sometimes think—until God sends his three witnesses. "Lift up your hearts!" he invites. "We lift them up to the Lord," we answer. "Oh, taste and see that the LORD is good!" (Ps. 34:8 NKJV).

Part 3

Our Reasonable Service: Getting Involved in the Drama

EIGHT

Tasting the Powers of the Age to Come

At a couple of points along our journey, we have recalled Hebrews 6 and its indication of the sort of thing that happens when God gathers his people into his church. Professing Christians, on the verge of apostasy due to persecutions, are solemnly warned about rejecting the covenant and its blessings. Here we learn that those who belong to the covenant community have been "enlightened"—the ancient church's term for baptism—"have tasted the heavenly gift" (the Supper), "have become partakers of the Holy Spirit," and "have tasted the good word of God and the powers of the age to come" (vv. 4–5 NKJV).

Tasting the powers of the age to come is a significant aspect of worship, as it is of the Christian pilgrimage itself. The church, through its divinely ordained means, becomes the locus for this remaking of sinners by the power of the Spirit. But what does it mean to taste the powers of the age to come? This is a question about what is often called "eschatology." While many standard theological texts tend to regard eschatology as the end of the book, since it is the end of history and the beginning of God's unchallenged reign forever, there has been a fresh appreciation for the importance of eschatology for our understanding of God's redemptive plan in general. In other words, eschatology is not only about what happens in the future but is concerned also with what has happened and is happening. Eschatology is attentive to God's unfolding plot from beginning to end, and it answers the question, For what can I hope?

In this chapter, I will try to demonstrate just how important eschatology is to our understanding of the most practical issues of worship.

Two Ages

"This age" and "the age to come" mark the two epochs of God's work in human history, the former lasting from creation to the return of Christ, when the latter will consummate God's everlasting reign. Too often, Christians have drawn too sharp a contrast between this world and the other world of heaven, as if the earth will be destroyed and believers will escape into a realm of pure spirit, with clouds and harps. This is a "spatialization" of heaven—in other words, thinking in terms of space rather than in terms of God's eschatological reign over all reality. Instead of pitting heaven against earth, however, Scripture contrasts reality under the present rule of sin and death and the coming reality in the consummation. Jesus uses this distinction. Those who forsake all for the kingdom will "receive a hundredfold now in this age [aeon] . . . and in the age [aeon] to come eternal life" (Mark 10:30 NRSV). Jesus speaks of the judgment "at the end of the age" (Matt. 13:40 NRSV) and refers to those who will not be forgiven "either in this age or in the age to come" (Matt. 12:32 NRSV). He distinguishes between "those who belong to this age" and those who have "a place in that age and in the resurrection from the dead" (Luke 20:34–35 NKJV). In fact, the latter are "children of the resurrection" who can never die again (v. 36). "The harvest is the end of the age." As "the weeds are collected and burned up with fire, so will it be at the end of the age" (Matt. 13:39–40 NRSV).

The writer to the Hebrews also employs this contrast in the text already cited (Heb. 6:4–5). Paul especially develops this two-age eschatology. He speaks of "the debater of this age" (1 Cor. 1:20 NRSV) and "the wisdom of this age" and "the rulers of this age" (1 Cor. 2:6 NKJV) as hostile to the gospel. Satan is "the god of this world [age]" (2 Cor. 4:4) only in an eschatological sense—that is, only in the sense that we still await the final judgment of Satan and his banishment along with all that is set in opposition to God's just reign over his creation. Demas is said to have deserted Paul because he was "in love with this present world [age]" (2 Tim. 4:10). At the same time, already—because of his victory in the cross and resurrection—Jesus is raised "above every name that is named, not only *in this age* but also in the *age to come*" (Eph. 1:21 NRSV, emphasis added).

In reality, then, there are three ages to Paul's eschatology: "before the ages" (1 Cor. 2:7), "in this age" (Eph. 1:21), and "in the age(s) to come" (Eph. 1:21). God's *eternal decree* ("before the ages") is realized *historically* in the other two ages. "In the present age" believers "wait for the blessed hope and manifestation of the glory of our great God and Savior, Jesus Christ" (Titus 2:13 NRSV).

So sin and evil cannot be attributed to the world itself, since that would be to impugn God's character as the good Creator of a creation that he pronounced good. Rather, it is the dominion of sin and evil as a result of human rebellion that marks this present age and its elimination that marks the age to come. We are not looking forward to the end of the world but to the end of the world *as we know it,* in its bondage to this fallen age, so that the whole creation will one day share in the bodily resurrection of Christ's co-heirs (Rom. 8:18–27).

Having said all of this, however, a tension begins to emerge. On one hand, Scripture assures believers that they have already passed from death to life, that they have already "put on Christ" in baptism and have been raised with him in newness, seated with him in the heavenlies. They were enemies, but now they are God's friends and children. They were in bondage to sin and guilt, but now they are liberated to serve God and are justified freely by God's grace. That future verdict of the day of judgment is announced already here and now, as believers are already declared righteous. Furthermore, they were characterized by unrighteousness according to the image of fallen Adam but are now being conformed to the image of Christ. This is the rescripting that has made believers definitively new. At the same time, they continue to sin and find unbelief, hypocrisy, and self-righteousness even in their noblest thoughts and deeds. In other words, they live in the wilderness, between the exodus and the Promised Land, redeemed but not redeemed, saved but not saved, liberated but not liberated. And despite the fact that their blindness has been healed, they still "see in a mirror, dimly, but then face to face" (1 Cor. 13:12 NKJV).

Biblical scholars call this liminal space in between these two ages the "already-not yet." The "already" aspect assures us that God's future—his "age to come"—has actually dawned even in "this present evil age." Jesus Christ has obeyed the law in our place, propitiated God's just wrath in his own body, and has been raised in victory on the last. Jesus' resurrection is the "silver bullet" in the heart of Satan, sin, and death. Or to push the analogy, it is the incoming missile from the age to come, exploding in this present age to begin the series of events that will conclude with our Savior's return in judgment and the restoration of the cosmos. The analogy that Paul uses above derives from agriculture. The "firstfruits" of the harvest were eagerly anticipated, since they would end months of wondering what the whole harvest would be like that year. Everyone would know whether it was a good or bad year. So Paul writes:

> But now Christ is risen from the dead, and has become the firstfruits of those who have fallen asleep. For since by man came death, by man also

came the resurrection of the dead. For as in Adam all die, even so in Christ all shall be made alive. But each one in his own order: Christ the first-fruits, afterward those who are Christ's at his coming. Then comes the end, when he delivers the kingdom to God the Father, when he puts an end to all rule and all authority and power. For he must reign till he has put all enemies under his feet. The last enemy that will be destroyed is death.

1 Corinthians 15:20–26 NKJV

Believers are already assured that they belong to the age to come— even now, because Christ's resurrection is the beginning of their own. This new life begins inside us, raising us from spiritual death, and then will reclaim us from physical death when we are raised on the last day. In Christ's resurrection, we recognize the first day of the age to come, and we are able to discern from the quality of his person and work what will characterize us as his body when that future age is fully realized.

But now it is the already and not yet, without any resolution into one or the other. This is where we are tempted to become lazy and reduce our eschatology to either pole. This affects worship tremendously, both in terms of the daily offering of our lives to God's service and the weekly worship in God's presence. Those who emphasize the already to the detriment of the not yet represent an "over-realized eschatology," while those who downplay the already in favor of the dominance of the not yet represent an "under-realized eschatology." The following section contrasts these extremes and tries to demonstrate how we can hold the two in better tension.

Contrasting Eschatologies and Their Implications for Worship

Worship encompasses so many different aspects of our faith and life that we can only briefly discuss a few of the most notable areas: how we understand the church as the kingdom of God and the individual believer as a citizen of that kingdom today; evangelism and church growth; the Christian life; and then finally weekly worship more specifically.

The Church and the Believer in the Kingdom of God

The age to come has broken into this present evil age in a definitive manner. John the Baptist came announcing, "The kingdom of heaven is at hand" (Matt. 3:2 NKJV). Jesus identifies the wheat as "the sons of the kingdom" in contrast to the weeds (Matt. 13:38). The new birth makes one a citizen of the kingdom (John 3:3, 5).

When the seventy who had been sent out returned to Jesus, they "returned with joy, saying, 'Lord, even the demons are subject to us in your name,'" to which Jesus replied, "I saw Satan fall like lightning from heaven. Behold, I give you the authority to trample on serpents and scorpions, and over all the power of the enemy, and nothing shall by any means hurt you. Nevertheless do not rejoice in this, that the spirits are subject to you, but rather rejoice because your names are written in heaven" (Luke 10:17–20 NKJV). This was one of those rare moments in our Lord's ministry when he was actually encouraged by his disciples. "Serpents and scorpions" refer figuratively to Satan and his minions. In the next chapter, Jesus tells the multitude, "But if I cast out demons with the finger of God, surely the kingdom of God has come upon you. When a strong man, fully armed, guards his own palace, his goods are in peace. But when a stronger than he comes upon him and overcomes him, he takes from him all his armor in which he has trusted, and divides his spoils" (Luke 11:20–22 NKJV).

Jesus has come to bind the strong man (Satan), scattering his armies (exorcism of demons), and will return finally one day to cleanse his temple fully so that the whole earth will be filled with the glory of God. His kingdom is present even now. And yet, it is not consummated. As real as it is in its present form on earth, it is still the kingdom present in the wilderness (like the tabernacle) rather than as a permanent settlement (like the temple). When Pilate demanded whether Jesus was king, the Lord replied in a manner that showed how different his dominion was from that which the Jews of his day expected: "'My kingdom is not of this world. If my kingdom were of this world, my servants would fight, so that I should not be delivered to the Jews; but *now* my kingdom is not from here.' Pilate therefore said to him, 'Are you a king then?' Jesus answered, 'You say rightly that I am a king. For this cause I was born, and for this cause I have come into the world'" (John 18:36–37 NKJV, emphasis added).

It is with this in mind that the risen Jesus commissions his disciples: "All authority in heaven and on earth has been given to me. Therefore go and make disciples" (Matt. 28:18–19). Jesus rules over a *kingdom of grace*, not yet a *kingdom of glory*. Just as he came in humiliation, suffering, and weakness, the kingdom advances not through the noisy or violent clashes of guns and tanks, nor through legislating the transformation of any earthly nation into God's chosen people. It does not come to earth in such a way that people can say, "Here it is! There it is!" Jesus cautions (Matt. 24:23–28). But when Jesus returns to earth, it will no longer be to offer his treaty of peace. The day of salvation will give way to the day of judgment. "Then they will see the Son of Man coming in the clouds with great power and glory" (Mark 13:26 NKJV), as the quiet kingdom of grace will become the ominous kingdom of glory, and the reign from heaven will be consummated upon the earth. God's will shall be done on earth as it is in heaven.

So this already-not yet eschatology regards the believer today as a pilgrim under the cross, walking toward the Promised Land. Before conversion, he or she was a transgressor rather than a pilgrim, living in a state of sin. Now, he or she is in a state of grace, awaiting the state of glory. There is the already: "For in that he put all in subjection under him, he left nothing that is not put under him," followed immediately by the not yet: "But now we do not yet see all things put under him," concluding with the already once more: "But we see Jesus, who was made a little lower than the angels, for the suffering of death crowned with glory and honor, that he, by the grace of God, might taste death for everyone" (Heb. 2:8–9 NKJV). Believers never live in either the already or the not yet by itself but always in that in-between world, moving back and forth between these two realities that mark our present travels.

In an over-realized eschatology, however, the believer is regarded not as a justified pilgrim under the cross, walking toward the Promised Land, but as a conqueror in glory, reigning over the Canaanites (unbelievers) in the New Jerusalem (often identified in history with one's own nation or group). Here, Christ's kingdom is entirely manifest, observable to the naked eye. It is not through the ordinary means of grace that he extends his kingdom, like a mustard seed's branches stretching around the world. Rather, it is through the immediate, obvious manifestation of God in his glory among us. The mission of the church today, in that perspective, is to "redeem culture" and make it subservient to God's reign. In this perspective, Christ is forced to recant and to tell Pilate that his kingdom now is very much of this world. Christians are not to view themselves as pilgrims in a weary land but as kings in the Promised Land, judging the world and ushering in divine government.

In an under-realized eschatology, on the other hand, the believer and the church generally are regarded neither as a pilgrim under the cross walking toward the Promised Land, nor as a conqueror in glory living in the Promised Land, but as defeated and awaiting escape from the world altogether. While the already-not yet eschatology recognizes believers in a state of grace (simultaneously justified and sinful) and an over-realized eschatology sees them in a state of glory (exaltation), an under-realized eschatology views them in a status quo (humiliation). If the already-not yet approach lives in the tension of cross and resurrection, and an over-realized eschatology lives in the resurrection without the cross, the under-realized approach lives in the cross without the resurrection. God's kingdom is viewed as an entirely future reality. One should only expect defeat and disappointment in the present, as it makes us long for the future. The kingdom's mission today, in this perspective, is survival.

Over-realized types tend to think that the judgment of the world begins now. They are the "sons of thunder," like James and John, who were rebuked by Jesus for wanting to call down fire on a Samaritan village for rejecting the gospel (Luke 9:51–56). The already-not yet perspective underscores Jesus' parable of the wheat and tares, in which he warns his disciples that the separation of believers from unbelievers and the judgment of the world is left for Jesus Christ himself when he returns in glory (Matt. 13:24–43). Until then, not only do believers and unbelievers live and work side by side as neighbors, but the church itself remains a field of wheat and weeds growing together. But if over-realized eschatologies are surprised that there are weeds among the wheat, under-realized versions are surprised to learn that there is any wheat at all!

Evangelism and Church Growth

It is not surprising in the light of the preceding that an over-realized eschatology will be triumphalistic, while an under-realized eschatology will be defeatist or pessimistic. An already-not yet eschatology, at its best, will be humble and recognize that Christ is even now reigning in grace and therefore has already empowered the church to be his witness and yet that "the gospel is foolishness to those who are perishing" (1 Cor. 1:18). Because Christ has bound Satan and reigns in salvation, the gates of hell cannot prevail against the advance of his kingdom. And yet, because of the reality of sin and the blindness of fallen humanity, the orientation must be toward faithfulness (already-not yet) and not toward success (over-realized) or failure (under-realized).

Consistent with a theology of the cross and resurrection, an already-not yet eschatology prepares us to serve God and neighbor, while an over-realized approach tends toward a theology of glory, regarding numerical growth and outward signs of prosperity as ends in themselves. An under-realized eschatology, however, makes the opposite mistake again, mistaking lethargy, pessimism, and a deadening kind of conservatism for faithfully defending the deposit entrusted to the church. For them, the end is not to grow (over-realized) or to serve (already-not yet) but simply to exist.

The Christian Life

It is not difficult to see how these contrasts can be applied to the Christian life. An over-realized eschatology will inevitably yield triumphalistic visions of the Christian life, as we see in the many forms of perfectionism, "victorious Christian living," the "higher life" of "sold-out, Spirit-filled Christians," as opposed to others. It is the imperative without the indicative, command without promise. There is nothing left for heaven, since we have everything now. It will almost always tend toward some program of works-righteousness, climbing a ladder of some sort into God's holy place through techniques, spiritual disciplines, sanctification methods, and other humanly devised rituals.

On the opposite end, the under-realized eschatology tends toward antinomianism. Fearful of any extraordinary claims to Christian growth in this life, it is actually a pious way of covering one's own refusal to live in the light of what Christ has accomplished. It is indicative without imperative, promise without command. While perfectionists are deluded in thinking that they can live above all known sin, antinomians are ignorant of the power of God's grace to break the back of sin's dominion. A proper eschatology will teach us to expect change because of the reality of Christ's work for us and in us by his Spirit, but it will also teach us to expect some disappointment and failure—not because we have lost but precisely because we do now belong to Christ and are therefore struggling with indwelling sin.

As the Scriptures reveal the Christian life, however—and as the already-not yet eschatology understands it—the indicative and the imperative are both equally real. Those who have been baptized into Christ really are new creatures—right now. They are defined by the resurrection as well as the cross and are no longer under the dominion of sin, Paul says in Romans 6. But lest anyone fall into the opposite error of some sort of triumphalistic perfectionism, chapter 7 reminds us that we are still sinners who do what we do not want to do and end up failing to do what we agree is good. Romans 8 ties it all up by concluding that one day we will not live in this in-between tension, but until then we patiently wait. "Who hopes for what he already has?" (Rom. 8:24).

Weekly Worship

Now let's pull these threads together in order to better appreciate how our eschatology drives our views on worship, even though we may not recognize it. I am convinced that our current debates over worship have little to do with "traditional" versus "contemporary," as though these were distinct styles or genres. Rather, I am inclined to see these two opposite poles as belonging to an under-realized versus over-realized eschatology. One type of worship tends to overstate the not yet, while the other tends to overstate the already.

An over-realized eschatology is marked by the announcement that Jesus warned us against giving in to: "Here he is! There he is!" The kingdom does not come with bells and whistles, with visibility—except through the preached Word, sacraments, officers, and the gathered saints in general. Over-realized eschatologies have always been responsible for idolatry. Impatient with Moses' mediation between them and God through the Word, the Israelites cajoled Aaron into allowing a golden calf to be forged. Impatient with hearing God, they decided to create a visual representation of God that they could control. Instead of being fearful, as they were when they heard God speak, we read that they now "sat down to eat and drink and rose up to play." An over-realized eschatology is a religion of the eye: Seeing is believing. An already-not yet eschatology is a religion of the ear: Faith comes by hearing. That is, in part, because seeing corresponds to the possession of something. That is why, for instance, Paul says, "Who hopes for what he already sees?" (Rom. 8:24). Hope corresponds to a promise that is proclaimed, while consummation corresponds to a vision that is seen.

The promise of Scripture is that one day the Lord will dwell forever among his people in a direct manner—even face-to-face. But an over-realized eschatology is convinced that this is the way things are at present. God is regarded as so intimate, so visible among us, so fully and directly experienced in our hearts, that there is often little sense of God's holiness, grandeur, sovereignty, and transcendence. Even otherwise sound Christians can then easily succumb to the logic of paganism, where it is supposed that god or the gods can be conjured by following certain procedures—new measures, a magical prayer, the foolproof evangelistic technique. An over-realized eschatology will tend toward being one-sidedly "this-worldly." In other words, it will focus on what is happening to us and in us, claiming more success for the church and for individual sanctification and experience of God than is appropriate to this age. And as long as these "new measures" make us feel that God's presence is extraordinarily experienced, we will keep coming. If they fail, however, they will leave disillusionment in their wake. Weary of waiting for the promise that we have heard to be fulfilled, we try to force the promised future to become a reality prematurely by "staging" our own spectacle, making our own golden calf.

An under-realized eschatology, however, will take the opposite tack. Instead of being this-worldly, it is utterly otherworldly. It is almost indifferent to the reality that God has come among us in Jesus Christ and remains with us until the end of the age by his Spirit. If the golden calf episode captures the over-realized eschatology ("Here he is!"), and the Word-and-sacrament ministry captures the already-not yet eschatology ("He is not here, for he is risen!"), the cynical wilderness generation reflects the under-realized tendency ("He is not here, period"). In under-realized eschatology, worship can only regard God as remote and irrelevant to us. His presence is rarely, if ever, felt and never expected. We cannot expect very much in the way of divine power and the joy that awaits us. The future "age to come" is *not* breaking in to "their present evil age." At this point, the problem is not even really "dead orthodoxy," since ignoring the reality of the Spirit's ministry in this age is hardly orthodox. Rather than demanding a sign (an over-realized "way of vision") or resting in a promise (already-not yet "way of hearing"), an under-realized eschatology accentuates the negative and can lead only to the deadening of a church.

Neither as a church nor as individuals, in our daily lives or in our weekly worship, are we entitled to be either triumphalistic or despairing. The realities of this new age of the Spirit are far too powerful and definitive to allow for the latter and are too often opposed not only by the world but by the church itself and even by our sinful hearts for us to think that we experience glory in this age. This is the age of grace, not of glory. If our worship is recognized chiefly by a steady diet of triumph, conquest, happiness, joy, the benefits and successes of being Christ's disciples, victory over sin, and attestations of our own faithfulness ("I will always praise you," "I just want to serve you," "I surrender all"), we are going to generate disillusioned and immature Christians. Even the praise choruses that draw on the psalms tend to excerpt only those stanzas that meet these criteria. Once the psalmist turns from joy to despair or sadness, the praise chorus is ended. If we were to find a contemporary musical style to fit the bulk of the psalter, it would not be Top 40 but the blues or the pensive adagio.

When the style of our music is always upbeat, loud, and ascending in enthusiasm, we miss the range of biblical teaching about God, ourselves, worship, and the Christian life. To be sure, the Bible in general and the psalms in particular include zealous praise and thanksgiving. But an over-realized eschatology has caused much of contemporary worship to get stuck in the "victory" and "excitement" mode that downplays the reality of ongoing sin, unbelief, and disappointment, as well as the attributes of God that are more disturbing to us. This cannot help but produce weak and immature Christians who cannot stand in times of trial and testing.

And yet, under-realized approaches to worship seem at times utterly indifferent to God's presence. I have been in "traditional" services that were little more than a classroom for doctrinal or moral instruction. Even if the sacraments were given a prominent role and the liturgy was centered on the divine drama, it was all often conducted in a flat, dull routine. There was practically no sense that God was visiting his people here and now, by his Spirit working through the ordinary means of grace, acting for our redemption. This dramatic sense of God's redemptive plot running through history and his presence now to rescript us and give us a new identity, a part in his play, is virtually absent from many such services. There is therefore little sense of the service being a stage upon which God is going to act here and now, personally for and with his people. It is not surprising that these churches tend to prepare a fresh generation for those churches that embrace an over-realized eschatology out of reaction.

A proper approach emerges not as we seek to find some golden mean between two extremes, an arbitrary "balance," but rather as a result of recognizing the characteristics of worship in this present age—after Easter and Pentecost but before the second coming. An over-realized eschatology produces a false immanence, an artificial sense of God's presence. The golden calf may have been called the presence of God, but it was in truth nothing more than a projection of the worshipers' felt needs. God is not present among us face-to-face . . . yet.

At the same time, he is not wholly absent either. An under-realized eschatology must be challenged as well. Although we do not see God face-to-face in worship, we do see through a blurry window—in other words, as he offers himself in his incarnate Son through the "treasure in earthen vessels" that is the ministry of Word and sacrament. False absence is no better than the false presence of trying to climb up to heaven to bring God down to us. With its already-not yet eschatology, Scripture points us to God with us, descending to us and seating us with Christ in heavenly places. It directs us to the in-breaking of the age to come through the preaching that makes a new creation, just as that Word gave birth to the first creation. It shows us God's signs and seals that prop up our weak faith and halting obedience. He is present, but on his terms and in the manner consistent with our time in between the times. And he is present because of his *promise,* not because of the skill of ministers or musicians.

As the church turns from user-friendly idols—a worship that promotes false intimacy and false victory—and from a self-serving conservatism that misses the reality of God's presence by the Spirit through the means of grace, we will do better to provide communities that reflect visibly the reality of the church and our own lives now. Although it is this present evil age, we are witnesses to the rending of that secular fabric by the entrance of the age to come in the person and work of Jesus Christ. Stanley Hauerwas summarizes this point well:

> God has not promised us safety, but participation in an adventure called the Kingdom. That seems to me to be great good news in a world that is

literally dying of boredom. God has entrusted us, His Church, with the best story in the world. With great ingenuity we have managed . . . to make that story boring. . . . God knows what He is doing in this strange time between "worlds," but hopefully He is inviting us again to engage the enemy through the godly weapons of preaching and sacrament.[1]

The Age of the Spirit

Throughout our study, we have referred to the person and work of the Holy Spirit, emphasizing the unity of the Trinity even when we speak of distinct actions of Father, Son, and Spirit. But we should not leave the topic of eschatology and worship without developing more fully an understanding of the Spirit's role in bringing the age to come into the present.

In the Old Testament generally, the Spirit would "come upon" those prophets, priests, and kings of Israel, authorizing and enabling these representatives of God to speak God's words. For instance, Othniel was made a judge only after the Spirit came upon him. Of the coming Servant God promises, "I have put my Spirit upon him; he will bring forth justice to the nations" (Isa. 42:1 NRSV). Ezekiel's calling to be a prophet was established in a vision: "He said to me, 'Son of man, stand up on your feet and I will speak to you.' As he spoke, the Spirit came into me and raised me to my feet, and I heard him speaking to me" (Ezek. 2:1–2).

This "coming upon" prophets is akin to the language of creation, in which the Spirit was working through the Word, hovering over the face of the deep in order to create an orderly world that would reflect his character, a realm full of his glory. After the fall, however, we see God coming to Adam and Eve "in the Spirit of the Day"—that is, judgment day. And yet God builds another holy city so that he can be present once more among his people. God so identifies with his people that the tabernacle and then finally the temple are actually small-scale copies of the Holy of Holies in heaven. Among other things, the Book of Revelation makes this very point, as the unfolding drama in heaven corresponds to the unfolding drama on earth, his kingdom advancing as its rider leads it into battle. That is why Jesus told his disciples to pray, "Our Father in heaven, hallowed be your name, your kingdom come, your will be done *on earth as it is in heaven.*" Just as there was a fall from innocence in heaven led by Lucifer, there was a revolt on earth led by Adam at the instigation of the serpent.

Throughout the history of Israel, God's battles on earth followed the earthly march against sin and oppression, just as he had won his heavenly battles. The seed of the serpent—in other words, those who join the conspiracy against God—is contrasted throughout the drama with the seed of the woman, who is the Messiah. That is why, for instance, we read the following concerning the correspondence of the heavenly and earthly war. David met the Philistines in the Valley of Rephaim for battle. And we read:

> Then the Philistines went up once again and deployed themselves in the Valley of Rephaim. And when David inquired of the LORD, he said, "You shall not go up; circle around behind them, and come upon them in front of the mulberry trees. So it shall be, when you hear the sound of marching in the tops of the mulberry trees, then you shall advance quickly. For then the LORD will go out before you to strike the camp of the Philistines." And David did so, as the LORD commanded him; and he drove back the Philistines from Geba as far as Gezer.
>
> 2 Samuel 5:22–25 NKJV

The kingdom was advancing, and God's will was being done on earth as it was in heaven.[2] Like two musical pieces that, when taken together, harmonize beautifully, God's victory on earth through David corresponded to his heavenly victory over Satan through the one who would eventually crush the serpent's head.

Precisely the same scene is discovered in Ezekiel: "Then the Spirit lifted me up, and I heard behind me a loud rumbling sound—May the glory of the LORD [the Holy Spirit] be praised in his dwelling place!—the sound of the wings of the living creatures brushing against each other . . . a loud rumbling sound" (Ezek. 3:12). So when we pray that God's will be done on earth as it is in heaven, we are, at least in part, praying, "May the people of God march on earth in step with the Spirit's march in heaven." And the day will come when the Spirit who is upon the Servant will be upon his people, keeping them in step with the Spirit's heavenly march. Ezekiel's apocalypse begins with a cloud rushing toward him, driven by a windstorm, the cloud filled with flashes of lightning reminiscent of God's voice at Sinai. A chariot is drawn by cherubim, with "one like the Son of Man" enthroned. The sound made by all of this was "like the roar of rushing waters, like the voice of the Almighty, like the tumult of an army" (1:24). One day, when sin and evil are banished and the whole earth becomes God's temple, there will be only one march—the march not of an army but of peaceful citizens who live in perfect righteousness and holiness before the Lord. The Spirit of the Lord has made us all witnesses of Jesus Christ and heirs with him of the kingdom of God. During this era, then, this kingdom below goes marching quietly behind the scenes as the pomp and show of this world's kingdoms rise and fall. And one day, as the announcement is made that the kingdoms of this world are now the kingdoms of our God and of his

Christ, those two marches—the heavenly and the earthly—will be in perfect sync, to form the consummate symphony.

In Genesis 11, at the Tower of Babel, the proud nations sought to reach God and perhaps even become gods themselves by building a temple to the heavens—out of reach, they thought, of God's floodwaters of judgment that came upon the world in the time of Noah. Instead of finding God, however, God himself descended in judgment, the Holy Spirit scattering the nations and confusing their languages. At Babel, humanity sought to usher in the kingdom of everlasting peace and righteousness by their own strength and for their own glory. But at Pentecost, the Spirit descended a second time—not in judgment, to confuse and to scatter, but in salvation, to save and to gather. Israel's designation, "a kingdom of priests and a holy nation" (Exod. 19:6), is now applied to the church, Jew and Gentile (1 Peter 2:9).

God declared through the prophet Joel, "I will pour out my Spirit on all people. Your sons and daughters will prophesy, your old men will dream dreams, your young men will see visions. Even on my servants, both men and women, I will pour out my Spirit in those days. . . . And everyone who calls on the name of the Lord will be saved" (Joel 2:28–29, 32). This is finally fulfilled at Pentecost, as Peter notes in his sermon. Just as in the roar of God's hosts "above the treetops," Acts 2:1–13 speaks of the Holy Spirit descending upon the followers of Jesus as he had upon Jesus himself at his baptism. The sound of rushing wind appears once again. At Pentecost, the heavenly and earthly march was wholly synchronized. Recall the imagery Ezekiel used of the coming of the Spirit as the sound of rushing wind and lightning. A chariot is drawn by cherubim, with one like the Son of Man enthroned. And instead of descending in judgment on proud humanity, dividing their languages and scattering the nations, the Spirit descended at Pentecost to unite a new humanity around the common language of redemption and to gather together Jews and Gentiles into one under Christ.

All of this underscores the role of the Spirit in this in-breaking of the age to come upon our own present age. While the Spirit's renewal of all things and God's full presence among us awaits us in the future, Pentecost is a present reality. "I say then: Walk in the Spirit, and you shall not fulfill the lusts of the flesh. For the flesh lusts against the Spirit, and the Spirit against the flesh; and these are contrary to one another, so that you do not do the things that you wish. But if you are led by the Spirit, you are not under the law. . . . If we live in the Spirit, let us also walk in the Spirit" (Gal. 5:16–18, 25 NKJV). The same Spirit who raised Jesus from the dead is now choreographing the rest of us to find our story in his story, dying and rising in him.

The worship that we find in the Book of Revelation not only repre-sents what is going to take place but what has taken place and what even now is taking place in the city of God. There the slain Lamb is enthroned in triumph, heel bruised but the serpent's head crushed. No wonder that heavenly worship centers around the concrete realities of Jesus Christ—his person and his work for sinners, just as it must here below. If the worship of the Lamb is all-consuming in heaven, then surely it must be in our churches: "on earth as it is in heaven."

As we look around, we do not see everything subject to Christ by the Spirit. However, we do see Christ ruling in heaven, riding his cherubim-drawn chariot to victory over all his enemies and ours. And there is a correspondence on earth, wherever the gospel is faithfully preached and the sacraments are faithfully administered. Here, we taste of the pow-ers of the age to come, and our hearts are gradually subdued. Our lust for this world and its "boasted pomp and show" yields slowly but surely to the "solid joys and lasting treasures" that "none but Zion's children know." While tasting is not the same as feasting face-to-face in our raised and glorified bodies at the Lamb's wedding reception, it fills us with gratitude and hope. Through these divinely appointed means, the Spirit breaks into our drab, one-dimensional, fearful, plotless world and sweeps us into his kingdom that is even now coming down out of heaven.

While we cannot expect to "hear the brush of angel wings" and know that "God is in this place" because we "see smiles on each face," we accept the testimony of those who have stood in the counsel of the Lord and have handed down to us what they received from him. More fully still, we see the glory of God in the face of Jesus Christ as he is pro-claimed to us. We can be assured that just as God rode into battle, lead-ing the Israelites to victory, the Holy Spirit even today moves his army below according to the steps of the heavenly hosts. Christ has conquered, and one day he will cleanse the land entirely of all rebellion and strife, war and poverty, pain, prejudice, sexual impurity, pride, and self-indul-gence. And then he will hand the kingdom over to his Father, with whom he and the Holy Spirit will rule forever, world without end. Amen. This is the "new song" that we are meant to sing—and the new power that we are meant to taste—until he comes in glory to make the world his dwelling place.

Heaven will not simply be an eternal version of one of our worship services. (Who would want to go?) Rather, it will be the real thing that our worship services—at their best—can only help us receive as a fore-taste. Jesus promised that he wouldn't start celebrating until we arrived at the party (Matt. 26:29). Through the preached Word, the Spirit ush-ers us into that heavenly celebration that is eternal for God and for all who are brought into his Sabbath "time." Through Holy Communion we "taste of the powers of the age to come" and share Jesus' own cup as he, both host and victim, grants to us the right to eat from that Tree of Life in the paradise of God that is his body. None of this is so realized that we have nothing to look forward to. In fact, "eye has not seen, nor ear heard what God has prepared for those who love him." But the same Spirit who indwells the heavenly city now indwells his church and takes from what is God's and makes it ours (Rom. 8:26–27). Not only "previews of coming attractions" but the actual *dawn* of the new creation itself is what the Spirit who raised Jesus from the dead brings through the ordinary ministry of Word and sacrament. What a difference it would make in our worship if people didn't simply think they were practicing for an eternity that they don't have any use for anyway but rather tasting the food on the table of a world feast that never winds down.

NINE

What Should Our Service Look Like?

Liturgy is a word that conjures up different images for different people. Some, reacting against being raised in formal churches in which nearly every word was scripted and carefully followed, view that word as a threat to the Spirit's freedom and an invitation to lifeless routine. Others place so much confidence in the formal liturgical patterns that they seem to diminish the role of the sermon and confuse human traditions with divine command. No term is neutral. Each is inevitably embedded in practices for which those using it are either grateful or suspicious.

I was raised in churches that were, on the whole, suspicious of forms. The more extemporaneous the actions in the service, the more genuine we felt ourselves to be. We were not "playing church" as others were. And yet, we too had our liturgical forms: We all knew when to stand and sit, and we all could anticipate what was coming next. Some take spontaneity to the logical conclusion of simply sitting and waiting for the Spirit to lead, as in Quaker practice, or sing until members feel led to express themselves in some manner, as in some charismatic churches. But even these become established forms and predictable patterns.

Regardless of where we find ourselves on the ecclesiastical map, it can hardly be disputed that all churches have some sort of liturgy. From the Latin word meaning "service," liturgy refers to the assembled gathering of God's people. Since, as we have seen, God is jealous not only that no other object be the focus of our worship but that our worship consist in nothing more or less than he has commanded, the character of our liturgy is of great importance. Since God is the director and playwright as well as the central actor, it is his skill and creativity and not ours that is normative for the service.

Although the tradition in which I now worship has stood guard against any attempt to impose liturgical obligations where God has not commanded them, it has also appreciated and appropriated many of the ancient forms and their basic structure. Despite their differences, the two sides of the magisterial Reformation, Lutheran and Reformed, have regarded the liturgy—that is, the actual elements and forms used in the service—as a carrier of the law and the gospel alongside the sermon itself. So, for instance, there is the reading of the law, confession of sin, and declaration of pardon. These are ways of preaching the Word even before the sermon begins. Even in the singing, the Word is carried along by the congregation's voices. The ministry of the Word begins not with the sermon but with the call to worship! If that is the case, it is particularly important that we go to the Word to discover what elements are required in it for the regulation of our worship.

One of the important practical issues that surfaces quickly in that kind of discussion, however, is how much of our service is dictated by tradition (whether ancient or recent). While there may be circumstantial aspects (the order of the various elements, what time we meet, whether we have communion every week, whether the minister wears a robe), there are clearly required elements that God has commanded for his worship. While one cannot point to a single liturgy and say that it contains the only form of genuine worship, some are clearly better than others in being faithful to God's regulation of his worship, which he has always taken very seriously. The point here is to be intentional, to at least attempt to think through what we do and why we do it, so that we can critique our practices and knowledgeably participate in the covenant renewal ceremony.

Discovering the relationship between Scripture and tradition is essential. One reason is that everyone belongs to a tradition of some sort—even an anti-tradition tradition is a tradition. So how can we avoid both starting from scratch with each generation and staying in our ruts? How can we be faithful to God's Word and to the body of Christ around the world down through the ages and into the future while also reaching out to a new generation in our own time and place? Does it matter how we worship, as long as we get the message right and our hearts are in the right place? Many people these days—pastors, music leaders, teachers, and laypeople alike—are asking about the nonnegotiable elements in worship. What should we expect—in fact, require—each Lord's Day?

One approach to this question is the minimalist view. As with debates over what constitutes the bare essentials in doctrine, minimalist approaches tend to focus on the least common denominator. This has its strengths, of course, but the maximalist approach is preferable. Even though readers may disagree with the precise form I advocate in this chapter, it is better to draw from the depths of "the whole counsel of God" than it is to try to make everyone happy. Only then can we engage in an open and fruitful discussion about the concrete details of the worship service.

Drawing on the distinction between "elements" and "circumstances," I will propose a rough outline of a typical worship service. Before doing so, however, I should disclose more explicitly where I'm situated. As a Reformed Christian, my theological, liturgical, and practical roots are in the line of the sixteenth-century Reformation, especially as it came to expression through the work of such leaders as Martin Luther, Martin Bucer, John Calvin, Zacharias Ursinus, and John Knox. And since the Reformers sought to return worship to the simpler liturgical practices of the ancient church, before the medieval innovations, my views are informed by the church fathers as well. This chapter argues from Scripture as its supreme court of appeal, and yet within a particular community that has shaped my reading of the Bible. Even if we do not arrive at common *conclusions,* I hope that at least our common *appeal* to Scripture as the only safe guide in settling these questions will make the discussion profitable. After addressing the question of worship elements, in the next two chapters I will examine briefly two topics related to style: the visual setting of worship and the music employed in that setting.

What Goes in the Service . . . and Why?

The first thing we should observe is that the structure and content of the service are never neutral, nor should they be regarded as matters of preference. Unlike the "gods of the nations," the God of Abraham and Jesus does not leave the matter of how we approach him in our hands. While there may not always be a clear black-and-white answer to all our questions about which style to use in a given context, it should be fairly obvious that liturgical style is more than the window dressing of worship. In fact, it is that which brings into an embodied form all our beliefs about God, ourselves, redemption, and the chief end of human existence.

By way of analogy, even architectural style can tip the scales toward transcendence (a cathedral with a towering nave) or immanence (a theater-style worship center), so we always have to think through the implications of style if we wish to support the biblical announcement of both God's majesty and nearness in Christ. Of course, that does not mean there is a divinely inspired architecture: As in creation generally, many styles could be appropriate—from neoclassical to postmodern. The real question, however, is whether thought has been given to issues of transcendence and immanence, the priority of the Word and the sacraments, and a host of other practical questions addressed by the theological convictions of a given church. At the same time, circumstances can make it difficult to make our services exactly what we might want them to be, although the necessary elements are present.

Sometimes we take style too seriously and end up worshiping a form rather than the God who seeks to reshape us through his chosen forms. "Going through the motions" can happen in "low church" traditions as well as "high church" varieties. One can sing the same praise songs repetitively and without much thought, just as one can say the Apostles' Creed each week without adequate reflection on what one is professing.

If style is not neutral, how do we determine the shape of our service, beginning with the liturgy or order of service? Non-Christian thought swings like a pendulum between hyper-transcendence and hyper-immanence. But as John Frame has noted, Christian thinking should take its direction not from the radical opposition of transcendence and immanence but from the biblical representation of God as covenant head of his people. As covenant *head*, God transcends his creation, and as *covenant* head, God is intimately involved with his people.[1] Although God "goes beyond" us, he has condescended to be "with us" as Emmanuel.

God has come close, but on his terms. It is therefore not left in our hands whether we will tip the scales toward either a sub-biblical transcendence or a sub-biblical immanence. Aaron's sons, Nadab and Abihu, served the Lord as temple priests, but when they offered a sacrifice that God had not commanded, God struck them dead. On one hand, they may have been looking for more transcendence—more ritual, another liturgical innovation. On the other hand, they may have had a desire for more immanence—a form of worship that seemed to bring God down to their level. In any case, they were sincere. They presumed to serve God in the way that they found "worshipful," but they were unwilling to regard God's commanded worship as sufficient. They thought this was the sort of business about which God might not care very much, at least as long as the worshiper's heart was in the right place. They learned otherwise—with tragic results, confirmed by the anguish of their father, Aaron, who had himself accommodated to the people in fashioning the golden calf.

I have labored to demonstrate from Romans 10 the logic of the gospel—God sending his emissaries to sinners rather than sinners trying to make their way to God by their own skill, cleverness, imagination, or efforts. God has already accommodated himself to our weakness. He is not far from us, if we will but attend to the ministry of the Word. Therefore, we must resist "the sky's the limit" when it comes to accommodation. The Bible must be read, sung, and preached in the common language of the people, but when we introduce skits, musicals, and puppet shows on the basis of wanting to bring God down to the level of the people, they can only conclude that God has not already accommodated himself sufficiently through the ministry of the Word. There is accommodation and there is accommodation. When Moses confronted Aaron about the golden calf, Aaron replied, apparently even without the benefit of marketing surveys, "You know the people" (Exod. 32:22 NKJV).

Ever since Cain—actually, ever since Adam and Eve—human beings have sought to worship God in their own way, on their own terms, in forms that seem "pleasing to the eyes and desirable to make one wise." We know that God clearly commanded every detail of worship in the Old Testament, but is it not one of the liberating aspects of the New Testament that faithful worship is a matter of the heart rather than outward form?

Old Testament versus New Testament Worship?

First, it is right to point out the break that occurred when the temple curtain was torn from top to bottom on Good Friday. As Jesus told the Samaritan woman, the time has come in Jesus, the true temple, when true worship is tied not to an earthly place but to the heavenly Zion. With Mount Sinai in mind, the writer to the Hebrews declares:

> For you have not come to the mountain that may be touched and that burned with fire, and to blackness and darkness and tempest, and the sound of a trumpet and the voice of words, so that those who heard it begged that the word should not be spoken to them anymore. . . . But you have come to Mount Zion and to the city of the living God, the heavenly Jerusalem, to an innumerable company of angels, to the general assembly and church of the firstborn who are registered in heaven, to God the Judge of all, to the spirits of just men made perfect, to Jesus the Mediator of the new covenant, and to the blood of sprinkling that speaks better things than that of Abel.
>
> 12:18–19, 22–24 NKJV

In fact, the entire Book of Hebrews is aimed at Jewish Christians who were turning back to the shadows of the old covenant with its ceremonies and sacrifices, when the reality to which they pointed had arrived. On this basis, Reformed Christians have rejected liturgical approaches that seek to base Christian worship on the shadowy worship of the Jewish theocracy, especially imitating its ceremonial, sacrificial worship of the temple period.

At the same time, too much can be made of the difference between testaments in terms of an alleged contrast between formal and informal, heartfelt worship. To be sure, Jesus castigates the religious leaders of his day for being so obsessed with the outward form and show of holiness that they could not even recognize their inward depravity. But this was not a New Testament critique of Old Testament worship. In fact, it differs little from the sort of rebuke that God gives Israel and Judah through the prophets: "For I desire mercy and not sacrifice, and the knowledge of God more than burnt offerings" (Hosea 6:6). Furthermore, judging by first-century Jewish prayer books, Jesus did not regard formal liturgies as inherently stultifying to a personal relationship with his Father. In fact, he tells his disciples not to be like the hypocrites who stand on street corners praying long-winded prayers of many words, and then gives them his famous form: "In this manner, therefore, pray: Our Father in heaven, hallowed be your name. Your kingdom come. Your will be done on earth as it is in heaven. Give us this day our daily bread. And forgive us our debts, as we forgive our debtors. And do not lead us into temptation, but deliver us from the evil one. For yours is the kingdom and the power and the glory forever. Amen" (Matt. 6:9–13 NKJV). Jesus not only did not abandon formal prayers but, as God in flesh, inaugurated one! Similarly, we read in Acts 2:42 that the early believers gathered for preaching, sacrament, and "*the* prayers." Although the definite article appears in the Greek text, it is often not included in English translations that have an anti-liturgical bias. Formal prayers were not viewed by our Savior as magical incantations but as disciplinary structures. Like a trellis, they taught wandering hearts to weave their prayers up to God in a manner that delighted him.

This is not meant to be an argument in favor of using only formal, written prayers but for structure in general. In conversations, my colleague D. G. Hart has compared liturgical structure to rules in baseball to which we gladly surrender our individual freedom and preferences in order to play a common game. Imagine what would happen if we all showed up at the baseball field and decided to do our own thing, enjoying the "baseball experience" in our own special way. There would, of course, be no game if that were the case.

Submitting to particular forms disciplines us not only as the congregation but also reins in pastors and worship leaders at whose mercy congregations too often find themselves. American sectarianism thrives on the unique charisma and personality of its leaders, and this is one of the reasons that worship forms always have to be changing, as a new entrepreneur comes on the scene. Slick services have slick preachers, and boring services have boring preachers. As I know from personal experience, the downside of having an active imagination is idolatry. The little thespian in me could easily construct experimental worship "experiences" for a living, but their very uniqueness and innovative cleverness would undoubtedly grow old fairly quickly, and there would be little similarity in worship over generations. More importantly, there is too much biblical history to remind us that God is pleased only with the simplicity of the worship he has prescribed.

Throughout centuries—in many cases, even millennia—God's people have sought to chain their worship to Scripture itself. In fact, the Book of Common Prayer (1552)—gem of the English Reformation—consists largely of biblical quotations. Also in the Reformed tradition is the Dutch Liturgy, adopted at the beginning of the seventeenth century, the Book of Common Order (commonly called "John Knox's Liturgy"), which is only slightly freer in style, and the Directory for the Public Worship of God, produced by the Westminster Assembly in the mid-seventeenth century. Luther's service was an evangelical revision of the Mass, and Calvin produced a simplified yet structured liturgy, as well as the Form of Prayers, for public worship. What the Reformers and their heirs opposed was the imposition of a particular liturgy on the church as a necessary form for the true worship of God.

Despite a rich Protestant liturgical inheritance, our churches (regardless of where they are on the spectrum) seem to give too little attention to why we do what we do. In many cases, hours are spent (hopefully) in preparing a sermon, but the rest of the service may be haphazard and lack a clear sense of a movement from point A to point Z. We are familiar with services that begin with miscellaneous introductions and announcements. Next, the choir sings and perhaps provides background to special music of some sort, followed by a congregational song, an offering, more singing, a sermon, more singing or special music, and a much anticipated benediction. When churches are contemplating moving from this to something else, like a seeker service or a high church service, we cannot help but be somewhat sympathetic to the reasons for their reaction. A worship service should be interesting—we are meeting with God, after all!—and it will be interesting if ministers and their congregations are intentional about its development and meaning. But whether contemporary or traditional, worship will become a boring, purposeless routine if that is in fact what is unintentionally conveyed in its preparation.

If worship is to be Christ-centered, then, we will not move beyond the types and shadows of God's commands in the Old Testament to our own types and shadows that lead us not to Christ but to our own creatively conceived images and "worship experiences." But while God has commanded us to gather together on the Lord's Day, he has not commanded us to meet at 10:00. Church services will vary in entirely appropriate ways; some things are necessary while other things depend on circumstances of time and place. The former we ordinarily call an *element* (i.e., it is necessary), while the latter is a *circumstance* (i.e., it is up to the church's discretion). Taking an offering is an element, while how it is taken is a circumstance. Following this logic, then, let's look briefly at what we may legitimately regard as a biblical liturgy, or order of service, in new covenant worship.

The Elements

The Invocation

Examples of formal invocations abound in Scripture. As indicated earlier, the Bible is a covenant charter and within it are smaller covenantal units. Just as a lesser king (a vassal) called upon or invoked the name of a greater king (a suzerain) when threatened by an invading power, "calling on the name of the Lord"—a form of expression that we find as early as Seth and his faithful line (Gen. 4:26)—was a political act. Invoking that line of the treaty was like pulling a fire alarm: The lesser king had better mean it and had better not craft secret treaties with other kings behind the suzerain's back. The covenantal or treaty structure of Scripture is clear, then, even in the opening of the service. God summons his people to gather before his court. All rise as the suzerain appears to take his throne. The stage is set and the opening act is performed. Invocations vary, but often they are taken from a psalm—often, Psalm 124:8: "Our help is in the name of the LORD, who made heaven and earth" (NRSV). Invoking the name of the one who has delivered us from Egypt, we are then met with God's gracious response, and the covenant renewal ceremony is underway.

God's Greeting (the Votum)

Sometimes called the salutation, the votum is God's response to the congregation's invocation. As God's ambassador, the minister raises his hands and blesses the people with God's promised rescue. The minister is not dispensing God's blessing in his person, as if he somehow had magical powers, but in his office. He is doing nothing more than acting as a divinely appointed emissary to speak for God where God has clearly spoken. In the churches with which I'm associated, the minister simply says to the standing congregation, "Beloved people of God, receive God's greeting: Grace and peace to you in the name of the Father, the Son, and the Holy Spirit."

God will not violate his oath but will descend in the power of his Spirit to take up his throne among us and to deliver us from the world, the flesh, and the devil. The only change in the New Testament is that the great liberation has already occurred and the agent of redemption has been revealed. Citing Joel 2:32, Paul declares, "For 'whoever calls upon the name of the LORD shall be saved'" (Rom. 10:13 NKJV). One of the greatest biblical testimonies to the deity of Jesus Christ is that God "has highly exalted him and given him the name which is above every name, so that at the name of Jesus every knee should bow, of those in heaven, and of those on earth, and of those under the earth, and that every tongue should confess that Jesus Christ is Lord, to the glory of God the Father" (Phil. 2:9–11 NKJV). What the apostle is saying here is that there is no suzerain— no great king—above Jesus Christ. Jesus of Nazareth is the protector of his people and the keeper of the covenant. So we call on him to be present among us by his Spirit, and we listen as Zechariah's prophecy is fulfilled in our presence: "They will call on my name, and I will answer them. I will say, 'This is my people'; and each one will say, 'The LORD is my God'" (Zech. 13:9 NKJV). The minister, acting in Christ's name and by his authority, declares God's goodwill toward the assembly.

The Reading of the Law

In any covenant, there is a reading of the terms of the treaty and its sanctions. Here assembled in God's courtroom, the people hear the commandments read and recognize their sinfulness. This reading of the law can be in the form of the Ten Commandments or in the form of Jesus' summary. Sometimes the minister reads from Galatians 5:16–26, where the apostle calls us to bear the fruit of the Spirit rather than the fruit of the flesh. Some churches are reluctant to read from anything but the Ten Commandments and Jesus' summary, but the reading of other obvious "law" passages (the Sermon on the Mount, Jesus' "Woes," countless passages from the prophets) may provide just enough variety to bring the law home in fresh ways each week. Doing so also teaches us to find the law throughout Scripture and not simply in the Decalogue.

Before we heard the reading of the law, we thought we were good people who could be better, but after hearing God speak, we are like the children of Israel hearing God deliver the commands: "You speak with us, and we will hear," they told Moses, "but let not God speak with us, lest we die" (Exod. 20:19 NKJV). Throughout Scripture, the reading of the law precedes repentance and faith, as well as instruction. After we flee its curses into the bosom of our elder brother, both the giver and the perfect keeper of that law in our place, he then sends us his Spirit to give us a new heart. While all of this happens definitively, once and for all, when we are converted, it is a lifelong process as well: We are always becoming Christians "again" every day, realizing afresh in our lives the power of Word and Spirit in our baptism into Christ. Repentance and faith are always renewed daily.

During periods in which this public reading of the law has fallen into disuse, so too has a genuine sense of what God requires of us and our standing before him as lawbreakers. We see a prime example of its liturgical place in the massive service that was conducted when God brought back a remnant from Babylonian captivity:

> So Ezra the priest brought the Law before the congregation, of men and women and all who could hear with understanding, on the first day of the seventh month. Then he read from it in the open square that was in front of the Water Gate from morning until midday . . . and the ears of all the people were attentive to the Book of the Law. . . . And Ezra opened the book in the sight of all the people, for he was standing above all the people; and when he opened it, all the people stood up. . . . Then all the people answered, "Amen, Amen!" while lifting up their hands. And they bowed their heads and worshiped the Lord with their faces to the ground.
>
> Nehemiah 8:2–3, 5–6 NKJV

We read that the Levites "helped the people to understand the law." "So they read distinctly from the book, in the Law of God; and they gave the sense, and helped them to understand the reading" (v. 8 NKJV)— equivalent to preaching today. Although this was a festival day, a day of great rejoicing, the reading of the law brought profound sorrow for sin: "This day is holy to the Lord your God; do not mourn nor weep," Ezra comforted. "For all the people wept, when they heard the words of the Law" (v. 9 NKJV).

We may not normally weep, as returning exiles did upon their first hearing of God's words, but we will recognize our sinfulness in fresh ways, as the Spirit uses his law—not only its explanation but its public reading—to convict us. The point is that we be brought humbly before God, to recognize again that we are even still, despite the work of the Spirit in our lives, not playing the part that we were meant to play. We agree again with his just sentence against us for our sins—were we not under his covenant mercies in Christ.

The Confession and Absolution

But those who call upon the name of the Lord *are* under God's covenant mercies in Christ. As the law slays, the gospel makes alive— and even in this scene in which Ezra addresses the remnant of Israel, we see that transition that we have known since God judged Adam and then clothed him: "Then he said to them, 'Go your way, eat the fat, drink the sweet, and send portions to those for whom nothing is prepared; for this day is holy to our Lord. Do not sorrow, for the joy of the Lord is your strength'" (Neh. 8:10 NKJV). This brings us to the transitional point in the service, from judgment to grace. Think of it as the turning point in a court trial, after the judge has convicted and sentenced the criminal only to find a way of acquitting him.

In our case, it is more than acquittal: God justifies the wicked by imputing Christ's righteousness to their account. Here we witness "the great exchange," as Luther called it. Jesus bears our guilt, and we wear his righteousness. As we publicly confess our sins together as God's people, we agree with God (that's what "confess" means, to agree with) that there is no way out for us, and we cry out for mercy. The covenantal character of this service once more underscores that although we confess our sins individually every day, we belong to the people of God. We are like the Israelites who "gathered together as one man in the open square" (Neh. 8:1 NKJV). For one-fourth of the day, the law was read "and for another fourth they confessed and worshiped the Lord their God" (9:3 NKJV).

Notice that this was not part of the temple worship. It actually had more in common with the synagogue worship that characterized Jesus' day. It can serve as a pattern for us—not as a pattern to be slavishly followed, as though it were commanded (if so, we would have to keep their schedule as well!). Rather, it indicates in public reenactment the cycle of salvation, obedience, disobedience, judgment, and salvation that characterizes the psalms that God's people sang and both the historical and doctrinal description of the Christian life that we find in both testaments.

The absolution is a public declaration that God has forgiven our sins. If we still have one eye on the pattern seen in Nehemiah, we notice that this is what Ezra does as God's prophet when the people confess and mourn their wickedness: "Do not sorrow, for the joy of the Lord is your strength" (Neh. 8:10 NKJV), he tells them in God's name and by God's own authority. It is similar to Jesus' declaration to the adulteress: "Woman, where are those accusers of yours? Has no one condemned you? . . . Neither do I condemn you; go and sin no more. . . . I am the light of the world. He who follows me shall not walk in darkness, but have the light of life" (John 8:10–12 NKJV). Similarly, Paul exclaims, "If

God is for us, who can be against us? . . . Who shall bring a charge against God's elect? It is God who justifies. Who is he who condemns? It is Christ who died, and furthermore is also risen, who is even at the right hand of God, who also makes intercession for us" (Rom. 8:31, 33–34 NKJV).

To many, the very word *absolution* sounds sacerdotal (i.e., according divine power to the minister himself). But it is part of the ministry of the Word. The minister has no inherent power to forgive sins, but Christ does, and he has called his ministers to proclaim in his name both law and gospel, to close the gate of heaven, and to open it by the ministry of the Word. The King of the New Israel declared to the Twelve, "I will give you the keys of the kingdom of heaven; whatever you bind on earth will be bound in heaven, and whatever you loose on earth will be loosed in heaven" (Matt. 16:19).

In contrast to the medieval church, which abused this authority and exercised tyranny instead of ministering to the people, the Reformers saw the authority given in Matthew 16 as a service rendered through the ministry of the Word and not through the "insider trading" of priests. This is why it is a fearful thing to be entrusted with this ministry. As exciting as it often is, it is also a two-edged sword that ministers wield. It kills and makes alive. Speaking in God's name is both a joy and a burden.

Just as God has given to his ministers the authority to preach, he has given the authority to proclaim God's curse and God's blessing in his name. They are like the prophets and apostles in this limited respect: In both cases, it is the king who is judging and forgiving through his ambassadors. They are authorized to curse and to bless in his name—an authority that they use as servants rather than as lords.

While the medieval church practiced private confession and absolution, requiring exact memory of particular sins and exacting often laborious penance (sometimes including money) to atone for iniquity, the churches of the Reformation returned to the ancient church's practice of public confession and absolution that was evangelical in character. While priestly tyranny had abused the office, the Reformers did not overreact by denying an important biblical teaching and comfort to believers. In recovering the apostolic and ancient church's understanding of "the keys" (Matt. 18:18; John 20:23; 2 Cor. 5:20), John Calvin, for instance, urged an evangelical practice of confession and absolution. For him, *private* confession and absolution were simply one-on-one versions of the same *public* confession and absolution: Both were a ministry of the Word and not a special "gift" or charism that the minister possessed beyond that ministry. It is not a different degree of forgiveness that one receives, as if this were a work that one might complete in exchange for God's favor. Rather, it is a greater, firmer sense of God's promise in the gospel that faith can grasp. "Unless this knowledge remains clear and sure," Calvin said, "the conscience will have no rest at all, no peace with God, no assurance or security; but it continuously trembles, wavers, tosses, is tormented and vexed, shakes, hates, and flees the sight of God."[2]

To be sure, we must exercise godly sorrow for our sins, confess them to God, and make necessary changes. "But if forgiveness of sins depends upon these conditions which they attach to it, nothing is more miserable or deplorable for us." Calvin says that at root is a misunderstanding of repentance. "Repentance is not the cause of forgiveness of sins," he argued. In the ancient church, confession to the minister was not a condition of forgiveness but an aid for those who needed to be convinced in private of that which ordinarily is sufficiently offered in public to God's people. Once the medieval abuses are removed, says Calvin, the practice is a marvelous gift of God to his saints:

> For this reason, the Lord ordained of old among the people of Israel that, after the priest recited the words, the people should confess their iniquities publicly in the temple [cf. Lev. 16:21]. For he foresaw that this help was necessary for them in order that each one might better be led to a just estimation of himself. And it is fitting that, by the confession of our own wretchedness, we show forth the goodness and mercy of our God, among ourselves and before the whole world.

Hardly an add-on for those weeks in which we feel particularly liturgical, "this sort of confession ought to be ordinary in the church." Calvin adds:

> Besides the fact that ordinary confession has been commended by the Lord's mouth, no one of sound mind, who weighs its usefulness, can dare disapprove it. For since in every sacred assembly we stand before the sight of God and the angels, what other beginning of our action will there be than the recognition of our own unworthiness? But that, you say, is done through every prayer; for whenever we pray for pardon, we confess our sin. Granted. But if you consider how great is our complacency, our drowsiness, or our sluggishness, you will agree with me that it would be a salutary regulation if the Christian people were to practice humbling themselves through some public rite of confession.

The practices of public confession and absolution were retained in Reformed and Presbyterian churches, in addition to Anglican and Lutheran bodies. "And indeed," Calvin adds, "we see this custom observed with good result in well-regulated churches; that every Lord's Day the minister frames the formula of confession in his own and the people's name, and by it he accuses all of wickedness and implores pardon from the Lord. In short, with this key a gate to prayer is opened both to individuals in private and to all in public." The Second Helvetic Confession presents the same view, as does the Westminster Confession: "To these officers the keys of the kingdom of Heaven are committed, by virtue whereof they have power respectively to retain and remit sins" (chap. 32).

Often, this practice was particularly linked with that marvelous moment when one who had refused Christ's reign in a deliberate and public manner, either in doctrine or life, came to repentance and stood before the church to be absolved from excommunication. John Knox's liturgy for Scotland gives us the following form of that absolution:

> In the name and authority of Jesus Christ, I, the minister of His blessed Evangel, with consent of the whole Ministry and Church, absolve thee, N., from the sentence of Excommunication, from the sin by thee committed, and from all censures laid against thee for the same, according to thy repentance; and pronounce thy sin to be loosed in heaven, and thee to be received again to the society of Jesus Christ, to His body the Church, to the participation of His Sacraments, and, finally, to the fruition of all His benefits: In the name of the Father, the Son, and the Holy Spirit. So be it.[3]

But in the ordinary public confession and absolution, we find the latter phrased in the following terms: "To all those who repent in this wise, and look to Jesus Christ for their salvation, I declare that the absolution of sins is effected, in the name of the Father, and of the Son, and of the Holy Spirit. Amen."[4] It was not merely the reiteration of certain comforting passages in Scripture, general announcements of God's gracious forgiveness, but a concrete, objective absolution in Christ's name for God's covenant people. Martin Bucer's 1539 *Strasbourg Liturgy* followed the recitation of 1 Timothy 1:15 with the statement, "Let everyone, with St. Paul, truly acknowledge this is his heart and believe in Christ. Thus, in His name, I proclaim unto you the forgiveness of all your sins, and declare you to be loosed of them on earth, that you may be loosed of them in heaven, in eternity. Amen."[5] "The substance of it is this," Calvin says of the "keys" in his interpretation of Matthew 18:18, "that Christ intended to assure his followers of salvation promised to them in the Gospel, that they might expect it as firmly as if he were himself to descend from heaven to bear testimony concerning it. . . . In a word, it is a wonderful consolation to devout minds to know that the message of salvation brought to them by a poor mortal man is ratified before God."[6]

Public confession and absolution follow the pattern of the prophets, and the latter marks the place where, as in Isaiah 40, God now turns the prophet from a ministry of binding to one of loosing: "'Comfort, yes, comfort my people!' says your God. 'Speak comfort to Jerusalem, and cry out to her, that her warfare is ended, that her iniquity is pardoned'" (v. 1 NKJV). Whereas ministers themselves might be inclined, depending on their personality, either toward legal rigor or sentimental leniency, this ministry of the Word guarantees that the people will receive God's appraisal and approval just as he has offered it in Scripture.

The Pastoral Prayer

As Calvin observed, after this public confession and absolution, the way is open to prayer.

> We can go boldly into the Holy of Holies to intercede for others, as well as ourselves, with the confidence that our Father hears us and delights in satisfying us with good things. Instead of wavering or dreading his presence, we are now confident that we are accepted children and co-heirs with our elder brother who is at his right hand.[7]

In the pastoral prayer, the minister intercedes on behalf of the church around the world, the secular rulers, and then on behalf of his own flock. I will again appeal to Nehemiah, this time chapter 1. Like Moses, interceding before an angry God on behalf of a wicked people, Nehemiah stands in the gap:

> I pray, LORD God of heaven, O great and awesome God, you who keep your covenant and mercy with those who love you and observe your commandments, please let your ear be attentive and your eyes open, that you may hear the prayer of your servant which I pray before you now, day and night, for the children of Israel your servants, and confess the sins of the children of Israel which we have sinned against you. Both my father's house and I have sinned. . . . Now these are your servants and your people, whom you have redeemed by your great power, and by your strong hand. O LORD, I pray, please let your ear be attentive to the prayer of your servant, and to the prayer of your servants who desire to fear your name; and let your servant prosper this day, I pray, and grant him mercy in the sight of this man [King Artaxerxes I].
>
> verses 5–6, 10–11 NKJV

Ministers intercede; they do not mediate. Like all believers, they have the privilege of bringing petitions before the covenant Lord through the only mediator, Jesus Christ. Just as they represent God to the people in proclaiming curse and blessing (law and gospel), they represent the people to God as one called to give a united voice to their requests. By praying for the needs of the world, the government's leaders, the church universal, as well as for the needs of a particular church, we learn in our public prayers what we too often neglect in our private prayers: to look beyond ourselves and the interests of our own family. "Therefore," Paul commands, "I exhort first of all that supplications, prayers, intercessions, and giving of thanks be made for all men, for kings and all who are in authority, that we may lead a quiet and peaceable life in all godliness and reverence" (1 Tim. 2:1 NKJV).

One of the most disappointing features of contemporary worship is the absence of prayer, and one suspects that few of the youth in evangelical or mainline churches today even know the Lord's Prayer, which covenant children have prayed—and used as a model for their prayers—for two thousand years. If corporate prayer does not play an important part in our worship, it should not be surprising that it is marginalized in the individual lives of Christians.

The Preached Word

As we have seen, the chief means of grace is the preached Word. A sermon is not only an exposition of God's Word but is itself God's Word. It is the Son of man preaching life into the valley of dead bones, wielding the two-edged sword that kills and makes alive. It is the Holy Spirit alone who is the effectual cause of the Word's work, but it is administered through preaching. This is why, according to historical practice, sermons begin with the invocation, "In the name of the Father, the Son, and the Holy Spirit," and end with "Amen," or its translation, "So be it." The sermon is the Word of God addressed to God's people.

Sometimes we see the sermon merely as an opportunity to make the Word effective. For some, it is an opportunity for mere reflection—data processing, to put it indelicately. For others, it is a chance to make a decision. Still others see it as a stimulation to emotional experience. But whether we make our intellect, our will, or our heart sovereign, we are exchanging the glory of God for that of the creature. As Scripture presents it, the Word itself—wielded by the heavenly agent (the Holy Spirit) and the earthly ambassador (the preacher)—does what it threatens in the law and promises in the gospel. The Word itself does this work, not because it provides an occasion for us to do something but simply by its being used by God according to his own sovereign will. It is not just the content of the Word but the preaching of the Word that is central in worship and is, strictly speaking, a means of grace.

To be sure, many other methods in our hi-tech era would appear to be more effective forms of getting us to do something. Drama can entertain and inspire, emotional choruses sung in ascending chords with growing instrumental intensity can alter consciousness and moods, while audiovisual sophistication can persuade people that the Christian message (whatever that may be) is relevant in our age. A booming anthem with a pipe organ and well-trained choir may stir us. But if the primary goal is not to get *us* to do something that will effect our salvation but for *God* to plant his Word in our heart, our criteria for effectiveness and success will be rather different. It is important for us to realize that it is not only the message of the Word but the method of preaching that God has promised to use for salvation and growth. It must, therefore, be central in worship.

The Ministry of the Lord's Supper

A regular feature of the assembly (Acts 2:46), "the breaking of the bread" was Jesus' first act at the resurrection day service with his disciples when they recognized their risen Lord (Luke 24:30–31). Frequent Communion fell into disfavor in some circles of the ancient church, however, when the emphasis on suitable preparation, introspection, and penance tended to obscure the evangelical character of the sacrament. As Orthodox theologian V. Palachovsky explains:

> It is indeed possible that the monks [of early Eastern orthodoxy], through the greater severity of their conception of preparation for the sacrament of the Eucharist, were in large part responsible for the sacrament's being received less and less frequently. The rarity with which communion was received was occasioned more by a spirit of rigorism than by indifference on the part of the faithful.[8]

Just as many believers delayed their baptism until their deathbed in order to clean the slate, a faulty understanding of sin and grace may have contributed to the decline in regular communion for fear of unworthy reception. (Protestant parallels, unfortunately, abound.)

In the West, the medieval church withdrew the cup from the laity. Since most laypeople received Communion only once or twice a year (Christmas and/or Easter), and then only the bread, this sacred feast had lost much of its practical significance by the time of the Reformation. At the heart of the Reformation was a practical renewal of preaching *and* sacrament as the divinely ordained means of grace and methods of drawing together the divine drama. Once again, the people received the Supper—both the bread and the wine—and did so weekly. At least that was the plan.

In Geneva, for instance, Calvin tried unsuccessfully throughout his entire ministry to implement weekly Communion, but the conservative city council thought it would be too jarring for a community that was used to infrequent Communion (Christmas, Maundy Thursday or Good Friday, Ascension Day, Pentecost). Just the same, Calvin's liturgy in Geneva was a service of Word *and* sacrament, and he always left the Communion part of the service in the liturgy each week, just to make the point, "This is what we're missing!" John Knox wanted such frequency in Scotland, but the burden of training and sending out new ministers was so overwhelming that it was often practically impossible. Few churches had the luxury of having their own pastor, and most had to make do with infrequent Communion. All of this was supposed to be provisional as they waited for better times. However, churches in the Reformed tradition have tended to call for frequent Communion in principle while going along with the practice of infrequency. Only now does a more frequent Communion in practice appear to be growing in conservative Reformed and Presbyterian circles, and it represents a convergence of practice with theory.

Typically, the ministry of Holy Communion in most Reformed, Presbyterian, Anglican, Lutheran, and Methodist bodies includes a number of common elements derived from the ancient church. First, there is the dismissal. "Ite misse," literally, "Go, it's over!" was declared by the minister when the unbelievers were dismissed after the sermon in the period immediately following the apostles. (The term "Mass" was derived from this expression.) This was carried over into the Reformed tradition by including Paul's exhortation, warning the unbelieving and unrepentant to stay away from the Supper. Everyone else, thus instructed, was to come to the Supper as believing and repentant sinners who sought strength for their weak faith by feeding on Christ and all his benefits. (See our earlier discussion.) In many churches in Africa and other parts of the world, the service of the Word actually ends, the people take a break, and then they return for the service of Communion without nonmembers.

While there is (and should be) diversity, many Christian bodies insert, before the reception of the bread and wine, the public profession of the Apostles' Creed, said or sung, as well as words of humble access and the words of institution that our Lord spoke and the apostle Paul repeated as a familiar part of the service: "For I received from the Lord that which I also delivered to you" (1 Cor. 11:23). Emphasizing the belief in the true presence of Christ with his people in heaven, where he is physically present at God's right hand, the Reformed emphasize that ancient part of the liturgy called the *sursum corda:* "Lift up your hearts," the minister invites, to which the people respond, "We lift them up to the Lord."

It is my purpose here not to prescribe the entire liturgy of Communion but to argue that this sacrament is an element—a necessary act in the *ordinary* worship service. Calvin's advocacy for Communion "every time the Word is preached, or at least weekly" is well supported by New Testament and ancient church practice. Some worry that such frequency would harm the Supper, that it would no longer be special. However, if it is, alongside the preached Word, a means of grace and a mark of the church—if, in other words, "The Holy Spirit creates faith by the preaching of the holy gospel and confirms it by the use of the holy sacraments" (Heidelberg 61), our "spiritual food and drink" and "a participation in the blood of Christ" (1 Cor. 10:3–4, 16)—why would we need regular preaching but not regular Communion? We could also say that we should have a sermon only monthly—or even quarterly!—because we are worried that it will no longer be special. But here, as elsewhere, it is simply not up to us to decide what we think makes something special. It is already special because God has promised to accompany its lawful administration with the reality that is promised—Christ and all his benefits, by the mysterious working of the Holy Spirit. Like the Passover, a type of both Christ's sacrifice once and for all and of our ongoing participation in and feeding on Christ, this is our covenant meal. Here Christ is both the priest and the food that he offers. And if unbelievers are present, will they not see the gospel that has been proclaimed in the sermon now visually enacted before their eyes as believers come forward to receive it? Will it not strengthen the sinews of fellowship that knit Christ's body together?

This issue of frequency is not a matter on which Christians should cause division or strife, but it does seem to demand attention. While we think through the implications of withholding the Word, and (hopefully) conclude that this would be disastrous, perhaps we should think through the importance of the Lord's Supper for nourishment in the wilderness of our pilgrimage. As with preaching, if this encounter with the Good Shepherd is lacking, the sheep will look for other means of nourishment.

Thanksgiving and Offerings

We do not offer a sacrifice for sin but a sacrifice of thanksgiving for sins forgiven in the one complete sacrifice of Jesus once offered on the cross. It is a "thank" offering that we bring. After a general prayer of thanksgiving, offered on behalf of the congregation, the minister invites offerings for the poor and the widows. Not only does the covenant meal signify and seal to us the union that we have in Christ but also the union that we have with the whole church in him. At this table, the rich and the poor come as needy beggars—needy not only of God's aid but of each others'. The poor need the aid of the wealthy, but the wealthy also need the poor so that they may minister to Christ (Matt. 25:31–46). As an extension of this "body life," the ancient church (and Reformed churches) would visit prisoners, the sick, and the shut-ins, bringing with them the Word, gifts from the offering, and the bread and wine from the public service, ministering the Word and sacrament to them as members of the same body with those who had just met.

Notice how this liturgical structure constitutes a play within a play, its own dramatic unity. It moves from invocation to confession, then to absolution and intercession; then the Word is preached and made visible in the Supper. God has been acting upon us, working repentance and faith in our hearts. What other response could we give than heartfelt gratitude and service to our neighbor in his name?

But God gets the last word.

The Benediction

Apart from the narrative structure of this covenant gathering, the benediction could easily become (and too often does become) little more than a way of saying, "The service is over, so good-bye." But here, one last time, *God* addresses his people. Grace has the last word, as the people receive God's blessing through the minister with raised hands. Not only do these benedictions appear throughout the Old Testament (chiefly the Aaronic form), but they are replete in the pastoral letters of the New Testament, closing these missives that were intended as apostolic sermons to be read publicly in churches throughout the Empire. The covenant people leave the courtroom bursting with thankful hearts because they leave with the assurance that God is on their side and that they stand under his blessing rather than his wrath.

Concluding Thoughts

Liturgies may be amended to better accommodate the *circumstances* of time and place, but the *elements* must remain intact. I have not proposed here a particular liturgy. I have merely outlined what I believe are the elements necessary for the right, biblical substance of worship, while also offering a bit of circumstantial context for how it may (not must) be practiced. Today, we are often told that an ordinary worship service consisting of a sermon, sacraments, prayers, and doctrines will not attract people. Enormous pressure is brought to bear, especially as some churches committed to a Word-and-sacrament ministry see members drift away to the megachurch down the street. Some of these churches fail to recognize the treasure that has been committed to their earthen vessels, relying on the safety of tradition instead of the power of the Spirit to transform sinners through his ordained means. And many of the megachurches and the churches that seek to imitate them have imbibed traditions of the last fifty years or so that have washed out much of the weighty and scripturally grounded aspects of historic worship. They too are often in the rut of a tradition, but one that is frequently determined by the spirit of the age.

But both "contemporary" and "traditional" churches often miss the real excitement. Both may easily fail to see where the action really is—the genuine "signs and wonders" ministry that God performs each week when the Word is rightly preached and the sacraments are rightly administered. Churches today are not more united in ministry but less, since they have jettisoned liturgies that are close to the biblical text and gave a certain amount of shared identity across denominations. We may not do everything that churches in the past did, but at least we should be as reflective about what we are doing in the light of Scripture. One of the most interesting trends today is that many pastors are crafting liturgies for their previously non-liturgical churches. In other words, they are now simply making their liturgical assumptions explicit. They are being deliberate and intentional, and many of them are more closely investigating Scripture and comparing their current practice to that of other traditions and other periods.

The important thing to see in all of this is that worship is the divine drama. In it, the drama of redemption that unfolds in biblical history now unfolds as a play within a play before us in a particular place and our own time. In it, we join Abraham and Sarah at the table with their greater Son through whom all the nations of the earth are blessed. With circumcised hearts, we join the cloud of witnesses who longed for Jesus' coming and the sending of his Spirit. Not just once but week after week, year after year, decade after decade, we are being reshaped by this counter-drama, as the plot of "this passing evil age" yields to "the age to come."

There should be a lot of freedom here, although eclectic experimentation, whether in a "high church" or "low church" direction, must be carefully checked. There will be a liturgy at everybody's church next Sunday. The question is whether it will be a good one or bad one, deliberately conceived and understood or followed out of unreflective routine. We should be delighted at the renewed attention being given to worship and liturgy. And above all, we should be encouraged by the church growth strategy of the apostles: "Then those who gladly received [Peter's] word were baptized; and that day about three thousand souls were added to them. And they continued steadfastly in the apostles' doctrine and fellowship, in the breaking of bread, and in prayers. . . . And the Lord added to the church daily those who were being saved" (Acts 2:41–42, 47 NKJV).

TEN

Is Style Neutral?

Theology is practical, which means that it cannot help but get drafted into the so-called "worship wars." The purpose of this chapter, as in the book generally, is at least to attempt to dive beneath the troubled waters of contemporary debates and find the deeper biblical, theological, as well as cultural currents that we often miss—whatever boat we find ourselves in at the moment. Does God care about style? Are the differences between traditional and contemporary worship equivalent to preferences for one spot over another on the radio dial?

Consider the following scenario from New York communications theorist Neil Postman:

> It is possible that, some day soon, an advertising man who must create a television commercial for a new California Chardonnay will have the following inspiration: Jesus is standing alone in a desert oasis. A gentle breeze flutters the leaves of stately palms behind him. Soft Mideastern music caresses the air. Jesus holds a bottle of wine at which he gazes adoringly. Turning toward the camera, he says, "When I transformed water into wine at Cana, this is what I had in mind. Try it today. You'll become a believer."[1]

Since Hebrew National frankfurters have already been sold with the slogan, "We answer to a Higher Authority," Postman, himself Jewish, concludes that the preceding scenario is not terribly far-fetched. "What we are talking about here is not blasphemy," says Postman, "but trivialization, against which there can be no laws."[2] As in the Middle Ages, people today are addicted to images rather than words—except sound bites, which are more like images than words anyway. "One picture, we are told, is worth a thousand words. But a thousand pictures, especially if they are all of the same object, may not be worth anything at all."[3] Postman's remarks remind us why God gave the second commandment, prohibiting images of God—not to mention the third, which prohibits misuse of God's name. It also reminds us why Christians are "people of the book," not "people of the image."

Style Matters

One problem that we need to take more seriously is the extent to which style not only reflects but actually shapes content. For instance, Postman notes that TV commercials rarely showcase products but rather those who consume them. Extensive marketing surveys determine profiles of potential consumers. "Images of movie stars and famous athletes, of serene lakes and macho fishing trips, of elegant dinners and romantic interludes, of happy families packing their station wagons for a picnic in the country—these tell nothing about the products being sold. But they tell everything about the fears, fancies, and dreams of those who buy them." In this kind of setting, says Postman, "The business of business becomes psychotherapy; the consumer, the patient reassured by psychodramas."[4]

But trouble comes when we see no harm in these psychodramas, no seduction that threatens to draw us back into "this passing evil age." After all, it's all about style, not substance, the tempter says in the sexy, sleek voice of our favorite movie star. In fact, we can easily work God into the psychodramas of worldly reassurance. Postman's example above is actually fulfilled in our hearing, as any visitor to a Christian Bookseller's Convention can attest. Slogans borrowing from these secular visions of salvation are slapped onto everything from T-shirts to music CDs to bedsheets, longer but only slightly more substantive versions achieving the status of books. The unintended effect is to empty our witness of its gravity. God's *weightiness* (that's what "glory" means in Hebrew) is sacrificed to the trite mediocrity that has come to characterize a world dominated by advertising and a church that tries to imitate it. In the style of the culture of marketing, there can be nothing serious or unsettling—people have a choice, you know, and have learned to switch channels over the slightest sign of a low entertainment value. The criterion for tuning in is whether it's interesting, not whether it's true.

Postman's use of the term *psychodramas* fits remarkably well with the "divine drama" scheme that we have been following. Both make threats and promises, offering curses for a missed opportunity and blessing to those who accept the vision of reality they enact. But they are bitter rivals locked in bitter combat. Contrary to the constant call to "translate" the gospel for our contemporaries, the psychodramas of our age and the drama of redemption cannot be transposed, since the divine drama assumes that the psychodramas of this fading age are the ephemeral candy—momentary felt needs—that Satan uses to keep us from the wedding supper of the Lamb.

Subverting the work of God does not require an explicit rejection of cardinal Christian doctrines, as many mainline churches have tolerated. All that would be necessary is that these truths become so trivialized as to be meaningless—one more passing image in a sea of passing images. And if we can raise the money to bring in an NFL starter who can give his testimony for the youth group, so much the better. As with TV advertising, it is not the product (or message) but the image of those using it that counts.

Style and the Character of God

As we have seen from the biblical examples of those who sought to worship God in their own way instead of in the manner prescribed by God, it is always dangerous to separate *how* we worship (style) from *whom* we worship (substance): The first and second commandments are inseparable.

But one more point bears mentioning in this connection and that is God's glory. Closely related to his holiness, God's glory distinguishes him from all that exists. *Kavod*, the Hebrew noun, means "weighty" or "heavy." We use these terms interchangeably in English as well: An accomplished composer is a "weighty" person (in public estimation if not in physical size), and when we are overwhelmed by a significant piece of news or a profound truth, we say, "That is heavy stuff."

This raises an important question then. If God is "weighty" and his name is "heavy," if he dwells in blinding majesty wrapped in a cloud, if his glory was so powerful that no one could see his face and live and high priests feared for their lives upon entering the temple's most sacred precincts once a year, what does that mean for the style in which we worship him today?

We are not living under the shadow of the ceremonial law but in the reality of our Savior's appearance. We have not come to the mountain of terror, says the writer to the Hebrews, but worship on Mount Zion (Heb. 12:18–24). Yet still, "our God is a consuming fire," and this is why we must come into God's presence through "Jesus the Mediator of the new covenant" (vv. 29, 24 NKJV). We come with confidence but not with glibness; with gladness but not with greasy familiarity. We cling to Jesus Christ as our go-between instead of skipping into God's presence directly, one-on-one, face-to-face, because we have been reminded of his fearful and holy splendor. This is a distinctly Christian worship experience.

In some Christian circles today, one actually hears comments such as, "I don't like church A because there's no life. It's way too heavy and overpowering. It's not heartfelt worship." It is quite possible, of course, that each of these accusations means exactly what it says and that it meets its target. But it is often the case that "life" in this context usually means a concert-like atmosphere in which volume, staging, and lighting play an enormous role. "Heavy" and "overpowering" mean that there is a sense of transcendence that is unfamiliar in our experience as secularized people. "Heartfelt" means casual. Cultural style is never wholly divorced from theological substance. This is why God, taking his glory so seriously, took his worship so seriously as well.

If we are worshiping the God of Abraham and Jesus, the style of that worship will necessarily be "weighty" or "heavy." And it is not that God's glory is merely one attribute, or that it is exclusively identified with God's holiness, justice, majesty, and power. God is glorious in his love, mercy, and tenderness as well. Thus, biblical worship entails the recognition that even when we are joyfully extolling God's nearness and kindness to us, it is always a weighty nearness and a heavy kindness that we admire.

We cannot praise God as he is while emptying the form of its corresponding seriousness. This does not mean, of course, that there is no joy in worship, but it does distinguish a peculiarly sentimental American view of joy from a biblical view of joy as a weighty surprise. While we must beware of legalism in applying this principle, it is important for us to realize as we plan services, church interiors, and sermons that a style dominated by "the lightness of being" is already a message received, often unwittingly, by the congregation.

The Role of Tradition

As evangelicals, we are committed to a high view of Scripture that subjects even the traditions of the elders, however ancient their pedigree, to the touchstone of biblical fidelity. And yet, many of those in evangelical leadership today who have decried the ascendancy in Washington of the sixties radicals are themselves curiously attached to rebellion against authority and tradition with respect to the Christian faith. At times, even the assertion of *biblical* authority in certain contexts draws the charge of legalism and authoritarian traditionalism. "Hey, hey, ho, ho, Western Civ has got to go"—that famous Stanford chant that rallied student revolt against the classics finds its ironic parallel in an evangelical world in which that which is past, just because it is past, is regarded as so many links in the chains that would bind our free, creative spirits.

While it is dangerous to generalize, my impression is that evangelicalism typically ignores tradition and embraces the secular culture, which is a rather unique approach in the history of Christianity. While no past age can be regarded as normative (or perhaps even helpful), according to many, the present state of "the culture" seems to have that position in discussions of evangelism, worship, and growth. No doubt, there are legitimate spiritual reasons for this, such as the recognition that the church is fallible and no period is golden. Dead traditionalism is more often than not a triggering mechanism for the rise of anti-traditionalism. However, we must not forget that this dismissal of tradition (or the *pretension* of dismissing it) reflects the spirit of the Enlightenment. "Enlightenment is man's emergence from his self-incurred immaturity," said Immanuel Kant. "Immaturity is the inability to use one's own understanding without the guidance of another." This immaturity is at the heart of religious appeals to authority external to the free and sovereign individual.[5] Kant contrasted "pure religion" (universal morality) with "ecclesiastical faith" (particular scriptures, creeds, and rituals), roughly corresponding today to the frequent contrast between spirituality and religion. Hardly "postmodern," this attitude of self-assertion against the authority or wisdom of others is the traditional position of modernity, and it permeates evangelical approaches to worship and church growth. Like the gnostics of old, many Christians today regard the history of Christ's body and its doctrinal consensus as little more than the prison house of the soul. Note Postman's analysis of the modern outlook and see if it helps us understand our own capitulation to the spirit of the age. "Technopoly" is the name for the new regime that controls all loyalties and enterprises in our day, and advertising is its chief tactic:

> "We are living at a time," Irving Howe has written, "when all the once regnant world systems that have sustained (also distorted) Western intellectual life, from theologies to ideologies, are taken to be in severe collapse. This leads to a mood of skepticism, an agnosticism of judgment, sometimes a world-weary nihilism in which even the most conventional minds begin to question both distinctions of value and the value of distinctions." Into this void comes the Technopoly story, with its emphasis on progress without limits, rights without responsibilities, and technology without cost. The Technopoly story is without a moral center. . . . It casts aside all traditional narratives and symbols that suggest stability and orderliness, and tells instead of a life of skills, technical expertise,

and the ecstasy of consumption. Its purpose is to produce functionaries for an ongoing Technopoly.[6]

Any particular, local culture must surrender to the global culture, as distinct forms of folk music give way to the more technologically available pop styles, the centuries-old patterns of town life (churches, shops, the courthouse and schoolhouse) around the village green dry up when the mall is built on the outskirts of the city limits. So why shouldn't the lifelong members of the small church where everybody knows each other (perhaps too much) surrender responsibility for anonymity when the megachurch takes its place next to the mall? One megachurch pastor is reported as saying, "What people demand today is probably more than what a small church can offer."[7] Technopoly so calls the shots these days that we cannot imagine why any but the most pedantic critics would question its wisdom and successful providence. Postman adds:

> In the institutional form it has taken in the United States, advertising is a symptom of a world-view that sees tradition as an obstacle to its claims. There can, of course, be no functioning sense of tradition without a measure of respect for symbols. Tradition is, in fact, nothing but the acknowledgement of the authority of symbols and the relevance of narratives that give birth to them. With the erosion of symbols there follows a loss of narrative, which is one of the most debilitating consequences of Technopoly's power. We may take as an example the field of education. In Technopoly, we improve the education of our youth by improving what are called "learning technologies." At the moment, it is considered necessary to introduce computers to the classroom, as it was once thought necessary to bring closed-circuit television and film into the classroom. To the question "Why should we do this?" the answer is: "To make learning more efficient and more interesting." Such an answer is considered entirely adequate, since in Technopoly efficiency and interest need no justification. It is, therefore, usually not noticed that this answer does not address the question "What is learning for?" "Efficiency and interest" is a technical answer, an answer about means, not ends.[8]

Parallels to the world of the church and its ministry are legion. As with Charles Finney's "new measures" in revivalism, those more sophisticated in the technology of church marketing today do not have to justify their efforts according to whether the average covenant child will be likely, at age twelve or so, to personally "own" the covenant. He or she may more likely be capable, as Gallup has repeatedly told us, of naming Santa's reindeer than the twelve apostles. Basic knowledge of the Bible—its main plot, much less its specific details—may be entirely lacking. Nevertheless, the beat goes on, since it has already justified itself in technical terms: efficiency and interest.

What they don't tell you is that the interest will wane just as soon as something "new" comes along and the excitement of the youth group wears off in college. The youth have been taught to value the new and improved over the tried and tested, so in some strange irony it may be the case that our youth groups are actually preparing lambs for the slaughter. It is no wonder that as they mature in their reflection on the world, they simply lose interest in what they thought was Christianity. The "unchurching" of the next generation is happening right under our noses, even in the very churches that pride themselves on reaching the unchurched.

Trivialization, in the name of evangelism, extends into the worship service itself, where shallow, repetitive jingles—many of them remarkably similar to popular advertisement jingles or pop music trademarks—slowly but surely erode the investment of generations of believing Christians throughout the ages and around the world. Eventually, we find ourselves stuck in that same narrow, superficial world of fleeting psychodramas that we were supposed to have left when we entered this place to taste "the powers of the age to come" (Heb. 6:5 NKJV). Ironically, much of contemporary worship has far less outreach potential, since it works within a quite narrow (though widely disseminated) style known as pop. Among churches outside the United States—especially in the less "developed" countries (notice the bias of the very term)—one is much more likely to see a greater unity of expression across denominational, geographical, ethnic, and socioeconomic lines.

Worship technologies increasingly replace the tough business of hearing the preached Word and joining the church in heaven and on earth in faithfully receiving it and sharing it with the world. Sometimes this is our fault as hearers and often, as pastors, we need to resist the temptation to capitulate to market trends. A friend who is a pastor recently told me that in his church, with a rather large university population, a self-appointed spokesman for this block reported to him that students can no longer give their attention to a half hour or forty-minute sermon. This pastor's response was interesting. "Isn't it still true that the university lectures are approximately an hour in length?" "Yes," the man replied. "And they still take notes all that time and then review those notes for an exam that will test their grasp of the material?" "Of course," the man answered, breaking into a grin as he realized where the analogy was going. If the medium of speech is still in regular use in the various departments of human interest and knowledge generally, why must it be obsolete in the church? Is it perhaps because we simply do not think that religion is as important as these other disciplines? It is not only university students who have been used to this format of public presentations. Think of the antebellum slave churches and the role of biblical preaching as the rhetorical center of black church life—even where few had the opportunity to receive a formal education.

Being stuck in a rut is an easy way to respond to this crisis, but lazy conservatism should find no safer haven with us than cultural captivity. We have to go back further and deeper than most conservatives are even interested in going—back not only before Nashville but before the gospel songs of revivalism, until we find deeper waters. Then we need to launch our boat there, searching for lost cities below. We need to get in touch with the church in past ages and learn from both its mistakes and its superior wisdom in the things of God. Fresh liturgical forms may have to be written, and many new arrangements for the psalms and hymns—including new hymn texts—are appearing even now that show appreciative familiarity with the heritage without being enslaved to it.

Style is not neutral. Cicero reminded us of what every Christian should know from Scripture, that "to remain ignorant of things that happened before you were born is to remain a child."[9] The marketing of youth, with its mechanisms of advertising ("This is not your father's Oldsmobile") and entertainment, both mechanisms using age segmentation as a means of creating two separate markets for products, are carried over into the church. This is not exactly what Jesus had in mind when he said that he came to set parents against their children. In fact, nothing could be more destructive to the covenantal fabric of the divine drama than to regard as neutral this pulling apart of the ties that bind us together as God's people called out of the world. Once more, style becomes a theological matter.

Statistical analysis of consumer trends is not neutral forecasting but is in danger of becoming a new master, dictating the terms of Christian discourse. "A bureaucrat armed with a computer," Postman says, "is the unacknowledged legislator of our age and a terrible burden to bear. . . . I am constantly amazed at how obediently people accept explanations that begin with the words, 'The computer shows . . .' It is Technopoly's equivalent of the sentence, 'It is God's will,' and the effect is roughly the same."[10] One of the reasons that mainline Protestantism fell to liberalism was the shift of authority from the church courts to bureaucrats. It is no wonder that the bureaucrats all moved in together on Riverside Drive in New York City, since they all tended to be the same kind of person anyway. It mattered little whether the bureaucrat was Presbyterian, Lutheran, Reformed, Episcopal, Baptist, or Methodist.

Today, it may well be not the frustrated social worker but the frustrated entrepreneur who will destroy what is left of American Protestantism if given the opportunity. It does not really matter to what theological tradition a denomination belongs, since they have all been de-theologized by those who have promised us all along that style is neutral and their church growth techniques are nontheological. What they meant was that their style would neutralize every distinctive feature of any particular church and make a distorted theology determinative.

Where the style of worship might immediately distinguish one church from another in past generations, given the different theological understandings, a visitor to an evangelical Reformed, Baptist, or Lutheran church today might think that he or she is in a generic spiritual mall. Style is not neutral, and if we all share a market-driven style, it may be because we are all market-driven in our theology, at least where it matters most—in our meeting with God. We are increasingly united not by our agreement in the truth but by the trademarks of the companies from which we purchase our common worship materials, many of them subsidiaries of secular corporations. Increasingly, our music, architecture, furnishings, and technology merge into one homogenous testimony to the trivialization of truth and the culture of entertainment and marketing, which have now become largely the same thing.

Some years ago, Marshal McLuhan made the famous observation that "the medium is the message." That is the point here. Style and content cannot be divorced any more than the body is meant to be divorced from the soul. In the case of the latter, the separation is linked to death, which is linked to sin. It is not the way things are meant to be in creation, and they will not remain so after the resurrection of our bodies. Like the physical body, style is a matter of sights, sounds, touch, gestures, postures. While it is true that worship cannot consist of prescriptions concerning each of these, they are not mere window dressing either. When the people of God were commanded to "worship and bow down . . . [and] kneel before the LORD [their] Maker" (Ps. 95:6 NKJV), they did. And when they were entreated to "present [their] bodies as living sacrifices" (Rom. 12:1), the possibility of separating style from substance was excluded. While this is not to suggest that we have to exhibit all the same physical movements that we find depicted in Scripture, it is to say that the gnostic temptation to pit spiritual worship against everything physical must be viewed with suspicion. The concrete way in which we worship God is not only an implication of the content of what we believe about God but is part of that content itself. To seek to separate style from content is not only like divorcing body and soul; it is as if to say that one may obey the first commandment while breaking the second.

Our situation resembles in some ways that confused era of Israel's history under the judges when "in those days there was no king in Israel" and "everyone did what was right in his own eyes" (Judg. 17:6 NKJV). But today, Israel does have a king who reigns over her, though she seeks out every high place for spiritual adultery, as the prophets charged. "Do not learn the way of the Gentiles" (Jer. 10:2 NKJV) does not strike us today as a direct warning, but perhaps it should.

The question is never between having a tradition or not having one: Everybody is "traditional" in the sense of being shaped by certain assumptions. But that's just it: They're assumptions, and as long as we are unreflective about them, we will end up living as if they were true even if they are ridiculous, while dismissing true ones as ridiculous. No one comes to the Bible neutrally, as an objective spectator. We all come with certain interests, fears, and a particular range of expectations as to what the Bible could or couldn't say. Scripture is good at tearing up our nicely arranged garden, but we do have a garden and we live in it. The real question then is *which* tradition, not *whether* tradition. Will we be shaped by a distinct biblical tradition or by the tradition of consumerism? That does not mean that every issue is settled once one has decided for the biblical tradition. There are still further qualifications: which tradition of Christianity? But these are not trivial, pedantic questions. They determine whether we will be passive or active in the Christian life and, for many readers, in the Christian ministry—whether or not we will be shaped by traditions, secular or ecclesiastical, that we have never actually understood, owned, and critically examined. Jaroslav Pelikan captures the essence of what I take to be the right kind of traditional thinking: "Tradition is the living faith of the dead, traditionalism is the dead faith of the living."[11]

What about the Setting?

I have labored the point that neither the content nor the style of worship is neutral; both will be shaped either by Scripture (which requires time and close attention to theological detail—the sort of thing that comes with centuries of Christian wisdom) or by the world (which in our day requires merely awareness of the latest longings and technologies for satisfying them). But what about the setting? As in any stage play, the set is important. It may not be essential to the successful performance of the play, but it provides the appropriate environment for following the lines and plot.

Similarly, particular architectural designs and furnishings are not essential to the very existence of the church. When the Samaritan woman asked Jesus whether the true "container" for God was there in Samaria or in Jerusalem, the true Temple who stood before her replied, "Woman, believe me, the hour is coming when you will neither on this mountain, nor in Jerusalem, worship the Father. You worship what you do not know; we know what we worship, for salvation is of the Jews. But the hour is coming, and now is, when the true worshipers will worship the Father in spirit and in truth; for the Father is seeking such to worship him. God is Spirit, and those who worship him must worship in spirit and in truth" (John 4:21–24 NKJV). "Spirit" in this passage should be capitalized, because it is the Holy Spirit who is in view. By this, then, Jesus did not mean our spirits, a view that has often been used to justify nearly anything on the ground that it helps us to connect inwardly with God. Rather, he is saying that the new covenant worship, in which the Holy Spirit will be poured out on the whole community, will not be tied to any particular place, as was the Mosaic theocracy. It will be a universal kingdom, where God will finally dwell among his people and his glory will extend to the ends of the earth.

This passage, then, should bar any hope of reentering the temple in Jerusalem to reestablish God's spatio-temporal domicile. Jesus Christ is the living temple in whom we as his co-heirs are living stones. God is not to be found in temples built with human hands; he is to be found wherever two or more are gathered in his name for Word, sacrament, and prayer. God's people have worshiped in caves and in cathedrals, and God's presence should never be identified with either.

But Word, sacrament, and prayer do indicate some sort of setting, especially when we look further into the drama that is being staged through these discrete actions. Here God is assembling his saints on his holy hill of Zion, regaling them with stories of victory over their foes—and even over their own rebellion. If the age to come is dawning here among us and in us, surely there are certain patterns and settings that are more appropriate than others. Here God raises his banner over them and claims them for his own possession, promising everlasting protection to everyone who calls on his name. As we have seen with the great service before the Water Gate upon the return of the exiles, Nehemiah had a massive pulpit erected high above the people, no doubt emphasizing that it was God himself who was gathering and addressing his people through Ezra. They gathered under the Word, not on an equal footing with it.

For centuries, churches across the denominational spectrum had raised pulpits. Even in Roman Catholic churches, where the high altar was the focal point, a high pulpit was raised above the people for the sermon. It is not surprising, then, that the Reformation, in its recovery of the preached Word, gave a fresh visual prominence to the pulpit. Along with the font (baptism) and the table or altar (the Lord's Supper), the high pulpit stood over the people as the minister himself stood under the Word that he preached. This practice enjoyed ecumenical support for centuries but has been challenged first by American revivalism, which replaced the chancel with a stage, and now by a more explicit use of the stage as everything its name implies.

In older churches, there is still the old furniture—heavy and difficult to move—for a reason. Those who do not look beyond their own prejudices will fail to ask what those reasons were, but whether one agrees or not, they were often important reasons. In *A Month of Sundays*, John Updike's character followed his father into the ministry but rejected his liberal Protestantism. It was the furniture that first made him rethink things, Updike writes. The very heaviness of the furniture suggested the truth of everything that liberalism regarded as too obsolete precisely for that reason—it was too weighty.[12] Certainly there is a danger in being so deliberate and opinionated about the "set" of worship that we lose sight of its real purpose and make life unduly difficult for others. (More church splits have probably occurred over building campaigns, music styles, and decoration committees than over false teaching.)

There will always be old church buildings that possess enormously attractive aesthetic features but inadequately "house" biblical worship. Still, we must recall that the Gothic medieval churches were *converted* to Protestant use by the Reformers; they were not *destroyed*. The same combination of theological and imaginative conservatism could provide enormous wisdom for us today, when architectural styles are tending to move in the direction of theater seating and stages. (Whatever one might say in its defense, the theater-style "worship center" is a radical break with church architecture in favor of entertainment architecture.) Furthermore, there have been some fantastic architectural designs of church buildings in a modern or postmodern style that continue to express faithfully in visual form the values of biblical, Word-and-sacrament worship. It is often difficult to distinguish exactly where theological values end and taste begins, and yet we must, it seems to me, steer a course between stylistic absolutism ("Only the Gothic style really captures transcendence!") and a general disregard for the set in which this divine drama is staged in its local weekly performance.

A setting in which the architectural prominence is given to Word and sacrament will reflect a different theological orientation than a setting in which the movie theater or concert hall predominates in influence. Despite its having unleashed a pogrom on historic Christianity, the Enlightenment obsession with wiping away the past and starting over with the insights of "modern man" runs deep in our veins as American Christians. Few devotees of the new and improved ever ask, "Now why is this here and that there?" They are like the radicals in the time of the Reformation who simply burned down churches and insisted on starting from scratch, following their own utopian visions. The generation that has torn down beautiful landmarks to make room for strip malls is now also in leadership in the church, and they pose a challenge to the ecology of God's covenant people.

Where the high pulpit, Communion table, and baptismal font are immovable and prominent, the furniture is there for a reason and should be changed only for an equally good one. The attitude that they are "in the way" may indicate that the ordained means are in the way of the extraordinary means that we have ourselves discovered. Whatever the design and style, a church interior should be distinguished from a theater and a stage as it is also from a temple of ritual sacrifice.

The furniture and design of churches, whether "traditional" or "contemporary," have theological assumptions, some of them implicit and others explicit. Some are obvious: One knows by walking into a traditional Roman Catholic church that the "main event" in the service is when the priest offers up Jesus Christ again as a sacrifice for the sins of the people. One knows by walking into a traditional Baptist church that preaching and the choir are important, and the distinctive practice of full immersion in baptism is front and center in the large baptismal tank behind the pulpit. One knows by walking into a traditional Lutheran, Reformed, Presbyterian, and Methodist church that preaching and sacrament are both important and central acts. Finally, one can discern whether an Episcopal church is "high" or "low" by where it falls on the preceding spectrum. It's not just a matter of style: "High church" congregations are identified by a more Roman Catholic theological commitment, while "low church" types are more likely adherents of the evangelical wing of the Anglican tradition.

One also knows when one is in the generic "New Church," regardless of formal denominational affiliation. Conspicuous is the stage, choir, instruments, projection screen, and theater seating. One is obviously in a building constructed for some sort of entertainment purpose, the setting suggests, regardless of intention. Preaching, if there is a standard sermon, is often delivered either from a music stand or by strolling casually through the audience. It is likely that the implied message is that preaching is not a means of grace, a divine summons and encounter in which God speaks death and life through the minister's words, but an occasion for the preacher to lecture, inspire, cajole, entertain, exhort, or lay out his opinions about dealing with life with God's help. In numerous church growth periodicals in recent years, the appeal to exchange pulpits for strolling is actually argued theologically, whether such advocates recognize it as such or not. People don't want to be "preached to." They want to feel that the pastor is one of them, vulnerable, a friend who has something to say that might help them along the way. But this theological rationale is at odds with the theological assumptions that have been outlined throughout this book. Agree or disagree with that outline, but we should all be able to recognize that style is not neutral.

Often, the "New Church" also shows little concern for the importance and character of the sacraments in the ordinary life of the church. Interestingly, while Baptists and those who practice infant baptism disagree rather strongly, for both the vessel of baptism is prominently displayed. But in the "New Church," ordinarily there is no visual sign that Jesus ever said, "Go therefore and make disciples of all the nations, baptizing them in the name of the Father and of the Son and of the Holy Spirit" (Matt. 28:19 NKJV) or that he instituted the Supper as a means of sharing in his body and blood (1 Cor. 10:16). Other symbols abound, giving evidence of the many other things not prescribed in Scripture that are nevertheless treated as means of grace. Style is not neutral.

Let me emphasize that I am not endorsing the "Old Church." There are old errors and new insights as well as vice versa. Further, some today defend the "Old Church" for reasons that are just as culturally determined as those of the new church. What *is* unique about our situation today, however, is the emergence of a new style that is self-consciously nontheological or at least not theologically deliberate about architecture, design, and furnishings. Even in churches in which theological distinctives are taken seriously, these decisions are often made for almost exclusively pragmatic reasons, drawing on the pastor's or building committee's experience. Conservative, traditional churches often underestimate the importance of these issues, counting on doctrinal instruction to carry all the weight. While "contemporary" staging is unabashedly theatrical, "traditional" staging is often anti-theatrical instead of being intentional about the sort of theater that is being performed on it. The choice is not between drama and no drama but which drama? Is it a drama that God is staging for the redemption of a people, or is it a drama that we are staging for God and for each other or for the unchurched? The show must go on, but whose is it?

Following are a few questions that we may not have thought about but that our forebears thought about and many of our brothers and sisters in other parts of the world continue to think about: Does the furniture, as well as its placement, announce that this is God's stage or ours? Why do we have flags up front where all the action is, especially the American flag? Is this a play about the legend of Christian America or the truth about and the effectual creation of the community of Pentecost, families of many tongues and nations who have come to the Jerusalem that is above? How is the roof pitched: too high to be capable of declaring that God has come near to us in Christ or too low to declare that God is holy and transcendent? Of course, opinions will vary widely—

and we must beware of becoming legalistic about what pitch, for instance, adequately testifies to God's nearness and transcendence. But we must begin to *ask* the questions again if there is to be a thorough reformation of worship in our day.

Music Matters

Having wandered now into the minefield of the worship wars, we might as well come to the front line. One of the ironies about the situation today is that while so much has been made of the importance of music in bringing God's people together, it seems to have been far more divisive than any doctrine, view of the sacraments, or liturgical position. There have been many tragic divisions in church history over secondary doctrines, but disagreements over worship—and especially musical style—have brought fresh wounds to the body of Christ. While before there were several major ecclesiastical traditions, now each denomination has its own internal division between "conservatives" and "progressives." In fact, many congregations are now divided along generational lines, each niche market having its own service each Sunday.

Many of the older hymns are just as contemporary as they ever were because they are richly scriptural, and the psalms that we use are divinely inspired, after all. But many of the older hymn texts as well as psalm texts, not to mention the music, need revision. In addition, we need new hymns altogether, and God seems to be sending us many, usually from outside the usual corporate channels in Nashville. For many of us, "traditional" versus "contemporary" no longer serves very well as a way of setting up the debate. We do not want to be "traditional" if that means nothing new, and we do not want to be "contemporary" if that means poor imitations of American Top 40 tunes with vacuous, repetitive lyrics. Furthermore, a growing number of Christians are impatient with a reactionary conservatism that refuses to utilize any instrument but the organ, even while accepting folksy gospel songs sung by soloists. Evidently, "traditional" for some means nostalgic, holding on to the "contemporary" songs of yesteryear that are often just as sentimental and us-centered as more recent ones.

Music and the Logic of Marketing

The point is that there is another way, beyond the traditional-contemporary impasse. But to move in that direction, we have to see what hinders us. The logic of marketing has particularly taken us hostage by employing market segmentation. When advertising first recognized radio and then TV as lucrative vehicles, American society was still somewhat connected generationally. Often, grandparents lived with their adult offspring and were linked to the future by the grandchildren at their feet. Even church burial yards were as yet preferred to the emerging cemetery industry, underscoring that communal link even to the dead who will one day be raised. Products were marketed by what we now regard as "cheesy" appeals to brand loyalty, a rather banal blend of traditionalism and sentimentalism: "It was good enough for your grandmother." "Give Me That Old Time Religion" hails from that same era: "It was good enough for grandma; it's good enough for me." However trite and shallow these expressions may have been, in its own way the advertising culture that helped shape them found *intergenerational* marketing still effective in making a sale.

However, an explosion of markets in subsequent decades has created the bewildering diversity of products and services we now see all around us. This is not wrong in itself, of course, but as sociologist Peter Berger has reminded us, it means that Americans have become obsessed with choice. As we noted earlier, he even calls this the "heretical imperative," since *haeresis* (meaning "choice") used to identify those who followed their own opinions and desires instead of God's Word. Everyone is a "heretic" today, Berger argues, because there is no longer a stable inheritance that passes from one generation to the next, any authoritative norm from which one could possibly deviate.[13] So instead of marketing to brand loyalty ("It was good enough for your grandmother"), products must appeal to the individual consumer's choice. It must be a statement of individuality, which is to say, one's identity (or hopeful identity) apart from any community: "This is not your father's Oldsmobile." How do advertisers know that this appeals to us? Because we are consumers who now prize choice over belonging, consumption over production, and image over substance.

It is almost inconceivable to many of us today that millions of people in America would spend an entire day together (sabbatarianism was the dominant practice across denominations) without being segmented into age groups. Children sat in church with their parents and grandparents and spent the day with fellow church members. Of course, children gathered together on their own, as did men and women. But this was all a natural sort of thing that just happened outside of organized gatherings, until the advent of "Women's Societies," "Men's Societies," and now—especially with the triumph of the post-sixties youth culture— "youth groups," with their own "youth pastors." When this phenomenon interacts with the culture of marketing (without which it would never have been born), "This is not your father's Oldsmobile" is translated, "This is not your father's church." The revivalist and the advertiser both agreed in substance on this point: Individual choice determines one's future—not *belonging* but *choosing*. But what church marketers fail to question is whether the culture of marketing should be allowed to dictate the terms of existence within the kingdom of God. Style is declared "neutral" and therefore entirely separate from the content—which is controlled by Scripture. And yet somehow, as enough time has passed, the evangelical movement has made sweeping concessions to modernity in theology and has become hostile to theological issues being raised in connection with practical questions about outreach, growth, and worship. One smells theological factors afoot after all. Form and substance are difficult, if not impossible, to separate.

Other lines of inquiry ought to be pursued in our discussions as well. For instance, we need to ask about the theological rationale for church music in the first place. What is its role? What is the significance of the shift from viewing music as a means of inculcating sound doctrine (Col. 3:16) and communal response to God's action (Eph. 5:19–20) to seeing it as "the worship time"? Is the implication that while we continue to tip our hat to the ministry of the Word, we believe that the main event is really about expressing ourselves, even if it is in an attitude of praise?

Far too many conservative critics of the contemporary worship style accuse those who favor it of shifting the focus from worship to entertainment. But this can easily become a cheap shot. After all, I've seen plenty of worship services in which the style of high culture provided the same entertainment value as the style of pop culture used in the church down the street. But even if one criticizes the CCM (Christian Contemporary Music) worship style for making the congregation an audience instead of the performers, this challenge fails on two counts. First, it does not fairly describe CCM worship, at least in most of the contexts in which I have witnessed it. I do not doubt that advocates of the pop worship style and their congregations see themselves as heightening congregational participation in worship. And, for the most part, they have achieved this. To be sure, the band up front is clearly in the lead, but there is often more congregational participation in the singing than I recall in my childhood with the big choir up front.

My second objection to this common criticism is that it's just not very good, even if it were true. If the service is primarily about us and what we are doing, then it makes sense that the congregation will be viewed as participants rather than as an audience. But I have argued that the service is chiefly a matter of who God is and what he is doing for us. He is not entertaining us, to be sure. We are not in that sense an audience.

But we are his covenant people, and his work for us in Word and deed is central; our response is just that—response—and should be treated as such in the service. Whether we are "traditionalists" or "progressivists," the deeper question is whether we regard the service primarily in terms of God's action and our response or in terms of our action and God's passive appreciation.

We do not come to church to affirm our faithfulness, our devotion, our praise, and our up-to-the-minute emotional state but to be addressed, undressed, and re-dressed by God. Only when this fact is central are we in any position to faithfully praise God as "our *reasonable* service." At this point, it seems to me that both traditional and contemporary parties miss the real point of singing as response and in both cases often place too much emphasis on *our* work in the service as if this were the main event.

What is the long-term effect of making the service predominantly a time in which we rather than God are "on stage"? And if we are doing all, or at least most, of the talking, where will God get in a word edgewise? Regardless of style, how long will believers last on repetitive praise without knowing what exactly God has done and is doing here, right now, in his Son and by his Spirit? Is this chiefly an opportunity for me to express my own individual choice of God—my love for him, my devotion to him, my thankful heart, my determination to obey him—or is it an opportunity chiefly for God to place me in a community of the redeemed who joyfully receive that glad announcement that he has acted for us on the stage of human history for our redemption? As in any play, the music cannot be the main event. It may assist the actors in performing their roles and us in listening better to the lines, but the real drama is in the story: its plot and its central character.

In recent months, I have observed a slight change on the music front of the worship wars, and I take it as good news. In between ads for synthesizers and PA systems are articles written by CCM industry leaders who nevertheless raise concerns about the directions of the last twenty years. *Worship Leader* managing editor David Di Sabatino observes, "Detractors of the contemporary worship movement have a legitimate complaint when they lament that current songs are devoid of theological acumen and have capitulated to the highly individualistic and commercially-driven *zeitgest* [sic] of our culture."[14] But that's not all. The next article calls our attention to the "quest of an ancient future: old hymns, contemporary context." This article cites Michael Card's observation "that the contemporary worship movement has simply capitulated to cultural trends." Card has discovered a new generation of young people for whom the old hymns are brand-new. And fresh features, such as new harmonizations, are breathing new life into these old texts. Various seeker-oriented pastors are quoted as suggesting that the superficial era of contemporary worship may be nearing its end. What was old is now new. "By exposing new people to many of these old classics in a way that is musically familiar but nonthreatening, we encourage a very healthy type of connection to our ancient faith."[15]

It is not surprising, then, that the so-called Gen-Xer is bored by CCM and is excited about liturgy and some intimation of transcendence. Donald C. Boyd recounts the story of a denominational official who led a focus group of twenty-something ministers. "While tossing on the table the idea of worship, one of the young pastors remarked, 'Well, I've been raised on traditional worship. You know, praise choruses, music projected on the wall, drama—that sort of thing.'"[16] Due to the breathtaking pace of change in music, pop-cultural taste is hardly a form that is likely to tie generations together and link God's people across the times and places of their common witness.

We need to get beyond the traditional/contemporary categories and rediscover the biblical, confessional, theological warp and woof of worship. This will mean that new thinking is in order, whether we're lazy praise-and-worship folks who are satisfied with a few chords on the guitar and undemanding content or lazy conservatives who just want to sing familiar tunes even if they have lost their freshness or have their own theological problems. Even now there are gifted pastors and musicians working in tandem to produce new lyrical texts and musical compositions. Every era of genuine reformation and awakening has generated a new era in liturgical and musical development, as the gospel is rediscovered in its astonishing depth. Like our forebears, we are reformers and not revolutionaries. We should seek to challenge ourselves and each other to greater biblical fidelity, but we should be suspicious of those who want to start from scratch. Reformation assumes change within continuity. In the late sixteenth century, both Rome and the Reformed churches considered prohibiting the organ's use in church, but it was gradually incorporated upon the condition, at least in Reformed churches, that it not be allowed to dominate (as, for instance, the praise band now does in contemporary worship). I would be among those who would be delighted to see a prudent use of the guitar and other stringed instruments in addition to or even in place of the organ. In fact, of greater concern than the use of a particular instrument should be the preference given to one form (pop music with its limited, upbeat range) and its physical prominence in the front of a theater-style church building where pulpit, font, and table have been eliminated as so much clutter on the musical stage.

Despite the challenges, the growing interest in reinvesting in historic Christianity represents an invigorating turn. It is quite ironic that more conservative Reformed and Lutheran writers defend the music of the Gaithers as "contemporary" and "seeker sensitive," while the coming generation of evangelicals finds this music far more alienating than the psalms of David and the great hymns that were written before the adoption of sentimental texts and tunes. While many evangelical pastors and writers are defending "Shine, Jesus, Shine," many of those on the vanguard of seeker churches are seeking refuge in the "Rock of Ages."

Frequently in the worship wars, both sides tend to think of traditional worship as involving classical music, while contemporary worship simply updates things. Favoring traditional or contemporary worship styles is largely a matter of the settings on our car stereo. But as Ken Myers explains, "Popular culture is not neutral regarding the sensibilities it encourages. Because of the centrality of commercial concerns, popular culture maintains a preferential option for the upbeat, the informal, the new and 'interesting.'"[17]

MTV represents not only a new technology (way of doing things) but a new epistemology (way of thinking). Instead of following and evaluating arguments, many people today see reality in terms of visual consumerism—fragmented images united by the thinnest of plots dangling precariously but interestingly before us. Precisely because these cultural habits are so pervasive and accepted, we are usually not even aware of them and treat them not as habits to be evaluated but as givens to be assumed. The same is true of the way we evaluate music.

But isn't it the case that the classical music of our day was the popular music of yesteryear? Bach was contemporary in his day, wasn't he? So why shouldn't we be contemporary in ours? This argument, however, confuses "contemporary" as a generic label for *the present* with a particular style in popular culture today that is called "Contemporary Music." To be sure, the common people in the eighteenth century were capable of being entertained by a higher quality of music than we typically are today. But that is not an argument in favor of Contemporary Christian Music. Although it is used to relativize music style, this argument actually supports the point that the pop music style of soft rock is inferior to the "popular" music of the Renaissance, baroque, and neoclassical eras. For one thing, contemporary pop music is inferior in its durability. Due to its inherently superficial construction, pop music captivates for the moment but, like fireworks, dissipates just as quickly. Does anyone really think that Bette Midler's "Wind Beneath My Wings" will be around in five hundred years, much less that it will be considered classical or high culture?

What the identification of today's classical music as yesterday's popular music proves is that there is an inherent quality in that music that simply does not exist in the pop style. The great psalms and hymns, just as the great folk music of diverse cultures, have been sung lustily for generations, by young and old, rich and poor, black and white. In fact, a number of our oldest (and newest) hymns were written by Africans and Asians as well as Europeans. There is a track record here. But we cannot help but notice how quickly a praise chorus or CCM song comes and goes. If church music has as one of its main objectives to inculcate the truth of God's Word, this creates problems. After all, even now a generation is being raised in our churches that has virtually no knowledge of even the best-known psalms and hymns—nor even a particular body of praise and worship music, since these songs often evaporate as quickly as they appear. Going, therefore, is another important means of passing down the Christian inheritance to our children at a time when they are trying to find a place to belong and a community that is deeper and wider than the present moment of individual inspiration. We no longer share a common body of church praise across the generations and around the world. We are stuck in the rut of the here and now.

Pop music is not simply the popular music of our day but a style all its own in history—the product of a convergence of many streams: marketing/advertising, the triumph of the therapeutic, and entertainment as stimulation rather than refinement. Common people today are not likely to find even new symphonic music appealing just as they are not likely to find recently written but sophisticated literature entertaining. This is not because 'N Sync and Barbara Cartland are the future's "high culture," just as Mozart and Dante are today's, but because there is something about the latter pair that is simply more enduring than the former. Television—its news, comedy, and drama—will never be regarded as an ennobling medium even five centuries from now. It is called the "boob tube" and "idiot box" today even by those who surrender large segments of their lives to it. As entertaining as he is, David Letterman will be forgotten while Homer's *Odyssey* will continue to be read by young and old alike.

Disdaining the sixties for the sexual revolution that leveled all prior moral norms, many conservative Christians today nevertheless embrace the same lust for innovation as an inherently superior category. *New* and *contemporary* are terms that refer not merely to works produced in recent years but the buzzwords for pop culture and its distinct musical forms. Arguments for contemporary music are far too simplistic when proponents say, in effect, that they just favor keeping up-to-date while opponents simply want to live in the past. Both living in the past and longing for pop culture are signs of worldliness, or at least laziness.

Freedom from the past and liberation from forms belong to the amorality of our relativistic culture. It is this individual freedom that absolves us of responsibility. So, for instance, homosexual couples are now identified as "nontraditional couples." Sexual orientation is no longer an ethical category but a matter of taste. No judgment or discernment is allowed—such couples are not wrong but different. This is just another illustration of how the terms *traditional* and *contemporary* miss the real issues involved. While we do not have to reject everything that is new, we do need to have a biblically informed wisdom that can assess the old and the new in the light of their use in certain contexts, such as worship.

I have no trouble admitting that I like certain alternative rock songs and I've watched enough television over my lifetime to confess my status as a debtor to my culture. But isn't there a balance between allowing for Christian liberty on one hand and embracing a reverse legalism that identifies Christian concern for the lost with total immersion in the wasteland of cultural nihilism? Why must a successful pastor be able to cite *Seinfeld* or *Touched by an Angel* in his sermons? Since when did the minister's authority among the young—and therefore over the congregation—rest on whether he was as addicted to sitcoms, movies, celebrities, sports, and other forms of entertainment as they are? (Citing *Touched by an Angel* will earn only a disparaging grin from the youth anyway and will give away the preacher's age profile.) In the past, in fact, ministers saw it as their business to encourage those under their care to greater maturity in their habits and desires, to give them a taste of nobler things. Those who cannot think deeply or feel deeply about much in general will never be able to think or feel deeply about God.

While listening to U2 or reading John Grisham is not sinful, such music and books cannot be regarded as the only sort of music and literature that are "contemporary." There is other music and other literature being produced today to which we might want to expose ourselves in order to live richer, fuller, more satisfying lives. Regardless of our own choices in that regard, which no church should dictate, it is a violation of the liberty of others that the choice for pop culture must dominate the corporate worship of God. In the past, traditional liturgies and music were sufficiently different from any particular cultural form (classical, jazz, blues, rock) that everyone could participate regardless of personal tastes. To the extent that pop culture dominates and that distinctive church culture surrenders to it, churches will become more bound to the inherently divisive nature of the culture of marketing.

Ken Myers, Leonard Payton, and others have made the point that until the invention of recording tape, there were roughly two categories of culture: high and folk. High culture is what an artist does simply for the sake of the art itself, while folk art is produced by and for a local community.

Switzerland's high-quality clocks were never high art or culture but belong to folk culture. Visitors would pick up a clock or two on trips. It was not only the mechanical products of the industrial revolution, however, but the processes of modernization, especially the routinization of labor, that converted small workshops into large factories. The mass production of these clocks on an assembly line parallels in some ways what happened in music. New recording technologies have made it possible for anyone almost anywhere to become a global citizen, a "nowhere man" who belongs to no particular place. While high culture and folk culture both were created by and for specific places, popular culture has created a global audience that enshrines choice, multiculturalism, and diversity even while it is bland, homogenous, and herd-like. This contradiction may have something to do with why pop culture artifacts rise and fall so quickly. Myers and Payton have observed that the main tradition of church music has been associated with folk music, not classical music as is often suspected.

Well into the beginning of the twentieth century, hymns were only included in the Presbyterian Church, for instance, with the codicil, "Permitted to be sung in the church by the General Assembly." Just as the minister was the "worship leader," the church was the patron and arbiter of church music. In nineteenth-century revivalism, however, there was a growing tendency to detach worship music from the church. The style of the "gospel song," sentimental and effusive (both musically and lyrically), borrowed heavily from the popular show tunes of the day's entertainment: vaudeville. But folk culture and an entertainment culture are two different things, each with its own set of values, goals, and means of attaining them. One need only thumb through a hymnal that predates D. L. Moody and Ira Sankey to notice how many tunes were taken from folk culture. These melodies were sung in Irish pubs and by Moravian farmers as they labored.

But a local pub is a very different atmosphere than a contemporary nightclub or stage. These folk tunes had both musical and lyrical character and depth. They were given not so much to self-referential expressiveness but to storytelling. What better vehicle to convey the drama of redemption than a storytelling idiom! But if they are quite different from popular culture, these folk melodies are also quite different from classical or so-called high culture. John Newton's "Amazing Grace" will be in use a lot longer than "Shine, Jesus, Shine!" but no one will confuse it with a Vivaldi concerto. The tune of "Immortal, Invisible, God Only Wise" was a Welsh folk song, not a chorus from one of Puccini's operas or a Mendelssohn symphony. Traditional church music for congregational singing, then, is (with few exceptions) not classical music. But pop music is neither classical nor folk culture; rather, it represents a new genre of mass-produced, market-driven culture. In fact, several of the largest contemporary Christian music companies in Nashville that supply transdenominational music leadership for churches are actually wholly owned subsidiaries of multinational corporations.

But a critique of pop culture is not the same as a rejection of cultural forms, which in any case is an impossible task. As embodied creatures of concrete times and places, our liturgical environment will surely display distinct marks. There is no reason why church architecture should adopt a neo-Gothic or neoclassical style any more than an eclectic or postmodern style. But neo-Gothic and neoclassical styles—and everything in between—reflect a degree of thoughtfulness and skilled labor that is missing from the stucco tract home in which my wife and I reside. I am always amazed, when visiting under-developed nations, at how much skill and energy could be discerned in many of the church buildings. Pop culture does not equal "contemporary" and "relevant" unless we have a simplistic view of our current options and are impatient with learning discretion in our cultural preferences.

Worship is not about cultural preferences, but we would be naïve to think that they play no role. By giving forms of culture that are not generated by the Disney Corporation a chance in our lives, we are more capable of developing discernment in a broader range of entertainment and enrichment. Does the literature we read enrich our lives? Do we ever listen to the kind of music that is richer in its variety than the routine patterns of mass-marketed songs? The better music (better according to the standards of music itself) is not more intellectual and less passionate but far more intense in its emotion because it delays gratification and then plucks chords deep in our souls that contemporary jingles cannot reach. Isn't this an apt analogy for what happens in the worship service? If the purpose of our singing in worship—at least one of the chief purposes cited by Paul—is to make "the Word of Christ dwell in us richly," then we need to be discerning enough about musical style to determine the most enduring, structurally rich, and edifying.

So Where Now?

Style is not neutral, I have argued. But I have not tried to make the case that God has delivered specific prescriptions that create a shortcut to serious reflection, study, and prayer. Moving beyond the cul-de-sac of traditional versus contemporary, we need to become more theologically driven as we come to a fresh analysis of where we have been, where we are, and where we are going.

Reductionism would extol the supposed virtue of either high or low culture. Instead, we should recognize that our lives are not that simple.

We live in a complex environment of overlapping spheres. A pep talk from one's spouse encouraging one to hang in there with a diet may be appropriate, but that does not mean that pep talks are appropriate for presidential inaugurations and state visits, live theater, or sermons in church. We need to embrace diversity and cultivate both tolerance and discrimination. Far from being antithetical notions, these skills are twin virtues sired by wisdom. There will be people on both sides of the debate who will want to make this easy: Just accept the new or just reject it; style has to fit the culture of marketing or style has to fit the culture of a bygone era. But we need to do some heavy lifting if we are to honor God's Word and serve his people in the past, present, and future. To build on the past, we need to understand the past—to appreciate it, at a time when this runs against the grain of our cultural sensibilities. We have to reject the market segmentation that sets father against son and mother against daughter not for the sake of the gospel but for the sake of target marketing. And at the same time, we have to understand our cultural habits. Some of these habits we may use to help us improve on the past, while others we will recognize as worldly accommodation of which we must repent. We will have disagreements about specific applications—and that is as helpful to future generations as it is frustrating for us. We cannot rush headlong into the future or hold nervously to the past. Those two options are no longer available to those who would be faithful today to God's drama of redemption.

ELEVEN

Taking a Break from the Buzz

"I wish I had more time to dig deeply into Scripture and solid Christian teaching, but my life is just too crazy." How many times have we heard that? *Said* that? And yet, deep down we know that we always have time for what we really want to do in life—because we make time.

The goal of this chapter is to show how God has made time for us and therefore expects us to make time for him. While many readers probably think this statement refers to a daily routine of private devotions, it doesn't. Though heartily in favor of such habits, I actually have in mind the Lord's Day, or the Christian Sabbath. For generations of faithful believers, Sunday was not about football or shopping but about God and feeding at his luxuriant table. But somehow, we got caught up in the buzz, and we wonder if we can ever get out. That's why we keep trying the latest spiritual diet plan—a new quiet time program, a new prayer, maybe even a spiritual director or a week in a monastery. But who suggests a recovery of the Sabbath? Irony of ironies, amid all the stress of "try this fad or feel guilty," a commitment to the institution that God has actually commanded risks being called legalistic. This chapter also suggests additional practical tools for escaping the relentless buzz.

Nobody needs to hear any more statistics on how much of the average American's life is spent watching television. In recent years, there have been a number of balanced and thought-provoking analyses of that phenomenon that Neil Postman calls "amusing ourselves to death." *New Yorker* writer John Seabrook calls it the "Buzz" that is produced by "the culture of marketing, the marketing of culture." Seabrook offers a snapshot of the Buzz from his own experience standing in the middle of Manhattan:

> The air was fuzzy with the weird yellow tornado light of Times Square by day, a blend of sunlight and wattage, the real and the mediated—the color

of Buzz. Buzz is the collective stream of consciousness, William James's "buzzing confusion," objectified, a shapeless substance into which politics and gossip, art and pornography, virtue and money, the fame of heroes and the celebrity of murderers, all bleed. In Times Square you could see the buzz that you felt going through your mind. I found it soothing just to stand there on my way to and from work and let the yellow light run into my synapses. In that moment the worlds outside and inside my skull became one.[1]

Listening is a difficult business these days. We belong to a talk-show culture that makes everybody's opinion as good as anyone else's, where the now arrogant vice of believing in the true, the good, and the beautiful has been replaced with the apparent virtue of following the useful, the preferred, and the stimulating. Is it possible that we in the church have mistaken our cultural obsession with this Buzz of the new and improved for the presence of the Spirit? And what can we do to become good listeners again? First, we will examine Seabrook's marvelous way of capturing the cultural shifts that have contributed to making our lives so noisy and dependent on the latest and greatest. Then we will return to Scripture and the wisdom of the faithful.

What's All the Buzz About?

Seabrook uses the "dumbing down" of the *New Yorker* as an illustration of the more general phenomenon, and much of what he says in this regard has easy parallels in the church. His project involved "wading a little bit deeper in the vast, tepid swamp of Buzz, with its surrounding cedar bogs of compromise."[2] Despite his analysis, Seabrook's book is not a Jeremiad against contemporary culture but an insightful and often sympathetic exposé. Turning each page, I found numerous applications to church life. For instance, he says concerning the changes in the *New Yorker* that "the real problem was that the culture of the writers and the culture of the ad people were too disconnected from each other to have much in common."[3]

Applying this insight to the church, we could say that we are used to blaming theology for differences and divisions among us, but theology has little to do with things these days, at least in explicit terms. The real problem is not that there are people who hold to this theology over that theology but that there is a hostility to any theology. The culture of the educated exegetes (the writers) is increasingly disconnected from the culture of the ecclesiastical entrepreneurs (the ad people).

Seabrook charts the seminal shifts: "The old cultural arbiters, whose job was to decide what was 'good' in the sense of 'valuable,' were being replaced by a new type of arbiter, whose skill was to define 'good' in terms of 'popular.'"[4] A "hierarchy of hotness" replaced the older hierarchy of value, and there was no such thing as poor taste anymore, just different tastes. Listing specific examples of the magazine's decline, Seabrook says, "Articles became much shorter, their deadlines were firm, and their publication was pegged to Buzz-making happenings." We could replace "articles" here with "sermons," especially in the light of his next sentence: "Doing stories that were topical, trying to get the public's attention, trying to be controversial, trying to sell magazines . . . became the norm."[5] Seabrook himself came to appreciate pop music even as he recognized its problems: "Pop was goofy, fun, sweet, open, honest, but at the same utterly fake."[6] "Without pop culture to build your identity around, what have you got?" Seabrook asks.[7] Buzz, otherwise known as pop culture, has "by its nature abhorred distinction and consumed all single points of view."[8] This is also readily apparent in contemporary church life.

Seabrook contrasts the world of the town house in which he was raised by "middle-brow" parents in New York and the world of the megastore. Again, as you read this, insert "traditional church" and "contemporary church" in the place of the town house and the megastore:

> In the town house was symmetry, in the megastore multiplicity. In the town house was quiet, in the megastore cacophony. In the town house was the carefully sequestered commercialism of my father's world, in the megastore the rampant commercialism of mine. In place of *New Yorker* distinctions between the elite and the commercial, there were MTV distinctions between the cult and the mainstream. In the town house, quality was the standard of value; in the megastore, the standard was authenticity. In the town house you got points for consistency in cultural preferences; in the megastore you got status for preferences that cut across the old hierarchical lines. In the town house there was content and there was advertising. In the megastore there were both at once. The music videos were art—music videos offered some of the best visual art on television—but videos were also, technically speaking, ads for the music, and the money to make them came from the music industry or the artist, not from MTV.[9]

Interviewing MTV president Judy McGrath for an article, Seabrook asked why, after her boss (the head of MTV Networks) raised concerns about gangsta-rapper Snoop Doggy Dogg appearing on the Video Music Awards, she went ahead with his appearance anyway: "But McGrath argued in favor of Snoop because, she told me, 'Musically, Snoop is happening now, and we have a responsibility to our viewers to show that.'" Notice the sense of fatalistic inevitability that also marks church marketing today when McGrath adds, "It is sort of scary that this is the direction the music is taking us, but we're not really in control of that, and if we try to control it, MTV is going to lose its edge, which is the thing that makes us great. Plus, it's a lot more meaningful to show this stuff—it's real. . . . You know, this is the world we live in."[10]

"You know, this is the world we live in": This is the solipsism that is supposed to make us accept the ruling order as our fate. Whether it happens at MTV or in the church, this sort of attitude reveals a serious case of nihilism. If nothing is intrinsically true, good, and beautiful—and therefore, superior to other things that are not quite as true, good, or beautiful—everything is a matter of taste. And in the culture of Buzz, taste is shaped by marketing.

> When you say about a painting, a music video, or a pair of jeans, "I like this," you make some sort of judgment, but it's not a judgment of quality. In Nobrow, judgments about which brand of jeans to wear are more like judgments of identity than quality. These judgments do not depend on knowledge of the canon, tradition, history, or some shared set-up standards about what constitutes "good taste" to give them weight; this kind of taste is more like appetite than disinterested judgment. Taste is the act of making the thing part of your identity. . . . Fanship, brandship, and relationships are all a part of what the statement, "I like this" really means. Your judgment joins a pool of other judgments, a small relationship economy, one of millions that continually coalesce and dissolve and reform around culture products—movies, sneakers, jeans, pop songs.[11]

Even Hollywood insiders concede that story line, plot, and characterization are fairly secondary these days. Lawrence Kasdan, author of the first *Indiana Jones* and cowriter of *The Empire Strikes Back* and *Jedi* scripts, says, "Narrative structure doesn't exist—all that matters is what's going to happen in the next ten minutes to keep the audience interested."[12] While most of us can't help but get caught up in the whirl of the Buzz, we also know deep down that there has to be something else. If even our stories don't have stories and our movies don't have plots, where will we find that "narrative structure" that makes our lives more meaningful than mere consumption and stimulation?

So what's the Buzz about? Nothing. Or, more precisely, it's about itself. The music video is about (i.e., an ad for) the product: the album. The evening news need not be about noteworthy events in the world but merely about the event of "reporting" it. Advertising need not be about products but merely create a consumer experience. And when the Buzz comes to church, worship need not actually be about God and what he has done, is doing, and will do to and for us but only about itself. "Let's just praise the Lord." What Lord? And why? Never mind all that theology: Let's just enjoy the "worship experience."

If the Buzz isn't about anything, what's the point? Stimulation. The consumption of experiences, audiovisual candy. What is the alternative? Let's turn from critique to construction as we attempt to answer that question.

Reel Time

When we think about who God is and who we are by comparison, it is remarkable that God not only has time for us but that he has invited us—uniquely among his creatures—to enter into his everlasting hours. This is not a flight from time or a flight even from time here and now in this world. Rather, it is a step into that time that God has set aside for our fellowship with him—as a foretaste of the renewed creation of which we are a part. As Gerhard Sauter expresses it:

> In this sequence, the forgiveness of sins is the work of the life-giving Spirit, who represents God before us and us before God. The Spirit places us before God and tears us away from all our relationships, considerations, and prospects with which we form our own lives, whether high-handedly, self-consciously, or powerlessly. This change through God's Spirit in no way leads to isolation and retreat into private life. . . . To take part in such actions means to pause from other activities, to step away from them for a time. Human beings are placed before God, and their community (not just their common fate) is constituted by that. To stand before God means that one is prepared for God's verdict and confident in God's grace.[13]

To stand before God as individuals incorporated into a body, condemned and justified, saint and sinner simultaneously, is to be made a new people by the Spirit. Contrast this image of standing before the presence of God with standing under the Buzz of our entertainment and advertising culture. With this contrast so sharp, why would we even want to make room for the latter in this space that God has carved out to begin his gracious reign among us? Why especially would we want to bring this market-saturated pop culture into the church's worship—that one break that we have in the week from the ephemeral, that which is even now decaying and passing away? And how can we actually "eagerly await" the coming of Christ and the consummation of his kingdom if we refuse to let go of "this passing evil age" and embrace "the age to come"?

In his helpful book on the Lord's Day, Joseph Pipa compared the inter-mittent strife over this topic to the face-off between environmentalists and developers over a piece of land.[14] "Often such controversy results in our losing sight of the beauties and pleasures of the day, so that the Lord's day is marred and disfigured much as it was in the days of the Pharisees."[15] The Lord's Day has always occupied a place of prominence in the piety of a wide variety of Protestant churches, although it has fallen on hard times in our circles as in others.[16] While not that long ago our great-grandparents probably lived in communities that took a break en masse from buying and selling and taking in ordinary amusements, regardless of their denomination, today it is difficult for us even to imag-ine surrendering a whole day every week for the things of God. This alone may measure the extent to which we all have become creatures of the Buzz.

Few subjects are more richly practical in the light of our concern for becoming better at hearing God and seeing his action in our lives. Chris-tians often say these days, "I know it's important to get to know God and to understand Scripture. I'd even like to dig into a bit of lay theology, but there's just no time." That is just the practical problem that this issue addresses: God has provided a time not only for us to enjoy him but for him to enjoy us. It is the glad day of rest in a restless world. After expos-ing to view the biblical-theological development of this theme, this chap-ter examines some concrete applications.

Rest for the Weary

The Sabbath was instituted by God in the Garden of Eden, where he invited Adam into his communion and to imitate his own reign. This is one of the most astonishing aspects of this institution. Transcendence is not aloofness. It is a property of God's very existence—he cannot help but be beyond anything we could imagine or think. Once God freely decided to create human beings in his image, he chose involvement over indifference. Far from being a distant deity, God is eager to be in the company of human beings whom he created in his own image. This is why he created Paradise, with its order, productivity, diversity, justice, and harmony—a "living room" where he could dwell with his image-bearers and they could dwell safely with him.

The Sabbath was the enthronement of the Alpha-Creator as the Omega-Consummator, the Beginning and the End.[17] As Meredith Kline observes concerning Genesis 1–2, "God sets forth his creative acts within the pictorial framework of a Sabbath-crowned week and by this sabbatical pattern he identifies himself as Omega, the One for whom all things are and were created, the Lord worthy to receive glory and honor and praise (cf. Rev. 4:11)."[18] Creation must not be viewed in static terms, as if there was nothing more, nothing better, ahead. This impression is often given when we think of the consummation (viz., the return of Christ and the new heavens and new earth) as a return to Eden. But Adam, as the federal head of the human race, was on probation in Eden. Although created righteous, he was capable of rebelling. Had Adam not sinned, he would have won the right to eat from the Tree of Life, but as it turned out, God posted heavenly guards at the entrance to that tree after the fall. No one but the true and faithful Adam could have eaten of that tree, for himself and those whom he represented.

Therefore, right from the beginning, all of history was moving toward the consummation—the state of living beyond the possibility of sin and death and sharing God's Sabbath rest with him forever. We see this fleshed out throughout the development of redemptive history, right up to the end, where in Revelation—because of Christ's fulfillment of the probation—all those who are in him are given the right to finally eat of that Tree of Life (Rev. 2:7; 22:1–5). It will not be a return to Eden—the beginning of the play—but an entrance with Jesus into a state more blessed than the first (innocence), which has yet to be played out on the stage of history (consummation).

In its character, therefore, the Sabbath is not cessation from activity but cessation from a particular kind of activity—namely, the six-day labor that is intrinsically good but has suffered the curse after the fall. God did not rest because he was tired; rather, it was the rest of completion, the rest of a king who has taken his throne. Representing the consummation, this sabbatical pattern was the way not only of hoping for the new creation but of experiencing it and participating in its peace.

Far from leading to a monastic renunciation of creation, the Sabbath affirms the natural world. Sabbath is to creation what cult (worship) is to culture (work): not intrinsically opposed but separated after the fall to be reunited in the new creation. Until then, the Sabbath is the in-breaking of the everlasting rest. The Sabbath gave a pattern, a measurable meaning, to human existence, just as the festivals in Israel's history annually impressed the vertical-horizontal development of redemptive history after the fall. These are not opposed: The resurrection, sufficient to move the Sabbath to Sunday, reverses the curse placed on creation because of man and represents the birthday of the new creation. Furthermore, it represents the privilege that we as creatures, not just as Christians, were meant to possess.

While the whole creation will with us one day be raised in newness of life, only human beings were created for fellowship with God. And one day, just as the kingdoms of the world will be made the kingdom of Christ, every day will be a Sabbath day, rest from sin, injustice, oppression, and suffering. One of Wendell Berry's "Sabbath Poems" captures this: "Make your land recall / In workdays of the fields / The sabbath of the woods."[19] The Sabbath gave rest to the land, to animals, to employees and employers and their families, anticipating the end of using the natural world and the beginning of our real enjoyment of it.

The ordinary week is a microcosm of God's "time," just as the temple in Jerusalem was a microcosm of God's heavenly "place." Like the week, history has a beginning and an ending. The Sabbath is the weekly link to both past creation and future consummation. Thus, it keeps us anchored to the order that God established before the fall as creatures who share his image as well as stretch our necks forward, longing for our full entrance into the Sabbath day that the Second Adam already enjoys with God. The Sabbath keeps us navigationally fixed to these two points—what is built into creation (Alpha) and what is still awaiting us in the future in the new creation (Omega). It gives us the tempo of belonging to the One *by* whom we exist and *for* whom our existence is directed. As the Sabbath is to calendar time, the temple was to temporal space— anticipating the day when "the glory of God shall cover the earth," bursting the dimensions of both days and places. Humans, having failed to enter God's rest in the beginning, will, because of Christ their forerunner, enter that rest at the last.

Unlike the temple worship, the Sabbath was not a sacrament of the church but an ordinance of creation (like marriage, vocation, and the state) and was not abrogated in the New Testament but strengthened and confirmed. The reinstitution of the Sabbath after the fall was actually very good news: It meant that God still held out the hope of entering his rest. There was still a promise out there on the horizon, which the people could taste weekly:

> Remember the Sabbath day, to keep it holy. Six days you shall labor and do all your work, but the seventh day is the Sabbath of the LORD your God. In it you shall do no work: you, nor your son, nor your daughter, nor your manservant, nor your maidservant, nor your cattle, nor your stranger who is within your gates. For in six days the LORD made the heavens and the earth, the sea, and all that is in them, and rested the seventh day. Therefore the LORD blessed the Sabbath day and hallowed it.
>
> Exodus 20:8–11 NKJV

As the fourth of the Ten Commandments that God gave his people at Sinai, the Sabbath institution was, after the exodus, anchored not only to creation but to redemption. Notice how the version of the Ten Commandments in Deuteronomy supplements the Exodus account. The prohibition is the same, but the rationale is slightly different: "And remember that you were a slave in the land of Egypt, and that the LORD your God brought you out from there by a mighty hand and by an outstretched arm; therefore the LORD your God commanded you to keep the Sabbath day" (Deut. 5:15 NKJV). The Sabbath is rooted in both creation and, for the believer, redemption. It is part of our story: "I am the God who brought you up out of Egypt."

Marriage remains a divine ordinance for Christians and non-Christians alike, representing God's claim upon all that he has made. Work and the existence of government also reflect God's common grace and our common creation. Likewise, the advent of the new covenant hardly abrogates the Sabbath. Jesus did not condemn the Sabbath but the parody of the Sabbath that the Pharisees had made of it (Matt. 12:2; Mark 2:24; Luke 14:5). Instead of announcing that the Sabbath had been set aside, Jesus gave its true interpretation. After Jesus healed a sick man, the religious leaders "sought to kill him, because he had done these things on the Sabbath." "But," we read, "Jesus answered them, 'My Father has been working until now, and I have been working.' Therefore the Jews sought all the more to kill him, because he not only broke the Sabbath, but also said that God was his Father, making himself equal with God" (John 5:16–18 NKJV). We can put this event together with that reported in Mark 2:

> Now it happened that [Jesus] went through the grainfields on the Sabbath; and as they went his disciples began to pluck the heads of grain. And the Pharisees said to him, "Look, why do they do what is not lawful on the Sabbath?" But he said to them, "Have you never read what David did when he was in need and hungry, he and those with him: how he went into the house of God in the days of Abiathar the high priest, and ate the showbread, which is not lawful to eat, except for the priests, and also gave some to those who were with him?" And he said to them, "The Sabbath was made for man, and not man for the Sabbath. Therefore the Son of Man is also Lord of the Sabbath."
>
> verses 23–28 NKJV

And Jesus confirmed this last remark by healing on the Sabbath (3:1–6).

The Pharisees had misinterpreted the Sabbath, since God had never prohibited works of necessity or mercy. The disciples were not working the fields but receiving God's provision to sustain their life—the very thing that the Sabbath itself signified. Any approach that turns the Sabbath into a slavish observance misses its point. Just as David was engaged in a redemptive mission when he ate the showbread, the Son of David was working the greater redemption promised. God's everlasting rest is not the cessation of activity, as the Pharisees seemed to view it: "My Father has been working until now," Jesus says, adding, "and I have been working." If God's "rest" is a royal enthronement rather than a cessation of activity, the same is true for us. As kings under God, we take our place with Christ in heavenly places, setting our minds on things above where our true inheritance lies. The Father and the Son are working redemption, which the healings represented. It is resting from creation-labor and from our sins, not cessation from activity, that the Sabbath envisioned for us as well as God.

Jesus audaciously (as far as the Pharisees were concerned) claimed that he was the Covenant Lord who instituted the Sabbath in the first place. He therefore offers the authoritative interpretation of the law. To turn the Sabbath into a burden is to utterly contradict its purpose, although to ignore it is surely to violate God's stated will. The Sabbath is not concerned with a slavish observance of the day, as in the Pharisees' practice. Rather, it focuses our attention on the gracious invitation to enter into the blessings not merely of Adam's once-a-week rest but also the Second Adam's eternal rest that is enjoyed "through a glass darkly" in this age through the Christian Sabbath.

This last point is made in Hebrews 4, where the unbelieving generation in the wilderness is used as a warning to those who were tempted, because of persecution, to abandon Christ and return to Judaism. We read:

> Therefore, since a promise remains of entering his rest, let us fear lest any of you seem to have come short of it. For indeed the gospel was preached to us as well as to them; but the word which they heard did not profit them, not being mixed with faith in those who heard it. For we who have believed do enter that rest, as he has said: "So I swore in my wrath, they shall not enter my rest," although the works were finished from the foundation of the world. For he has spoken in a certain place of the seventh day in this way: "And God rested on the seventh day from all his works"; and again in this place: "They shall not enter my rest." Since therefore it remains that some must enter it, and those to whom it was first preached did not enter because of disobedience, again he designates a certain day, saying in David, "Today," after such a long time, as it has been said: "Today, if you will hear his voice, do not harden your hearts." For if Joshua had given them rest, then he would not afterward have spoken of another day. There remains therefore a rest for the people of God. For he who has entered his rest has himself also ceased from his works as God did from his.

> verses 1–10 NKJV

"Today" is "the day of salvation," not simply one solar day but "this age" in which the Spirit has reinstituted the Abrahamic covenant through its New Testament administration. This "today" is the time that God has allotted for us to enter into God's seventh day through the door that Jesus Christ has thrown open by his resurrection and ascension. He who is "the resurrection and the life" calls for his brothers and sisters to join him, to move beyond the six days of work into the seventh day of rest. And the sign of this was his resurrection on the day beyond the Old Testament Sabbath. Matthew's Gospel seems to go out of its way to make this connection: "Now *after the Sabbath,* as the *first* day of the week began to dawn, Mary Magdalene and the other Mary came to see the tomb," but they were greeted by an angel's glad announcement, "He is not here; for he is risen, as he said" (28:1, 6 NKJV, emphasis added). Instead of pointing forward to the new creation, as the Old Testament Sabbath did, the arrival of the new creation in Jesus Christ signaled the beginning of God's everlasting week. What the Romans called Sunday was in fact the birthday of the new world. Each Lord's Day is a "little Easter."

So decisive was this event that it shifted the Sabbath from Saturday to Sunday and was now acknowledged as "the Lord's Day." It was on that first Easter Sunday that Jesus proclaimed the Word and celebrated the Supper (Luke 24:13–35). After the ascension, the disciples were assembled in the upper room for the celebration of Pentecost, the Old Testament "Feast of Weeks" or "Feast of Harvest" that anticipated the ingathering of the full harvest from the nations (Exod. 23:16; Num. 28:26). Thereafter, we learn that the disciples met regularly on "the first day of the week." "Now on the first day of the week, when the disciples came together to break bread, Paul, ready to depart the next day, spoke to them and continued his message until midnight" (Acts 20:7 NKJV). "On the first day of the week," Paul commanded the Corinthians, "Let each one of you lay something aside, storing up as he may prosper, that there be no collections when I come" (1 Cor. 16:2 NKJV). Explaining the context for his heavenly vision in Revelation, John says, "I was in the Spirit on the Lord's Day, and I heard behind me a loud voice, as of a trumpet, saying, 'I am the Alpha and the Omega, the First and the Last'" (Rev. 1:10–11 NKJV). Imagine that! The Lord of the Sabbath, exalted to the right hand of God, visits the apostle on the Lord's Day and announces that he is the Alpha-Creator and Omega-Consummator, the source and the goal of all creation.

The Lord's Day, or the Christian Sabbath, reiterates continuity not only between Old and New Testaments but between creation and redemption. The world does not finally belong to Satan or to rebellious humanity—"this present age"—but ultimately to the Creator who has redeemed the world and even now introduces "the age to come" in a preliminary way. The Lord's Day is the festival of the new creation to be treasured, a day not only that we set aside but that sets us aside. As children of this day, we proclaim that we are not our own but are bought with a price—the very rationale given in Deuteronomy. It is a weekly Easter Day, transforming our identity and relation to this age by that power of the Spirit who raised Jesus from the dead.

Who would want to miss this day or crowd out the in-rushing of God's eternal rest by surrendering it to the twisted, plot-less, pointless, and powerless forces of consumerism, greed, ambition, and self-assertion? Do we not believe that God provides for us? That is the assumed question in the wilderness, when God provided manna for the unbelieving generation. They gathered the manna.

> Then [Moses] said to them, "This is what the LORD has said: 'Tomorrow is a Sabbath rest, a holy Sabbath to the LORD. Bake what you will bake today, and boil what you will boil; and lay up for yourselves all that remains, to be kept until morning.'" So they laid it up till morning, as Moses commanded; and it did not stink, nor were there any worms in it. Then Moses said, "Eat that today, for today is a Sabbath to the LORD; today you will not find it in the field. Six days you shall gather it, but on the seventh day, which is the Sabbath, there will be none."
>
> Exodus 16:23–26 NKJV

But the Israelites violated God's command and gathered more manna on the Sabbath, implying that what God provided for them during those six days was insufficient. In their greed, they focused all their energies on their stomachs and showed no signs of confidence in God. God had provided not only their daily bread but the day of feasting in his presence, yet they were unbelieving. Similarly, John warns us, "For all that is in the world—the lust of the flesh, the lust of the eyes, and the pride of life—is not of the Father but is of the world. And the world is passing away, and the lust of it; but he who does the will of God abides forever. Little children, it is the last hour" (1 John 2:16–18 NKJV).

It is no less true in our day than it was in Israel's that the knowledge of God and participation in his covenant is easily crowded out by a love of the world. Now, as then, the church loses its vision, its mission, and its power when it surrenders the Sabbath to "the world [that] is passing away" instead of to "the age to come." It is no wonder that children of evangelical parents today know considerably less even of basic Bible stories than the children of unbelieving parents in previous generations. God has given us six days a week to labor and to participate in the good gifts of creation along with non-Christians, but the Sabbath belongs to the Lord. It is the Lord's Day, and the miracle is that we, who were once not his people, are invited to enjoy it with him in his presence.

At the same time, there is a ceremonial part and a moral part to this commandment, the former having been fulfilled and therefore no longer in force. While it is to be observed, it is not to be observed with rigor but with gladness. B. B. Warfield captured this transformation of the Sabbath by its fulfillment when he wrote, "Christ took the Sabbath into the grave with him and brought the Lord's Day out of the grave with him on the resurrection morn."[20] Warfield observes the stress especially of John on Jesus' appearance to his disciples on "the first day of the week." There were four Sundays before the ascension. "But there is an appearance at least that the first day of the week was becoming under this direct sanction of the risen Lord the appointed day of Christian assemblies."[21]

But what of the passages that tell us not to set one day above another? "One person esteems one day above another," Paul says, "another esteems every day alike. Let each be fully convinced in his own mind" (Rom. 14:5 NKJV). But notice that Paul does not say, "One person esteems the Sabbath above other days," while others don't. Since the church's first converts in a given center were often Jews, Paul labors in each of his epistles to keep the Jewish ceremonial law from becoming a test of fellowship. Since Paul mentions this in the context of eating meat sacrificed to idols, it is most likely a reference to the feasts of the Jewish calendar, not to the Sabbath itself. After all, if the Sabbath is an ordinance of creation, how could it be a matter that is simply left up to individual conscience? The same interpretation could be offered of Colossians 2: "Therefore let no one judge you in food or in drink, or regarding a festival or a new moon or sabbaths, which are a shadow of things to come, but the substance is of Christ" (vv. 16–17 NKJV). Again, the pastoral context involves those Jewish Christians who had, in essence, required Gentile believers to become Jewish. Jewish ceremonial laws concerning food and drink, the old covenant festivals and sabbaths (note the plural, referring to the monthly and annual sabbaths), are obsolete because each pointed to Christ and passed away with his arrival. But not so the Sabbath, which has become the Lord's Day. It not only points to Christ but announces his arrival.

Let me conclude this defense of the Christian Sabbath with Richard Gaffin's marvelous summary. God saw that all he made was "very good." "But he did not yet see the 'very best.' That was because even before he created, God had decided that 'the best of all possible worlds' was not to be at the beginning but at the end of history."[22]

The Lord's day is about worship because it is first of all about the gospel. It is a sign, to the church and a watching world, that we "are not our own" (1 Cor. 6:19) but are depending on our God, not ourselves, to provide for us. It is a sign that our trust is not in ourselves and our own efforts as fallen sons and daughters of Adam, but in the perfect righteousness of the last Adam and in God's faithfulness to his covenant promise to do for us what we are unable to do for ourselves. . . . The pattern of six days of activity interrupted by one of rest is a reminder that human beings are not caught up in a meaningless flow of days, one after the other without end, but that history has a beginning and ending and is headed toward final judgment and the consummation of all things.[23]

In other words, the regular observance of the Sabbath keeps us oriented to God's drama of redemption and catches us up into it as the Spirit reconciles us to God through Word and sacrament. On this day, we announce that we are expecting the redemption of the earthly creation and not merely of individual souls. The creation that has been in bondage to decay because of us will be liberated because of Christ. On this day, we announce to the world that when our Savior cried out, after his perfect works throughout his earthly life, "It is finished!" he had finally obtained for his new humanity admission to the Tree of Life. The workweek completed, he now calls out through his ministry in this age, "Come to me, all you who labor and are heavy laden, and I will give you rest. Take my yoke upon you and learn from me, for I am gentle and lowly in heart, and you will find rest for your souls. For my yoke is easy and my burden is light" (Matt. 11:28–30 NKJV).

Structuring Our Sabbath, or Being Structured by It

Imagine a whole day of Christian proclamation, instruction, praise, fellowship, and edification. Our callings in the world often require occasional day-long or even week-long "continuing education" seminars, and similarly, Christian conferences in theology have sprouted up across the landscape in our time. But what if each week we could really "taste of the powers of the age to come" by sustained attention to what God has done, is doing, and will do for us by his Spirit in Jesus Christ? Wouldn't we become better parents without hit-and-run sermons on parenting? Wouldn't we become mature worshipers without having our theological education crammed into a morning lecture? And wouldn't we develop deeper, richer, and more lasting relationships without requiring banal tips on making friends? Christianity cannot be inculcated merely through moral aphorisms or even merely through the statement and restatement of true propositions. It must be experienced regularly in a community that is in it for the long haul. There must be actions and not just words.

We can rail against consumerism even as we belong to the teeming masses whose cars flood shopping mall parking lots on the Lord's Day. Isn't this precisely the sort of activity that God forbade the Israelites from engaging in, when six days of gathering the manna were, to their mind, not enough? One trend in some churches (especially megachurches) is actually to bring the mall to the church, suggesting unwelcome parallels to the temple that Jesus cleared of money changers. "This Sunday morning, when Sandra Whitman goes to church, she will kneel down, pray—and then do a little Christmas shopping," a newspaper article reports.

We could also mention sports entertainment. Why is it that we eagerly watch hours of a game on television but consider God lucky to have had us for an hour on that same day? Imagine how revolutionary it would be if a majority of Christians stopped shopping, working, or watching TV on Sunday. "I'd love to dig into the Scriptures, but I just don't have time—what with work and all," again assumes that we are entirely at the mercy of forces beyond our control. Given the statistics, many of us who say this have plenty of time for entertainment, shopping, sports, and the like. We would have to do no more than recover Sabbath practice in order to have enough time for growing in the grace and knowledge of our Savior.

This sort of observance would be a witness to the world that we are not slaves in Egypt, in bondage to the priorities of a greedy culture of marketing and entertainment. It would also be a kindness to our fellow creatures. There can be no doubt that the stress placed on marriages and families these days has a great deal to do with the pace of work and also the web of activities that keeps the household scattered to the four winds. Again recall the version of the fourth commandment found in Deuteronomy, applying the commandment not only to God's people but to "your stranger who is within your gates, that your manservant and your maidservant may rest as well as you. And remember that you were a slave in the land of Egypt, and that the LORD your God brought you out from there by a mighty hand and by an outstretched arm; therefore the LORD your God commanded you to keep the Sabbath day" (Deut. 5:14–15 NKJV).

We can take a break from consuming and engage in works of mercy. In fact, a practice in many churches is to visit the elderly in a nursing home on Sunday afternoons. As we refuse to surrender this day to the tyranny of the clock and the gods who amuse us, we enjoy a foretaste of heaven and also proclaim to the world that God is our refuge. Take the family on an afternoon walk and have them recite a psalm that they have memorized while you point out to them the concrete beauties of God's creation, the signs of the fall, and the promise of redemption. Why not ask each of them to explain the sermon and then discuss its implications. You are teaching your family to turn off the Walkman and the whirl of the week, to stop and listen. They are becoming listeners of God's Word, integrating faith and life.

This day was given to us not because we are strong but because we are weak. Many who might respond to the preceding arguments with the objection, "But every day is the Lord's Day," do not actually set aside every day for sustained attention to the things of God. To be sure, there may be a brief moment of daily devotions and periodical prayers, but every day does not belong to the Lord, at least in part, because we have not discovered the enormous power of the Lord's Day to reorient our ordinary workweek. "But every day is the Lord's Day" often leads to the unintentional consequence that no day is the Lord's Day. As Dorothy C. Bass writes concerning the Lord's Day, "No other days can be the same, after this one."[24]

We Have Time

One of the assumptions of our age is that this life is all there is, so we'd better enjoy it. Richard Bauckham and Trevor Hart write:

> Like visitors to an art gallery who arrive 20 minutes before closing time we rush from exhibit to exhibit, fearful that we shall miss something worthwhile. The horizon of our own finitude haunts us, and we rush to cram as much as we possibly can into the available space, travelling ever faster and further, seeing and tasting more, trying out as many options as we can while we have the time and, ironically, as a consequence having time for very little at all. Has there ever been a generation with so little time actually to take time and enjoy the world? Always craving the next thing we so often fail to savour the moment offered to us.[25]

The weekly Sabbath is a flag planted in the middle of Times Square where we gather to protest this way of life. It is a contradiction of what appears to be an obvious fact of life. "No," we are saying, "we have time to do this." Friends, family members, employers, and employees will doubtless look at us much as a dog hearing a siren. They don't have time. Isn't that what they (and we) say all the time these days? The more time that technology promises—and even delivers—the more of a slave we seem to become to the clock. Secretly, we love it. We wonder what we would ever do with our lives if we didn't have our work. Church bores us for the same reason that heaven bores us: It's a distraction from the work that really gives us pleasure. To reverse Augustine a bit, "We were

created for work, and our hearts are restless until they find rest in it."
The Sabbath controverts all this and says, "You think that God's 'time'
is rest in the sense of immobility? Angels with harps bouncing from
cloud to cloud? On the contrary, the only rest is the cessation of warfare, temptation, doubt, fear, insecurity, distance from God, condemnation. Otherwise, it's about the busiest place there is." So, the Sabbath
should not be treated as a blank space in the week but as the one space
that is filled and overflowing with the richest gifts of divine activity.

As those who love life precisely because we do not have to hoard it
(it's been given as a free gift, not as an object to be greedily consumed),
we are also those who know a little bit about what death means. It is
not the last act. Evil as it is, tragedy will be swallowed up in comedy.
God will get the last laugh. People who live life hurriedly and greedily
may well have a problem accepting "the resurrection of the body and
the life of the world to come." In other words, an inability to stop for
the Sabbath may reveal a deeper problem of far more serious consequence; namely, that one really believes only in this life and that the
only thing that survives us are our legacies: children and memories of
us and our accomplishments.

In addition to recovering the Lord's Day, there are ways of taking
back territory we've surrendered and making a place in each day for
training ourselves and our families in the things that matter most.

"Home Schooling": Recovering the Disciplined Art of Catechism

Regardless of where we send our children to school, surely we can
agree that their spiritual development is chiefly a responsibility of the
home. Even when churches are doing what they should be doing, they
cannot make up for a disconnect (let's just call it hypocrisy) at home. If
God does not matter there, he will not—at least in the minds of our children—matter anywhere.

But let's take it one step further. Imagine that you and your family
had a "big picture" grasp of the whole Bible. You knew pretty well how,
say, the Bible's teaching on the prophetic office of Christ related to the
question of ongoing revelation today. When you heard someone say
something that seemed to contradict the doctrine of the Trinity, a bell
would go off. You would know that something was amiss, and you could
articulate a response to help out a friend who was a new Christian. You
could discuss rather fluently the great truths of Scripture and support
those basic beliefs with reference to particular passages. This was pre-

cisely what the ancient practice of "catechism" provided for generations of Christians.

Historically, many Christians have thought that the main context of religious and moral instruction takes place in the home, not in the church. That is why the Protestant Reformers prepared catechisms—manuals of instruction summarizing the Bible's basic teaching to be learned by rote in the earliest years (like a new language) and then investigated, elaborated, and even tested by mature scriptural reflection in later years. There was a time when an average Christian young person knew by heart the questions and answers of the Westminster Shorter Catechism, the Heidelberg Catechism, or Luther's Small Catechism. A few years ago I recall a woman returning to church after she had abandoned it for a life of immorality. "I just couldn't get those questions and answers or the Bible verses I had to memorize along with them out of my head," she said concerning the catechism of her youth.

Not too long ago, it was still common for parents to drop off their children after school or on Saturdays for weekly catechism classes, supplemented by the parents around the evening meal. To be sure, it was a matter of going through the motions for many kids, but that was the fault largely of the parents who sent them. The kids returned home and found little of the practical, living reality of the truth, and they learned from the home to separate theory from practice. But hypocrisy can happen quite apart from catechetical training. Imagine the enormous practical difference that recovery of this practice could make on so many levels—practical differences that a month of "practical" sermons and programs have fallen far short of matching.

Richard R. Osmer, a Princeton Seminary professor, points to the declining use of the catechism as a major source of mainline disintegration. "Somewhere along the way, the church failed these people," and now they are out the door—attracted to exotic religions or none at all. "It failed to provide them with the intellectual and spiritual resources needed in a postmodern world."[26] In addition to public worship, Osmer observes, catechism shaped generations of believers who—even in their early youth—had a better grasp of Scripture and its teachings than many pastors today. "The sequence of infant baptism, catechetical instruction and then admission to the Lord's Table provided a structure for education that dominated most Protestant churches from the Reformation period through the 19th century."[27] Osmer summarizes the changes:

> The earliest of these was the Enlightenment's critique of dogmatic authority. In some corners, teaching of the catechism came to be viewed as the epitome of authoritarian indoctrination. More important in the U.S. was

the challenge of the Sunday school movement. Lay-led and evangelical in its theology, this parachurch movement came to shape congregational life over the course of the 19th century and pushed catechetical instruction into a secondary position. By the turn of the 20th century, moreover, the language of the catechisms seemed increasingly archaic; and questions were being raised about the viability of the theology expressed in the catechisms. . . . But these programs were undermined by two further developments. The first was the rise of modern educational and psychological theory that attacked the basic assumptions of the humanistic education program with which catechetical instruction had long been associated. Briefly put, these emerging fields placed far more emphasis on the active role of the learner in the construction of knowledge and advocated a teaching style that was oriented toward the emerging experience of the child. The text-based methods of humanistic education, which stressed internalizing classic modes of speaking and writing, were portrayed as antichild and authoritarian.[28]

According to Osmer, restoring catechism is essential particularly because the average young person today is now speaking multiple "languages" and living in multiple worlds of thought and action. He or she needs to have fluency in Christian speech. While in the past a number of public and private institutions combined to inculcate some knowledge of Scripture, today that simply is not the case. If churches and homes will not catechize the next generation, it will not happen at the YMCA or Boy Scouts, much less at the arcade or the mall.

> If Paula [a young woman who illustrates this trend] follows the pattern of the average American child, she will watch 30 hours of television a week and by the age of 12, will have viewed on TV approximately 100,000 violent episodes and 13,000 people violently destroyed. At her public school, she will receive no Christian education and little moral education. If she follows trends found in every major study of higher education since the 1950s, Paula's experience of college will have a secularizing impact on her faith, mediating the intellectual relativism and cultural eclecticism that is so much a part of her postmodern world.[29]

Furthermore, the modern educational and psychological theories have only made education more difficult:

> After almost a century of experiential religious education, with its heavy emphasis on process over content, personal creativity over communal identity, and emergent experience over biblical-theological knowledge, it is safe to say that the members of mainline Protestant churches know less about the faith, are more tenuously committed to the church, and are less equipped to make an impact on the surrounding world than they were at

the turn of the century. . . . Teaching of the catechism is not a cure for the ills currently besetting the church, but it can represent the starting point of movement toward reforms that are desperately needed.[30]

Growing interest has assisted a virtual cottage industry of new guides to catechism for all ages, with curricula for both church and home. Again we are reminded of the importance of church practice. It does not matter if we assent to all the right doctrine, unless we really believe it. And we can enter into personal confidence in the truth of God's Word only by growing up into it, as we experience it in community as the people of God. We are shaped in our beliefs as much by concrete worship practices and decisions about what we sing over many years as we are by the propositions to which we yield assent.

A revival of traditional Christian practices whose practical success has the record of impressive centuries of vital witness will not look—should not look—like the first century, fifth century, twelfth century, sixteenth century, or eighteenth century. But it must not look like the twenty-first century stripped of these antecedents. We will, no doubt, find our way back to these resources as people of our time and place. In doing so, we will be surprised at how similar some of our problems are to those faced by our brothers and sisters in other times and places. We will be lifted out of our snobbery toward the past, as if our generation were the only important one in the history of the church. And we will also encounter new questions that they will help us answer: How can we enjoy the Sabbath in our day of commuter churches? What will regular catechism practices look like in today's overcommitted and often broken homes? Is there an emerging approach to church music that reaches beyond the dead end of traditional-versus-contemporary and contemporary-versus-traditional? If style isn't neutral, what criteria should we develop so that God's Word may dwell in us "richly in all wisdom" (Col. 3:16)? But these are all exciting questions, if we have already accepted the challenge to move in these directions. We can expect variety as we step up to the plate ourselves, in our time and place, understanding and incorporating, but not slavishly imitating, that which has gone before.

The Buzz is claiming us—though we are claimed already by Another—and it will increasingly come for our children and grandchildren. But we don't have to accept this as a fate, any more than we simply accept any other truce with worldliness. And while our responses will not only be varied but characterized by faithfulness and unfaithfulness—even simultaneously—may God give us the grace that will help us shake off the fake yellow glow from the Buzz of a fading age and lustily sing:

Savior, if of Zion's city I, through grace, a member am,
Let the world deride or pity, I will glory in Thy name.
Fading is the worldling's pleasures, all his boasted pomp and show;
Solid joys and lasting treasures none but Zion's children know.

John Newton, "Glorious Things of Thee Are Spoken"

TWELVE

Reaching the Lost
without Losing the Reached

Here is the dilemma. There are many churches these days that instead of reaching the unchurched are unchurching the churched. Modernity has already done a great deal to tear apart the generational fabric and rootedness that comes with long-term commitments. According to some statistics, the average candidate for a "seeker" church is not an unbeliever but a lapsed churchgoer or a churchgoer who has been so uprooted and transplanted in his or her life that belonging to a deeply rooted community can only appear ingrown.[1]

No real growth in the number of conversions to Christianity has occurred during this period of the megachurch, so we might be justified in concluding that the growth is the result of smaller, more rooted churches gradually losing their membership to megachurches.[2] Many of these people are not necessarily unbelievers who need to be reached but professing Christians who do not want to commit to anything beyond themselves and who insist on not limiting their options. How can we reach the lost without losing the reached?

Seekers or Tourists?

A good deal has been written and said in recent years about the remarkable rise in tourism. Every summer, Europeans experience mixed emotions as the American and Japanese tourists arrive, cameras hanging from necks like pendants. "See Europe in Ten Days" is actually taken seriously by us because we don't intend to get to know the culture—we just want to take pictures and experience the experience. Perhaps that is a bit cynical, but it is nevertheless worth asking whether the blending of consumerism and tourism might be evident in the way contemporary Americans approach religion and spirituality. We call them seekers, but "tourists" might be more apt. The term *seeker* conjures up notions of destination. One has to be looking for something in particular in order to qualify as a seeker, but we are all used to being consumers and voyeurs of other people's experiences. Unlike seekers, tourists have no intention of committing themselves once they find that for which they are looking. They are fascinated by nearly everything, just as "doing Asia" is fascinating, even if it is seen through the tinted glass of trains and posh buses. This does not spell defeat, however, because we believe that the gospel is "the power of God unto salvation." It can arrest people in their tracks and end their spiritual tourism. But if that arresting truth is lacking in the churches on their itinerary, they will remain tourists and voyeurs—connoisseurs of religious experience along with everything else.

Former labor secretary Robert Reich notes, "Instead of liberating us, the new world of choice is making us more dependent on people who specialize in persuading us to choose this or that."[3] In relation to the church, I would argue, that makes pastors travel agents. Reich is right on this point: We are so burdened with small choices that we have little time to invest in long-term community, instruction, relationships, and obligation. Any notion of a covenant community gets lost in the deal. As Deborah Stone explains, ". . . true freedom is something more than no one interfering with her personal will."[4] She adds:

> Lately, freedom has taken on a new consumerist cast: being able to choose from an array of goods in every aspect of our lives. . . . There's only one problem with this vision of the good life as being set loose in a superstore: Most of us, as we begin to fashion our life plans, want some things that can't be had off the shelves. We want to roam in our imaginations and to create things that don't yet exist. We want connectedness as well as autonomy. We want to love and be loved. We want understanding, loyalty, and compassion. We want the pleasures of working with others on some larger project. No one—least of all the market or anyone in it—can produce and package any of these things for us. These aren't things we can choose. We have to make them, and we can't make them alone. Why can't we make these things in markets? Because markets are designed to disconnect people at the first sign of trouble. When we're disappointed with something we purchase in the market, we don't go back. We don't bother to tell anyone why we're unhappy. We find another supplier. Like a child with her toys, when we get tired of something or it fails to please us, we up and leave.[5]

Market-driven church growth principles cannot help but loosen and then disrupt entirely the interconnectedness of Christian communities.

Not only does such an approach lead churches to promise what they cannot deliver, but it is intrinsically resistant to the values that preserve a community over the long haul, during trials as well as triumphs. What Deborah Stone here says of markets is true of most churches in America today: "We don't bother to tell anyone we're unhappy. We find another supplier. Like a child with her toys, when we get tired of something or it fails to please us, we up and leave." While market principles, including the greatest possible freedom of choice, may be valuable economic goals, they become utterly corrosive when allowed to establish the criteria for the things that matter most in our human existence: relationships, civic institutions, education, the arts, and churches.

David Brooks explores this cultural phenomenon of unlimited choice in his acclaimed *Bobos in Paradise*.[6] Having realized that New Age spirituality and smorgasbord religion "can lead to lazy spirituality," the new upper class ("Bobos") has realized that "the toppling of old authorities has not led to a glorious new dawn but instead to an alarming loss of faith in institutions and to spiritual confusion and social breakdown. So if you look around the Bobo world, you see people trying to rebuild connections."[7] At the same time, they still value their own personal freedom of choice as the nonnegotiable commitment. Although he is a nonpracticing Jew, Brooks observes, "The life of perpetual choice is a life of perpetual longing as you are prodded by the inextinguishable desire to try the next new thing. But maybe what the soul hungers for is ultimately not a variety of interesting and moving insights but a single universal truth. . . . Maybe now it is time, the Bobo says, to rediscover old values, to reconnect with the patient, rooted, and uncluttered realms."[8] Brooks cites a *New York Times Magazine* issue on religion with the headline "Religion Makes a Comeback (Belief to Follow)."[9] One cannot live on hype and personal taste forever:

> Their souls being colored with shades of gray, they find nothing heroic, nothing inspiring, nothing that brings their lives to a point. Some days I look around and I think we have been able to achieve these reconciliations [between choice and meaningfulness] only by making ourselves more superficial, by simply ignoring the deeper thoughts and highest ideals that would torture us if we actually stopped to measure ourselves according to them. Sometimes I think we are too easy on ourselves.[10]

When Relevance Becomes Irrelevant

Dean of Duke University's chapel, William Willimon, is among a growing number of "postliberal" mainline Protestants who have recognized that they've reached a dead end. Having sold the uniqueness of Christian faith and practice for a mess of cultural pottage, all in the name of "relevance," the result has been the very opposite. He writes:

> I'm a mainline-liberal-Protestant-Methodist-type Christian. I know we're soft on Scripture. Norman Vincent Peale has exercised a more powerful effect on our preaching than St. Paul. . . . I know we play fast and loose with Scripture. But I've always had this fantasy that somewhere, like in Texas, there were preachers who preached it all, Genesis to Revelation, without blinking an eye. . . . I took great comfort in knowing that, even while I preached a pitifully compromised, "Pealed"-down gospel, that somewhere, good old Bible-believing preachers were offering their congregations the unadulterated Word, straight up. Do you know how disillusioning it has been for me to realize that many of these self-proclaimed biblical preachers now sound more like liberal mainliners than liberal mainliners?[11]

While evangelicals and other conservative Protestants hold to a high doctrine of Scripture in principle, the last two decades have especially seen a growing disregard for making their sermons expositions of Scripture; rather, it's often the case that the Bible is used as a sourcebook of quotations for what *we* really want to say.

It is difficult to challenge the assertion that the mainline Protestant churches have become trivial, irrelevant, and are losing their membership rapidly. But Willimon also cautions evangelicals that they appear to be repeating those mistakes, assuming that our task is to make Christianity relevant to contemporary men and women rather than causing our contemporaries to critique their beliefs and commitments in the light of the Christian narrative. By the time we "translate" Christianity in terms that are comfortable for contemporary people, we have emptied it of all its meaning, its sharp edges, and the radical dissonance that is supposed to exist between the city of God and "this passing evil age." Willimon writes:

> Lacking confidence in the power of our story to effect that of which it speaks, to evoke a new people out of nothing, our communication loses its nerve. Nothing is said that could not be heard elsewhere. . . . Unfortunately, most of the theology I learned in seminary was in the translation mode. Take this biblical image and translate it into something more palatable to people who use Cuisinarts. The modern church has been willing to use everyone's language but its own. In conservative contexts, gospel speech is traded for dogmatic assertion and moralism, for self-help psychologies and narcotic mantras. In more liberal speech, talk tiptoes around the outrage of Christian discourse and ends up as an innocuous, though

urbane, affirmation of the ruling order. Unable to preach Christ and him crucified, we preach humanity and it improved. . . . Most of our people are under the impression that we preach what's on our mind. They say, "Well, he's often a bag of hot air, but he visited Mama this week in the hospital, so we allow him twenty to thirty minutes to vent his political opinions each week in exchange for his being so nice." ("He's full of hot air, but he's *our* hot air.")[12]

Arguing for the authority of the biblical text in preaching, Willimon insists that churches stop preaching to the masses and start preaching to the baptized: "Baptism asserts that we meet and speak under an identity that challenges and endangers all other identities."[13]

Not long ago I ran across an interesting discussion in *Leadership Journal* in which Lee Strobel, then a teaching pastor at Willow Creek Community Church, expressed the commonly held view of preaching as "translation":

> John Stott once said that good preaching begins in the Bible and then builds a bridge to the real world, which I think is true for believers, because they trust the Bible. Often for seekers, however, I find that the reverse works: I begin in the real world, connecting with their needs, and show them that I do understand where they've been and where they are. Based on that, I show the relevance of Scripture. I build a bridge from the real world into the world of Scripture.[14]

But that is just the question, isn't it: Do we even know what the "real world" is apart from its divine description? The world is a marvelous creation of God, in bondage to sin, suffering, evil, and pain because of human rebellion, redeemed by Jesus Christ, who will come to make all things new. Furthermore, hasn't God built that bridge from the Word to his hearers by sending us preachers who announce his judgment and pardon?

In the "hermeneutics of translation," the culture takes over, usually in the idiom of the therapeutic, and instead of preaching being linked to baptism (buried with Christ and made new in him as we are members of his counterculture), it is linked to whatever "point of contact" might be out there in the world. God's Word must name "this present evil age" for us, an age that is both under God's common grace and yet still participates in the common curse.

Increasingly, we hear that what unites us is mission, not theology. Doctrinal diversity is encouraged, as long as we can all agree on the mission and its methods. "Mission" and "evangelism" are in danger of being exploited as "get out of jail free" cards for any capitulation to the culture that we can imagine. How can this fail to bring an end to the fruit itself in due time? William James's suggestion that the best religion is not the truest but the one that produces the most favorable results in one's life and in the world (defined, of course, by the individual and the world) ends up being endorsed by the churches themselves.

It is impossible to limit these criticisms, however, to one particular part of the visible church today. I am increasingly unsure what I will find when visiting a church today, regardless of its name, denominational affiliation, or confessional position. More often than not, the preaching that I expect to hear from nearly any quarter, despite nuances of style (traditional or contemporary), politics (Republican or Democrat), and illustrations (pop culture or high culture), is unhinged from the text of Scripture. Whatever the theoretical commitment to a high view of Scripture in conservative churches, they are as likely today to give the impression that what the preacher had to say today was more important—at least more interesting—than what God might have said. It seems that very little serious exegesis is done in sermons today, and that can only encourage a subtle but effective process of secularizing our churches in the very act of "preaching." There is hardly a sense that God's Word opposes anything in our exciting age, except the moral crises that nearly anybody who would show up at our churches would already oppose.

Often the assumption is that it's fine to talk about God, sin, grace, redemption, justification, sanctification, and so on, as long as the emphasis falls on application. *Leadership Journal* asked Lee Strobel and retired New York City pastor Gardner Taylor the following question: "Thirty years ago a sermon on Elijah and his desert experience at Horeb would have emphasized God's sovereignty and provision. In today's therapeutic climate, often the application is how to cope with burnout or depression. Is that a legitimate switch in emphasis?" Taylor responded, "Any type of preaching that does not bring in the vertical aspect of the sermon—the impact of God upon human life—cannot be called a sermon. There's no excuse for the preacher if he or she is not speaking to people for God—a presumptuous undertaking, to be sure, but one that we are called to do. And unless that is done I don't think preaching has occurred." Strobel, on the other hand, sought middle ground. "On the one end are extremely vertical messages that emphasize doctrine or the nature of God but, unfortunately, lack application. These sermons generally don't accomplish what I think the goal of preaching is, which is life change. . . . The answer is in the middle."[15] But is it not the assumption here that God's revelation of himself and his mighty acts in history is not in itself life-changing?

If God is no longer the focus and main actor in this drama, it is not surprising that "vertical" preaching itself should fall under criticism as a medium. Surely we can accomplish "life change" in more effective ways. In fact, the very act of preaching—not to mention the office of preacher— is increasingly diminished in importance as the minister, both literally as well as figuratively, steps out from behind the pulpit and stands not in his office as ambassador of God but in his own person.

Strobel typifies the logical conclusion that evangelicals, despite their theory of Scripture, seem to be practicing these days:

> Nor do I think it's necessarily whether the message is expository, topical, or textual. I did a message once that was unbiblical in the sense that I didn't quote Scripture. I wanted to preach a simple message on the gospel, so we created a forest scene on the stage of the church. A little girl sat on my lap, and I read her a children's book called *Adam Raccoon at Forever Falls*, a powerful allegory of the gospel. . . . I read the story, and then I closed the book; the little girl jumped off my lap. Then I looked out over the audience and said, "What you just heard was the gospel of Jesus Christ told in a story form."[16]

Although he surely does not intend it, the implication is that Scripture is not sufficient for preaching and evangelism. "I wanted to preach a simple message on the gospel, so we created a forest scene on the stage of the church" raises the important question as to whether we can still count on God's Word to give us a simple gospel message. Furthermore, what does this say about the authority of God's Word in the service, when Adam Raccoon can be regarded as a worthy substitution? Why is it exceptional to announce to the audience, "What you just heard was the gospel of Jesus Christ told in story form," as if the vast tracts of Old Testament narrative and the New Testament Gospels now belong to the image of a bygone era that couldn't tell stories. (In actual fact, the art of storytelling belongs to the past far more than to the present.) Does this not create the impression that the Bible is above the people, too tough for them to understand? That is already the impression of most people on the street and a growing number of people within the church.

As these practices become more acceptable to people, the role of the pastor and the place of preaching will become more ambiguous. Generations ago, the pastor would stand behind his pulpit, knowing that he was preaching not himself but Christ. He was not there to pontificate, hypothesize, or moralize. There was some sense that the minister was not up there because he was such a fantastic person or had a lot of great insights or wanted to sell a product but because he was thoroughly trained in the original languages, exegesis, and theology, and had been called to the pulpit as God's emissary. As revivalism spread, the preacher moved from the pulpit to the stage and paced back and forth. Today, the preacher may often be found strolling through the audience, much like a talk-show host. Unintentionally, we are sending the signal that God's chief means of grace is merely a method that we could take or leave. "I do try to think through every sermon," Strobel says, "to see if I can supplement the boring image of a lone preacher standing and speaking. I try, for example, to integrate video into my preaching when I can."[17]

I cannot help but observe the similarity between the practical denial of the sufficiency of Scripture in our day and in the medieval church. "But may not images be permitted in the churches as teaching aids for the unlearned?" the Heidelberg Catechism asks. "No, we should not try to be wiser than God. He wants his people instructed by the living preaching of his Word."[18] Contrast this "swim against the tide" attitude with the following thoroughly un-heroic fatalism I came across in a newspaper interview with a pastor: "Evangelical churches have thrived on careful exposition of the Scriptures, and lengthy sermons. But we are approaching the place where there is no intellectual content left in the sermon. *So we will be driven* to the power of liturgy and the communication of the gospel through the arts" (emphasis added).[19] Why answer a dearth of intellectual content in the sermons by turning to golden calves? Is this really an inexorable, ineluctable destiny? Why not answer the problem of shallow sermons by suggesting substantive ones? Is this all that we can expect from today's preachers, and we'd just better find a different medium?

Advocates of seeker-driven approaches are to be commended for their missionary zeal. Furthermore, I, for one, am grateful to have been challenged to consider some of their arguments. Nevertheless, "we should not try to be wiser than God," who has already accommodated to our weakness. We must stop assuming that we are reaching the lost if we are not clearly proclaiming God's justice and mercy in the Christ-centered drama of redemption as it is scripted by Scripture. Stanley Hauerwas makes this point in striking terms. "We accepted the politics of translation," he says, "believing that neither we nor our non-Christian and half-Christian neighbors could be expected to submit to the discipline of Christian speech."[20] This is precisely the assumption, he rightly contends, that must be challenged.

An advertisement keeps popping up for a new paraphrase of the Bible. It's a full-page, color photograph of a woman who appears to be young, sophisticated, well educated—with a hint of cynicism. "Pastor," the caption reads, "if you want to reach me, you better watch your language." The inside copy elaborates: "Distracted by deadlines and bills, this is the only time she takes to nurture her spiritual life. You can't afford to lose her attention when you reference Bible passages that are too lofty and obscure." We take such advertising copy almost like tomorrow's sunrise, as a given. If this woman is at all representative of how many people in our churches think and live, then surely we ought to follow this ad's advice.

But that is just what we are challenging here. Why can't a good pastor respond, "No, this isn't about making things comfortable for you. If you are baptized, then this speech that the Bible uses is your language. You have to make an effort to understand it, to live in its world, and to breathe its air. If you are too distracted by deadlines and bills to take any time outside of this one hour a week for your faith, then you'll pardon me for not losing the rest of my congregation to the world just for you."

To be sure, there are convoluted ways of speaking that stick out like a sore thumb even to those who are well studied in the Scriptures, and we ought to avoid pseudo-intellectualism and affectation. But let's face it: Preaching and sacrament are "insider communication." People cannot just walk in off the street and expect the nurture of the covenant community to be quickly accessed without any effort at learning a new language. We do this all the time when it matters: learning the language of computers, the peculiar speech of our own field, the stories and inside jokes of our family. I know pastors who make fun of memorizing the catechism in these times of "short attention spans" but rattle off baseball statistics from the sixties. Imagine football games in which nothing could be said that an outsider to the game might not conveniently understand. This ad assumes not that Christianity must be translated but that it need not be communicated at all, unless it can be immediately understood by a non-Christian or a professing Christian who does not actually practice his or her faith outside the church building.

D. L. Moody once quipped, "I can write the gospel on a dime." Similarly, I've been asked what I would tell a person in an elevator if I were explaining the gospel, as if my answer—which was extremely brief and simple—justified shallow Christianity. Those who belong to the church—and it is they who are the chief concern in the service—should expect to spend more time mining the riches of God's grace than someone stuck in an elevator for a minute and a half.

It is not the purpose of the church to merely enlighten or to say essentially what people already know or can find somewhere else in the culture, but in this case with quotes from Jesus and his friends. We should recall Paul's appeal to new Christians in Rome: "I beseech you therefore, brethren, by the mercies of God, that you present your bodies a living sacrifice, holy, acceptable to God, which is your reasonable service. And do not be conformed to this world, but be transformed by the renewing of your mind, that you may prove what is that good and accept-able and perfect will of God" (Rom. 12:1–2 NKJV).

This, it seems to me, is one of the most exciting as well as challenging aspects of our witness today—recovering the story that can make sense of our sound-bite existence. Genuine relevance is found not when the church tries to be relevant, since repeating what people already think is rather boring. Genuine relevance is found in contradicting the wisdom of the world that we entered the church with on Sunday morning. We should share the hope in Stanley Hauerwas's conclusion: "May our preaching be just as terrible" as the truth itself. "Indeed, may we preach so truthfully that people will call us terrorists. If you preach that way you will never again have to worry about whether a sermon is 'meaningful.'"[21]

Fatalism or Reformation?

One of the reasons for a proliferation of images in the medieval church (against the decisions of early church councils) was purely pragmatic: They were the "books" of the unlearned. The Reformers, however, asked why pastors should cater to the weakness of the people, as Aaron did, rather than leading them to greater Christian maturity. Today we face this same problem of cultural accommodation.

First, it is important to observe from the outset that everybody is sit-uated in a particular culture. We have learned in recent decades that we are not disembodied minds floating above the particularities of time and place; rather, we are shaped by our location. At the same time, this can be used by some as an impetus for a fatalistic embrace of contemporary culture. Ironically, this passive acceptance of everything new is similar to the traditionalist's "we've always done it this way." In both cases, the historical-cultural situation becomes normative. Second, it is important to recognize that in every "translation" something gets lost. This does not mean that we should not attempt simple clarity, but it does mean that we have to ask ourselves in each case whether we are distorting the con-tent in the process. Language and concepts cannot be separated, since the words we use shape our understanding of what it is we are trying to say. Sin is not "dysfunction." "Sin" needs explanation not translation.

Third, there are many church practitioners today whose somewhat superficial understanding of "postmodernism" has led them to adopt a crude type of cultural relativism. However, this is not postmodern at all but modern to the core. Throughout the nineteenth century and much of the twentieth, a philosophical hermeneutics dominated known as *his-toricism*. According to this view, every epoch has its own form of life and is essentially self-contained and inaccessible. In this way of thinking, there are no values or truths that transcend all ages and places. Similarly, many evangelicals who have recently read summaries of postmodernism assume that this is true even though they might reject cultural relativism if asked directly. It is just part of the air that we breathe. But what does this do to the unity of the human race, the image of God in all human beings, and the deeper unity that God has established in Jesus Christ among his children? God prophesied through Zephaniah of a coming day:

> Then will I purify the lips of the people,
>   that all of them may call on the name of the LORD
>   and serve him shoulder to shoulder.
> From beyond the rivers of Cush
>   my worshipers, my scattered people,
>   will bring me offerings.
> On that day you will not be put to shame
>   for all the wrongs you have done to me,
> because I will remove from this city
>   those who rejoice in their pride.
> Never again will you be haughty
>   on my holy hill.
>
>   3:9–11

Notice the obvious parallel with the Tower of Babel (Genesis 11) and the haughtiness of the nations in their proud tower—their self-created "holy hill" from which they could thwart God's purposes.

This passage and its New Testament fulfillment at Pentecost indicate that there are ties that bind us to the characters in this divine drama that are far tighter than the cords of blood and culture. It was this stand that was taken by the Confessing Church against the capitulation of the German Evangelical Church to Nazi ideology, and it needs to be taken again against the more subtle forms of cultural captivity. We do not have to give in passively to the cultural temper of the times. God's Word is not remote, locked in its own time and place, in need of being made relevant to Boomers. It continues to affect the new world it describes—if we would just turn off the TV for a minute and listen.

Ministers are not free to choose their story; nor are hearers. This is a startling assertion in evangelical as much as mainline circles today. In fact, it could be argued that evangelical preaching today—in sharp contrast to that of only a generation ago—is at least as eager to sound and look like the world as the liberals of yesteryear, just as Willimon suggested above. C. Peter Wagner argues, "Traditional church models no longer work in our fast-changing world. A commitment to reaching the lost is driving new apostolic churches to find new ways to fulfill the Great Commission."[22] In this outlook, "our fast-changing world"—that which the Bible knows as "this fading age"—becomes the norm, and church models are viewed in thoroughly relativistic terms, as if God had left the twenty-first-century church to find "ways to fulfill the Great Commision" other than Word and sacrament.

According to George Barna, it is "critical that we keep in mind a fundamental principle of Christian communication: the audience, not the message is sovereign."[23] Is this the same evangelical movement that castigated the World Council of Churches for its slogan, "The church follows the world's agenda"? In actual fact, the current trends that are touted as "unique" and "unprecedented" have marked declining civilizations (and churches that follow them) throughout history. Near the beginning of the twentieth century, writer and social commentator Walter Lippman wrote, "The philosophy which inspires the whole process is based on the theory, which is no doubt correct, that a great population under modern conditions is not held by sustained convictions and traditions, but that it wants and must have one thrill after another."[24] Steiner Kvale has written more recently, "Fascination may take the place of reflection; seduction may replace argumentation."[25] From political campaigns and TV "news" to our church life, our culture is surrendering to nihilism—even if it appears dressed in cheerful pastels instead of Gothic black.

When we read in media reports and sociological studies that contemporary services are increasingly targeting those who want "spirituality" but not "church," we are back to our original question: So what? Should this surprise us—hasn't it always been that way? Is it not simply part and parcel of rejecting God's authority? Why accept the preferences of a lot of especially white, middle-class, suburban Americans as a fate? Is the sociological "is" equivalent to a theological "ought"? Who determines the church's mission, message, and methods? Those whom Scripture describes as "hostile to the things of God"? Most Americans—professing Christians—for a fairly long time thought that slavery was simply "where people are these days." Is it really loving to set aside the truth about sin and judgment and even to downplay the person and work of Christ as its answer simply because these are not the questions that are being asked by unbelievers? Imagine our elementary school teachers deciding that they will no longer teach the alphabet because the children aren't interested in learning it.

"Where once a community of believers shared a common vocabulary, many feel free to define God by their own lights," we read in a *USA Today* cover story, "In Search of Faith." Do we read that as a reality to which we must submit or as a challenge that might afford an opportunity for the church to say something interesting for a change? Does anyone see this self-created spirituality as a species of idolatry, a proud threat of an ungodly generation shaking its fist in God's face, declaring, "We will not have him reign over us"? Why is sexual promiscuity viewed as a more serious threat than the swelling tide of arrogance against Christ, his Word, and his church?

Another evangelical pastor announced in an interview that his goal is "to make the church adjust and fit in with modern society." "Society reinvents itself every three to five years," he says—as if this hyperbolic and otherwise banal observation could lead to only one conclusion. After all, why couldn't we interpret the data differently and say that precisely because society is so plastic and relationships as well as structures of meaning so fragmented the church has a marvelous opportunity to provide a space for continuity and community with a divine drama? "The churches are really cross-denominational," the same pastor says. "The blur of all that is consistent with the age we're living in."[26] Again, why does the blur (i.e., confusion) of our age have to shape the church, when the church has a chance to be a place of clarity and direction at such a time? We simply must resist the fatalistic logic that would have capitulation as the only relevant response to our context.

One last example of what I perceive as fatalism is the following statement, typical of some church marketers: "The data shows a continuation of the pattern that first emerged more than a decade ago, in which Americans feel tremendous freedom to construct their own religious perspectives and practices, regardless of traditions and time-honored teachings.... The American public is sending a clear message to Christian leaders: Make Christianity accessible and practical or don't expect our participation."[27] First, there is that preface, "The data shows," which, as Neil Postman reminded us, has come to serve the same function that "thus says the Lord" used to have. But more importantly, how does Mr. Barna get from data indicating a generally pagan American populace to the imperative that churches therefore adapt in order to benefit from their participation? A church filled with pagans is in worse shape than a small country church that has faithfully shepherded God's children for generations. The data does not indicate what we should do but only what may be happening at a given moment in the fickle world of public opinion.

And Now for Something Completely Different

While the enormous size of the "Boomer" generation has elicited a great deal of attention, and the seeker spirituality especially associated with that generation has received a lot of press, that is hardly the whole story. We have already seen such signs of change among advocates of CCM worship who have now called for greater theological reflection. In *soul-Tsunami,* cultural historian Leonard Sweet says that the so-called "Busters" (1961–81) "will keep the past and the future in perpetual conversation."[28]

Lynn Smith cites Karen Neudorf, publisher of *Beyond* magazine, targeting Generation Xers and Busters. "'A concern I have is that the Busters are biblically illiterate,' says Neudorf. 'While people are hungry for experiential faith, where will our doctrines come from? Who will teach us our doctrinal roots? Young adults need to be mentored.'"[29] "A hunger for roots will characterize the 'ancientfuture' churches, and this will have an enormous effect on worship. To be 'radical' in the postmodern era means not to tear up the roots, in the root canal fashion of the '60s," says Sweet, "but to 'go to the roots' and there find the direction, energy and nutrients necessary for growth and development."[30] The so-called "Millennials" (born since 1981) get even more interesting. Robert Webber tells us, "Millennials are looking to the past to find old ways to cope with the world situation. For them, old is better. They have a newfound love for the classics and a deep interest in things medieval. In worship, this is evident in the millennial disdain for contemporary worship for its lack of form and beauty."[31] In fact, Webber says:

> I am less enthusiastic than church growth prognosticators and predictions about the future of the church being in the megachurches. I firmly believe that the small church will continue to play a key role in handing down the faith from one generation to the next. Nor do I embrace the idea that contemporary worship is a style of the future. Contemporary worship lacks depth and is generally not connected with the history of God's worshiping community. It seems unlikely to me that a market-driven church and worship will survive. It will eventually be swallowed up by the culture it embraces.[32]

Growing numbers of younger people are dumping these lowest-common-denominator approaches, either for no church or for churches that have some substance. A letter to the editor in the *New Yorker* caught my attention recently along these lines:

> I was once drawn to the faith of my father, a devout Lutheran, out of a sense of comfort in the familiar. But I didn't find spiritual fulfillment until, after years of trying on other religious identities, I turned to Eastern Orthodoxy. I agree with John Updike that Christianity, seen strictly as a religion and not as a political movement, seems to be fading. Could that be because many denominations have diluted sacredness out of the faith? Church services have become hug-thy-neighbor group-therapy sessions, confir-

mation classes bear the moniker "Deviating for Christ" in an effort to attract teenagers with "cool" language, and important religious services, like those at Easter and Christmas, include bunnies and Santas. Where is the sense of awe—even a touch of fear—of the Divine that I felt in the cathedrals of Europe or the church of my youth? God seems to have become a benign friend on whom one can call when needed, and Christianity merely a long-distance carrier to make that call. No wonder so many of us search for more.[33]

This person is not alone. In fact, scores of younger evangelicals, many of them prominent, have left for Eastern Orthodoxy or Roman Catholicism, in an effort to find something that transcends the shallow narcissism of cultural Christianity. Both "high church" mystery and contemporary familiarity easily pave the way for idols, as we try to force God to put in an appearance and allow us to experience his majesty on our terms. Christians are discovering in their own circles of confessing Reformation churches a remarkable growth of interest among young people who are fed up with fast-food religion. Some traditionalists will risk squandering this moment with a "See, we were right all along" smugness that ignores the contribution that their own laziness and thoughtlessness have made to the crisis. But if we really understand what is going on here, it will be not only a chance for numerical growth but for a rediscovery of what we believe, why we believe it, and what we do and why we do it in our worship. Conservatives have as much to learn about what really animates the evangelical tradition as those who might visit our churches. Our commission is to be guided by Scripture and not by conservatism or progressivism. God's Word will always shake us up, wherever we are on that spectrum.

Sarah E. Hinlicky speaks for this growing trend when she writes the following suggestions about how to reach her own over-stereotyped Generation X:

> We know you've tried to get us to church. That's part of the problem. Many of your appeals have been carefully calculated for success, and that turns our collective stomach. Take worship, for instance. You may think that fashionably cutting-edge liturgies relate to us on our level, but the fact is, we can find better entertainment elsewhere. The same goes for anything else you term "contemporary." We see right through it: it's up-to-date for the sake of being up-to-date, and we're not impressed by the results. . . . We know intuitively that, in the cosmic scheme of things, the stakes are too high for that. . . . On the other hand, you shouldn't be excessively medieval and mysterious, either. Mystery works up to a point, but it's addictive, and once we get hooked on it, the Church won't be able to provide enough to support our habit. We'll turn instead (many of us already

have) to Eastern gurus and ancient pagan spiritualities. . . . The Church
has fought against that gnostic impulse from the start: Christianity is explo-
sively non-secretive, God enfleshed for everyone to see, the light shining
in the darkness. We're much too comfortable alone in the dark; we need
the light to shake us up.[34]

Hinlicky and her cohorts are weary of platitudes and ideological fads.
"We see complicity in the Church where you want us to see stability,
moralism where you want us to see righteousness. The ultimate difference is that where you see the City of God we see only the City of
Man." She also rejects the spiritual marketing that makes Jesus the
answer to everything. "Our stumbling block is Christianity presented as
a panacea."

> So you're in quite a pickle: you can't tell us that the Church has "the Truth"
> and we know that the Church won't miraculously cure us of our misery.
> What do you have left to persuade us? One thing: the story. . . . You won-
> der why we're so self-destructive, but we're looking for the one story with
> staying power, the destruction and redemption of our own lives. That's to
> your advantage: you have the best redemption story on the market. Per-
> haps the only thing you can do, then, is to point us towards Golgotha, a
> story that we can make sense of. Show us the women who wept and loved
> the Lord but couldn't change his fate. Remind us that Peter, the rock of
> the Church, denied the Messiah three times. Tell us that Pilate washed his
> hands of the truth, something we are often tempted to do. Mostly, though,
> turn us towards God hanging on the cross. That is what the world does to
> the holy. Where the cities of God and Man intersect, there is a crucifix-
> ion. The best-laid plans are swept aside; the blue-prints for the perfect
> society are divided among the spoilers. We recognize this world: ripped
> from the start by our parents' divorces, spoiled by our own bad choices,
> threatened by war and poverty, pain and meaninglessness. . . .
>
>   One more thing. In our world where the stakes are high, remind us that
> all hope is not lost. As Christians you worship not at the time of the cru-
> cifixion, but Sunday morning at the resurrection. Tell us that the lives we
> lead now are redeemed, and that the Church, for all her flaws, is the bearer
> of this redemption. A story needs a storyteller, and it is the Church alone
> that tells the story of salvation. Here in the Church is where the cities of
> Man and God meet, and that is why all the real spiritual battles, the most
> exciting adventure stories, begin here. We know that death will continue
> to break our hearts and our bodies, but it's not the end of the story. Because
> of all the stories competing for our attention, the story of the City of God
> is the only one worth living, and dying, for.[35]

Not long ago, the *Wall Street Journal* published a report by Eric Felten on the use of demographic marketing for churches. According to

recent studies, those who identified themselves as "Educated Working Families" "want Adult Theological Discussion Groups." Furthermore, they prefer "'Traditional/Formal Worship' held in churches with 'Somber/ Serious Architecture.'"[36] While there are plenty of surveys to indicate that many people out there want or even demand seeker-driven worship, a growing number of studies is showing quite different trends. This has been my own experience, and I've seen it confirmed in numerous places. As the emptiness of market-driven churches is realized, many people are looking for some depth and accountability—not only their own accountability but that of the church and its ministry to the wider church of Christ.

But it doesn't matter what the trends are or what they indicate. They may be helpful and even interesting, but they cannot be normative. Felten concludes:

> But is slick "ethnographic" marketing the answer? Or does it suggest that preachers are succumbing to temptation? Are they giving in to the sort of poll-driven waffling that long ago denuded the public square of political leadership? In short, will they tailor their message to the whims of their "constituencies"? Even if there weren't something fundamentally disturbing about this effort to enlist Madison Avenue on behalf of the Word, how much use are religious demographics? It is somehow hard to imagine a firm religious conviction, or reliable moral compass, issuing from marketing tactics. . . . A church confident of its message doesn't need to massage it with marketing studies. God help the prophet who polls.[37]

So why do we continue to accept the logic that contemporary worship "experiences" are overcoming the divisions of Christ's body? That they are reaching the unchurched? That they are revitalizing churches and uniting all of God's people around mission? At least one reason, I'm convinced, is that we are in bondage to the logic of marketing. For instance, how many innovations have been introduced in the interest of "keeping our young people"? Just last week, at a Reformed church of largely postwar Dutch immigrants, the young people selected all the psalms and hymns—and their selections were "A Mighty Fortress," "Psalm 9," and "Jerusalem the Golden." These young people don't look very different from other people's kids, but they think differently. There is a sense of integration between the generations. It is a genuine community, and in recent months a growing number of younger couples and singles have come from other churches. Some of them enter with leather jackets and tattoos, long hair or buzz cuts, and they still get invited by some older couple in the church to dinner at their house after church.

In 1994, Dr. Kim Riddlebarger and I planted a church in a Reformed denomination and watched it grow rapidly. Again, the growth was largely from younger couples and single people who were burned out on the megachurches in the area. Since most of them are right in the middle of contemporary American (in fact, Southern Californian) culture, they have seen what modernity has to offer and have become disillusioned "mall rats." This church is not a model by any means, nor are Reformed churches, generally speaking, in any better condition right now than anybody else's. But it is an example of what can happen when we provide an alternative drama, a different theater in which God and his action takes center stage. We have crafted a contemporary version of a Reformed liturgy based on past patterns, and we try to find the best music to assist the people in cherishing God's Word in their hearts and in expressing their gratitude to him. Our experience confirms the reports that the coming generation wants more than pop religion.

William Willimon gives the following challenge and illustration: "We need biblical preachers now, more than ever, to remind us that 'He who sits in the heavens laughs' (Ps. 2:4) over our kings and kingdoms. God, not nations, rules the world!"[38]

And as we have been observing, there is some good news on the horizon. While we must risk falling into the marketing trap ourselves simply because some of the data seems to put wind in our sails, marketing and demographic studies are yielding some surprising information. Michael Sack, marketing consultant to Fortune 500 companies, says, "Today's young people see almost 1,000 percent more images than 55-year-olds saw in their youth. Surprisingly, though, they don't have a corresponding understanding of the images they see. The ability to find meaning in print or video is much greater in people over 50."[39]

At this point, we would expect many evangelical church marketers to conclude that we therefore need more video, more sound, more lights, more action. But Sack takes it in a different direction: "For X-ers, those ages 16–25, the images have no symbolism, no moral value. They choose images for color or movement or entertainment. Inanimate messages—anything other than person-to-person speech—lose value as you get younger in this culture." His interviewer asks, "Many would assume it's the other way around. Isn't it the MTV generation that deals in images?" Sack replies:

> For X-ers, the media are flashing two thousand images a day. They can't deal with that, so they ignore the images. As a result, young people are a hundred times more sophisticated in handling images, but not in attributing significance to them. The young eat images like popcorn; older adults eat them like a meal. . . . When pastors . . . ask people to watch a video,

they need to know it will be less effective for those who are young. The impact of anything that hasn't been personally delivered is going to go down by about 25 percent for each ten years an audience is below 50.[40]

These statistics are substantiated by others. A recent *Christianity Today* survey found that "Pastors were more likely than listeners to think their sermons should be shorter. . . . About 75 percent of pastors said it's important to tailor sermon length to congregational expectations, while only half (53 percent) of listeners felt the same. The Builder generation, those 55 and over, wanted preachers to cater to their sermon-length ideals more than did Boomers or Gen-Xers."[41] And then here is a real surprise:

> Interestingly, in our survey, Gen-Xers seemed to have longer sermon attention spans than Boomers. Perhaps the effects of our fast-paced, media-oriented culture are not as severe as supposed. Sermons just may get a little longer in the future to satisfy the younger generation's desires. Few listeners thought multimedia presentations or drama would make their pastor's preaching more effective. Only 20 percent of listeners said that their pastor's sermons would be improved by using multimedia, while 63 percent of pastors said this would help. Other techniques that pastors were two or three times more likely than listeners to believe would help their preaching included story-telling, narrative, or dramatic techniques (60% vs. 17%); illustrations (46% vs. 14%); movement outside the pulpit (37% vs. 14%); personal stories (25% vs. 12%); references to popular culture (22% vs. 11%); and gestures (32% vs. 9%).[42]

As for the Boomers, "The god they don't believe in revolves around discomfort rather than truth and evil. Their idea of evil is irritation. . . . The inability to look into the eyes of suffering, into the negative side of things, limits boomers' ability to appreciate the positive side of things. In that regard, research indicates Christians are no different than the rest of the culture." Sack says that Generation X "has almost no concept of evil" but is looking for something to make sense of it. "I've never seen a group of people anywhere," he says, "including people in absolute poverty in the Philippines, who have a greater urgency to hear good news than the under-25 generation in this country. They long to hear that there is hope."[43]

Gen-Xers need "written reinforcement of key concepts." Theirs is the "feed me" generation, according to Sack, whereas the Boomers are the "entertain me and earn me generation"—"faddish, intellectually lazy."[44]

Already we see Gen-Xers investing more of their time in finding meaning and community, often in sharp contrast to their parents. Their attention spans are not short—as long as there is something worth listening to. This generation may be the most representative of those who are swelling the venues where theology conferences are held across the United States and Canada. I run into them all the time, and they are eager to learn and grow, to find themselves by reference to Christ and his people. All that Sack mentions here concerning Gen-X identity indicates that there may well be more interest among this coming generation in embracing the discipline of Christian faith and practice. Bored by simulacra and surface, their "feed me" attitude and their need for "written reinforcement of key concepts" suggest that they may find serious biblical preaching, teaching, worship, and community more attractive than the more self-obsessed and anti-intellectual generations.

At the end of the day, however, God's kingdom does not fall and rise according to the demographics of a given generation. Vital Christianity will probably never dominate the American landscape and exercise power over the nation's institutions, but God will always reserve for himself seven thousand who have not bowed their knee to Baal.

A Few Ideas

This chapter has attempted to distinguish genuine seekers from "tourists," urging us to recover our confidence in the power of the gospel to make itself relevant rather than placing our confidence in the power of our own "translation" (i.e., transformation) of the message. The way forward is neither a lazy conservatism nor an equally lazy fatalism about the way the culture happens to be right now and how we have to accommodate to it. And new statistics on the coming generation are encouraging.

If we are to grow our churches God's way, it seems to me that we have to define more carefully such terms as *mission, outreach,* and *evangelism.* As noted above, these terms often serve as unwitting euphemisms for cultural accommodation. So a seeker-driven church with four thousand members (or at least people in the audience) will always be able to lord it over a smaller church that pretty much does the same thing it has been doing for generations. But it will be able to do this only if size and busy programs define success, and the present rather than the past or the future is the standard. If one's definition of success is the size of the audience at present, then the smaller, more traditional churches will have to bear the moral superiority of the more seeker-driven argument.

If, however, one's definition of success is growth (both in depth and breadth) over several generations of faithful preaching, teaching, outreach, and discipleship, there is no longer a basis for saying that the megachurches are actually successful in mission while traditional churches are not. Many advocates of the church growth movement just assume a definition of success that is in dispute. While megachurches come and go, there are many small, deeply rooted churches across the country—many of which would receive from their critics the designation "dead orthodox"—that have in fact made more disciples over the long haul. It all depends on definitions.

But this is not to say that more traditional churches do not have anything to learn from the church growth literature. The greatest strength of many traditional churches is also potentially their greatest weakness: the tendency to focus almost exclusively on the nurture of the covenant people within the local church to the exclusion of knowing or even caring about what is happening to the people beyond their walls. One may be forgiven for having the impression of some conservatives that they just don't get out much. In addition to the central mission of the church—making disciples through Word, sacrament, and nurture—there are extensions of that ministry that should be considered. The following ruminations are nothing more than considerations, and they are largely limited by my own experience and reflection.

1. *Daily instruction of the youth.* First, there was a generation that knew proof-texts without really knowing the divine drama—sort of like memorizing a lot of lines from Shakespeare without knowing how one of the plays actually goes. I've already referred to the practice of catechism, which was followed in the home, in church, and at Christian schools for generations. This use of a catechism is being revived in many quarters.

But wouldn't it be plausible also to reintroduce the practice of daily instruction before or after school—either at someone's home or in a room at school or church? Growing up in a small town with a rather large Mormon (Latter-Day Saints) population, I occasionally visited "seminary" with my friends (friendship evangelism, of course!). Every day before school they would meet for an hour of religious instruction and prayer. The dedication of both students and teachers to this practice doubtless plays some part in the commitment that has made Mormonism one of the fastest-growing and closely knit communities in the world. If even weekly instruction is considered taxing on our hectic lives, daily instruction will seem thoroughly implausible. But in a time when the next generation of even churched young people is largely ignorant of the basic teaching and practice of Christianity, we might want to reconsider our priorities. Remember, the best evangelism occurs through long-term relationships, as well-informed believers confidently articulate their faith and demonstrate its importance over months and even years. People, not programs, evangelize.

2. *Word-centered innovation.* At Tenth Presbyterian Church in Philadelphia, associate pastor Richard Phillips introduced a question-and-answer box and answered one of the questions just before the beginning of the evening service. This is a type of innovation that is quite useful. God does command teaching to take place in worship, and this parenthesis in the service is part of the ministry of the Word. Although Pastor Phillips did not do so, this could even serve as an opportunity for the pastor to walk among the congregation, providing a stark contrast between this type of teaching and the preaching that occurs when he mounts the pulpit.

3. *Distinguishing between the covenant renewal ceremony and outreach.* Both worship and outreach are tasks given by Christ to the church, and neither should be used to marginalize the other. Examples abound of strong teaching churches offering lunchtime "Christianity 101" chats in the heart of a business district, Friday night seeker meetings at which a brief exposition of a challenging Christian teaching is followed by lively discussion and even debate, and soup kitchens and other diaconal services that offer financial counseling free of charge. Meeting in a pub with men who do not attend church but are open to an extended conversation, hosting luncheons for professional women or parenting classes—all of these are fine pre-evangelistic strategies. Child care is another outreach option that has proven valuable in enhancing a church's connection with its community. None of these outreach activities should get in the way of the Word-and-sacrament ministry at the heart of the church's life, but when the latter is thriving, the former adorns the gospel with the fragrance of communal discipleship and an outward-looking interest.

4. *Radio.* It may surprise many pastors to learn how inexpensive radio broadcasting can be, depending on the size of the market. While a preaching format (viz., "live" or recorded worship services) reaches older people—often those who cannot make it to church—other formats work better for younger audiences. Once again, here there is liberty while the worship service has fixed elements. One would not want to replace a sermon with a panel of several pastors talking about a particular topic, or with clips from movies and songs in the popular culture as a way of drawing people (especially the unchurched) into the conversation. And yet, all of these are appropriate in a nonofficial setting. If a church has the resources to produce a high-quality program locally, it could have a good deal of drawing potential. For well over a decade now, I have watched our nationwide broadcast, *The White Horse Inn,* attract many new members and inquirers to churches across the country that place an advertisement at the end of our program. A church in a university town may consider buying airtime on the school's station on Sunday, a church in a rural area may find that the local Christian station is effec-

tive, and an inner-city church may find a secular station more useful for its purposes.

5. *New attitudes toward the believing community.* Many traditional churches are ingrown, exhibiting little concern for evangelism, discipleship, and fellowship. We might call these churches seeker-resistant. Churches definitely must be seeker-sensitive, warmly welcoming unbelievers and inviting them into the circle. But there must still *be* a circle into which they are invited! We should be sensitive to the off-putting quirks that have nothing to do with faithful worship. At the same time, seeker-*driven* churches have gone too far in this direction, viewing the generations of faithful believers gathered by God as little more than mini-ministers who have failed if they haven't filled the church with visitors. Many churches are missing the gold under their nose. They have all these people who want to be nurtured over a lifetime, who know that their baptism obligates them to disciplined Christian instruction and practice, and who are nevertheless candidates for being *un*churched if their seed is never planted in the depths of scriptural teaching and practice. We must stop thinking of communicant members as beasts of burden (under the guise of "finding their ministry" or "discovering their spiritual gift") for outreach and instead regard them as the precious treasure that God has entrusted to a church's care. In all the frenetic business of our over-programmed churches, many parishoners do not have the time to *receive* adequate instruction and care, for themselves and their families. Let me unpack this one a bit.

Reaching the Reached

In many churches, believers have brought their children to the Lord and are raising them in the fear and knowledge of God. But instead of feeding them and fulfilling its covenantal obligations, the church too often redirects the supply to the unchurched. And the sad reality is that the unchurched are often professing Christians who are in many cases returning to church only if there are no obligations placed upon them. It is church members who first need to be regularly evangelized, regularly brought low and raised up, regularly fed on God's great work in Christ throughout redemptive history. Well-taught, well-connected, and well-cared for congregations will be outward-looking, eager to reach others with the gospel, and dedicated to acts of service toward neighbors. They will not need canned evangelistic speeches. They will be able (with their newfound time as a result of fewer church programs) to express their faith confidently and with a genuineness that comes from having been liberated by learning more about God and his Word.

We should ask ourselves what happens when the teen becomes a parent. Growing out of a youth culture of one generation, he or she outgrows his or her most direct religious environment. On the other hand, a practice that unites the generations is sure to provide continuity and relevance in every phase of life. We have a marvelous opportunity to re-evangelize those whom God has already placed in our midst, and we should not take their Christian knowledge or practice for granted in an age in which anything serious or lasting is regarded as boring. We need to be willing, as parents, pastors, and parishoners, to accept the fact that we will be bored sometimes—even with good sermons, strong teaching, robust worship, and effective elders and deacons. It is okay to be bored sometimes: "No pain, no gain."

Still pilgrims in the "in-between" time, we are simultaneously saint and sinner. But if we don't do anything that sometimes bores us, we will miss out on some of the most important things in life! Think of the daily experience at home. Although we like to be entertained, we know that our parents, siblings, or children will render us disillusioned if we thought for one moment that they existed to keep us occupied. And yet, few of us would suggest that the family institution needs to be radically altered in order to make it more interesting. Or consider education. Whether we were learning the alphabet or chaos theory, how many hours of boredom were involved? Was it worth it? Or should we have been allowed to have that extra recess we would have opted for? Too often we are impatient with progress and we have come to expect worship to be exciting, so if it isn't, we are disappointed. The fault must lie with the service and not with us. Perhaps we need a new sound system, a new choir, a new pastor. Radical moves may be necessary, because I'm losing my interest. But what if the problem is with me? And what if, by virtue of our continuing struggle with sin and the fact that we do not yet behold God face-to-face, excitement in worship is the exception rather than the rule? Many of the most exciting things in life are the ephemeral, bubbles that delight only to disappear when captured, while many of the most enduring and ennobling ventures are driven along by quite ordinary habits—commitments—of mind and body.

The most valuable things in life must be won by active struggling, not by passive stimulation. Whether due to the weaknesses of our finitude or our own sinful hearts ("prone to wander, Lord, I feel it, prone to leave the God I love"), our boredom must be acknowledged as a real struggle and yet as a doomed foe because we will not surrender the gold for the glitter.

Yet this should not give comfort to the pastor who is on his third rep-
etition of his Sermon on the Mount series that everybody seemed to
appreciate in 1963. In far too many conservative churches with which
I am familiar, boredom is practically considered a virtue. But a minister who is dry and prosaic, pedantic and repetitive in his style may easily, over time, alienate the younger people under his care from the Word
of God. A minister must keenly appreciate that part of his role is to main-
tain the interest of the young people. This does not mean pandering (for
one thing, young people see through patronizing appeals to the "youth
culture"), but it does mean spending time with them, asking them questions, and trying to discern where they are in their Christian understanding and experience so that one is able to keep them in mind when
writing a sermon.

Seeker-driven preaching (which dominates today even in churches
that might not designate themselves as seeker churches) not only impov-
erishes believers but also undermines genuine evangelism of visiting
unbelievers. In an article titled "Dumbed-Down Preaching Fails," the
editors of *Current Thoughts and Trends* summarized the thoughts of
James Troop.[45] The summary reads, in part:

> Unfortunately, the anti-intellectual thrust in many of today's pulpits cer-
> tainly isn't communicating that fact [of Christianity's profundity]. Instead,
> like Tweedledum and Tweedledee, simplicity and stupidity reign, unchal-
> lenged by tired and immature laity. "The status quo is simple sermons for
> simple Christians, as the world looks on." Pastors complain that their dis-
> interested congregations don't wish to be challenged. Indeed, today's laity
> is so ill-informed that classical and literary illustrations and quotations
> often go right over their heads. . . . Yet milk-based congregations aren't
> seeing examples of preaching like that set by the Apostle Paul in the pul-
> pit either. Today's pastors don't defend the gospel strongly and boldly as
> did the apostle, and with a "lack of any magnificent obsession in the min-
> istry," uninspired preachers content themselves with pulpit mediocrity
> and complacency. . . . The gospel is the most important and compelling
> news preachers have to give the world, and adults need to be educated as
> to their need to hear what their preachers need to say.[46]

Outreach begins with a well-taught laity, stirred by the great truths
of Scripture. If the preaching is consistently Christ-centered, it will evangelize the church and visitors who, as the quote above indicates, are
looking for some clear direction when they finally get up the courage to
visit. Another thing: In a talk given at Westminster Seminary in California, New York City pastor Tim Keller made the point that, in contrast to gimmicky "Bring-a-Neighbor-to-Church-Sundays" or canned
evangelistic pitches, what really works is when parishoners bring friends,

relatives, and coworkers to church *because they can count on the message*. When parishoners are embarrassed by their church or are convinced that it will not effectively reach their neighbors or will somehow not faithfully present the gospel, they lose their interest. An evangelistic, growing church is one in which the members are convinced that it is faithful in its shepherding of the already persuaded.

But it is not only the view of the pastor and preaching that needs to change. If the first evangelistic audience—the current members of a church—is to be reached and kept, we need to rethink how we view the other church offices. "Let the elders who rule well be counted worthy of double honor," said Paul, "especially those who labor in the word and doctrine" (1 Tim. 5:17 NKJV).

In far too many cases, at least in my experience, elders are chosen because of their general leadership skills, success in business, high position in the community, and other worldly considerations. Surely an elder is not disqualified for possessing these gifts, but they do not necessarily qualify him either. If churches are increasingly run like businesses, we may inquire as to whether we have bought a corporate business paradigm of leadership in the church. Elders should be chosen not for their worldly accomplishments but for their ability to "labor in word and doctrine" and for their success with their families, their friends, and their brothers and sisters in the church. In the denominations with which I am most familiar, the elders visit every family in the church regularly and provide spiritual guidance to those who are suffering.

Deacons, too, are needed in any congregation—as we are reminded in Acts 6:

> Now in those days, when the number of the disciples was multiplying, there arose a murmuring against the Hebrews by the Hellenists, because their widows were neglected in the daily distribution. Then the twelve summoned the multitudes of the disciples and said, "It is not desirable that we should leave the word of God and serve tables. Therefore, brethren, seek out from among you seven men of good reputation, full of the Holy Spirit and wisdom, whom we may appoint over this business; but we will give ourselves continually to prayer and to the ministry of the word."
>
> verses 1–4 NKJV

The apostles, finally, were no longer distracted by the immediate temporal needs of the people and could concentrate on the ministry of Word and sacrament. "The word of God spread, and the number of the disciples multiplied greatly in Jerusalem, and a great many of the priests were obedient to the faith" (Acts 6:7 NKJV). Could it be that reforming our church polity to reflect more closely the biblical pattern would have a much greater impact on evangelism and church growth than would distracting our pastors and elders from their mission by burdening them with administrative programs and a business paradigm of ministry?

Calvin's Geneva was a model city, historians say, in part because of the effectiveness of its restored diaconate. As refugees fled persecution from all over Europe and arrived in Geneva with nothing but the shirt on their back, the deacons in Geneva established an enormous network of service institutions. With each office performing its function well, the church in Geneva was a powerful witness in a difficult period of history, and Christian leaders came from great distances to experience and take the model back to their own countries. Leaving the inner city has been a trend among evangelical churches. Yet, there are notable exceptions, and among these are strong churches with a faithful preaching ministry, a wise ruling ministry, and an effective diaconal ministry. Examples of the latter include services to AIDS victims, soup kitchens, thrift stores, medical clinics, schools, and other ministries of mercy. As these offices are performed according to God's revealed will, unbelievers cannot help but see the *kavod*—the weightiness—of God among us, even through the weakness of the church.

A renewal of the inner life of the church—from worship to teaching and church discipline—is the most pressing need today, not only for the church's own health but for genuine outreach to take place.

The Theology of the Cross

In a few places I alluded briefly to a contrast that was drawn sharply first by Martin Luther and then by the other Reformers. It is a contrast that is easily discerned in the Scriptures, especially in Mark's Gospel and in Paul's epistles: the theology of the cross versus the theology of glory. This relates to the present topic in several ways, as should become apparent.

One of the most interesting subplots running through Mark's story of Jesus is the intensification of death's steps. The trip to Jerusalem is the story line. The closer Jesus and his disciples get to Jerusalem, the more Jesus talks about his impending crucifixion. Repeatedly, the disciples grumble at these moments until finally, close to the city of David, Peter rebukes Jesus for talking about the cross. After all, they were thinking that this was going to be the big entrance. With the people behind them, Jesus would enter as a conquering Messiah to throw off the Roman bondage and institute his kingdom.

Right after Peter's magnificent confession of Christ, Jesus talks again about how he must "be killed, and after three days rise again." "Peter took him aside and began to rebuke him. But when he had turned around and looked at his disciples, he rebuked Peter, saying, 'Get behind me, Satan! For you are not mindful of the things of God, but the things of men'" (Mark 8:31–33 NKJV). The last time someone tried to throw Jesus off his path and to exchange the way of the cross for the way of glory was when the devil tempted Jesus in the wilderness, precisely where Mark begins his Gospel. Peter is therefore treated here as an unintentional ambassador of Satan. He cannot think about the cross—defeat, sorrow, the anger of the crowds. He can only think of the positive: the triumphal entry of Jesus to take his throne. Jesus follows this episode by teaching about taking up his cross.

Then, one chapter later, Jesus raises the subject again: "The Son of Man is being delivered into the hands of men, and they will kill him. And after he is killed, he will rise the third day." And the response? "But they did not understand this saying, and were afraid to ask him" (Mark 9:31–32 NKJV). The very next section relates the debate that the disciples were having along the road. It was about positions in the new order. The Twelve were giddy with excitement about getting closer to Jerusalem: the coronation day of their hero, who would also raise them from obscurity to success and prosperity. They were ready to capture the culture for Christ. Talk of the cross and God's judgment of sin were distractions from the Big Thing that was about to happen: the Buzz of a glorious reign in Jerusalem. Jesus rebukes them (vv. 33–36).

A third time, one chapter later, Jesus announces his impending death (Mark 10:33–34). Will they get the message of the cross now? Or will their hearts be so prepared for triumph that they cannot talk about the wages of sin and Jesus as the Lamb of God who removes the curse? Here is the result:

> Then James and John, the sons of Zebedee, came to him, saying, "Teacher, we want you to do for us whatever we ask." And he said to them, "What do you want me to do for you?" They said to him, "Grant us that we may sit, one on your right hand and the other on your left, in your glory." But Jesus said to them, "You do not know what you ask. Can you drink the cup that I drink, and be baptized with the baptism that I am baptized with?" And they said to him, "We can." And so Jesus said to them, "You will indeed drink the cup that I drink, and with the baptism I am baptized with you will be baptized; but to sit on my right hand and on my left is not mine to give, but it is for those for whom it is prepared."
>
> Mark 10:35–40 NKJV

The disciples could not even for a moment take their eyes off the thought of immediate glory, power, success, and victory. It was beyond their comprehension that the glory would come later—because of the cross that Jesus, as well as they, would endure now. They wanted to be enthroned with him, one on his left and the other on his right. But they were asking for the spots that would be taken by the two criminals on Good Friday. Jesus' anticipated throne was quite different from that which swelled the ambitions of the disciples. "And when the ten heard it, they began to be greatly displeased with James and John." But, of course, James and John had just verbalized what the rest of the disciples were thinking—and what we are likely to be thinking as well. "Even the Son of Man did not come to be served, but to serve, and to give his life a ransom for many" (v. 45 NKJV).

Paul's division of things into "the wisdom of God" and "the wisdom of the world" followed this theology of the cross and the theology of glory pattern. "The message of the cross is foolishness to those who are perishing," he said (1 Cor. 1:18). People may be looking for a god who will serve them and help them get what they want out of life, but nobody is looking for God on the cross. "For Jews demand signs and Greeks desire wisdom, but we proclaim Christ crucified, a stumbling block to Jews and foolishness to Gentiles, but to those who are the called, both Jews and Greeks, Christ the power of God and the wisdom of God" (vv. 22–24 NRSV). If sin is no longer the problem, then how could the cross be the solution? By nature, we are glory-seekers, but when the Holy Spirit buries us in Christ's death and raises us with him in newness of life, we are marked with the cross and see all of reality through it.

In his Heidelberg Disputation, Martin Luther said that a theologian of the cross "says what a thing is," while a theologian of glory calls the bad good and the good bad—whatever it takes to have popularity. No one has described and applied this contrast with respect to our own day better than Lutheran theologian Gerhard Forde. He writes:

> It is evident that there is a serious erosion or slippage in the language of theology today. Sentimentality leads to a shift in focus, and the language slips out of place. To take a common example, we apparently are no longer sinners, but rather victims, oppressed by sinister victimizers whom we relentlessly seek to track down and accuse. . . . We no longer live in a guilt culture but have been thrown into meaninglessness—so we are told. Then the language slips out of place. Guilt puts the blame on us as sinners, but who is responsible for meaninglessness? . . . Since we are victims and not really sinners, what we need is affirmation and support, and so on. The language slips and falls out of place. It becomes therapeutic rather than evangelical. . . . A theologian of the cross says what a thing is. In modern parlance: a theologian of the cross calls a spade a spade. One who "looks

on all things through suffering and the cross" is constrained to speak the truth. . . . It is curious that in spite of attempts to avoid offense, matters don't actually seem to improve. We seek affirmation, but we seem to experience less and less of it. . . . Perhaps a return to calling a spade a spade has its place.[47]

But the theology of the cross involves more than refusing to dress the wound of the people lightly. It imposes a certain lens on reality that fundamentally alters not just a few doctrines here and there but how we think, act, worship, and reach out to the world. It is not that the theology of the cross is simply negative; rather, it cannot help but recognize the divine judgment standing over us—over our self-righteousness, our pretentious plans of ushering in God's kingdom by our grand efforts, our preference for our methods over God's. And it is a judgment that stands not only over others but over us—crucifying us with Christ, the one who at the cross bore the curse for our delusions of grandeur.

Although the gospel will always at first be foolishness to those who are perishing, I cannot think of anything that intersects more obviously with the experience of younger generations today. They are not optimists, like the Boomers, but suspicious of sales pitches for "revolutionary" products. They will doubtless jibe more with Paul's experience in Romans 7 than with sermons on how to access God's power for victory. At the same time, they are craving hope—that is what every survey mentions about the Xers. The theology of the cross looks beyond the cross to the resurrection as the cruciform shape of victory—a hope that is not based on that which is accomplished by us but is the climax of the Jesus story. While many among the older generations have tended to expect everything now, Xers take seriously a message that holds out the restoration of the whole creation and then recognizes that this hope is not consistent with what we see or experience right now. "For we were saved in this hope, but hope that is seen is not hope; for why does one still hope for what he sees? But if we hope for what we do not see, we eagerly wait for it with perseverance" (Rom. 8:24–25 NKJV). To be sure, there is still Romans 6, declaring to us our definitive, once-and-for-all newness. And there is still Romans 8, with its sweeping panorama of a restored creation. But in between is a theology for pilgrims.

A theology that starts from the premise that we are sinful and weak rather than basically good and strong is in the best position, ironically, to provide a realistic basis for hope. We know that the latter is rubbish. We've seen too much selfishness, greed, ambition, anger, pride. Our homes have been living witnesses to total depravity. Victorian moralists who sentimentalize "home life" and "virtues" can't survive in these times for very long. Their cheery optimism toward human ability rings hollow.

At such a time as this, will we, like the disciples, demand that only smooth doctrines and triumphalistic plans guide our paths? Or will we embrace the truth about life, ourselves, and God—even when the polls and church marketers suggest otherwise? Calvin's assertion, "Whomever the Lord has adopted . . . ought to prepare themselves for a hard, toilsome, and unquiet life, crammed with very many and various kinds of evil,"[48] obtains a new kind of credibility in our day. It has the ring of truth, far more than the "before" and "after" testimonies and choruses with which many of us are familiar. The theology of the cross, however, does not leave us with a dark pessimism. "Now we see," Calvin says, "how many good things, interwoven, spring from the cross. For, overturning that good opinion which we falsely entertain concerning our own strength, and unmasking our hypocrisy, which affords us delight, the cross strikes at our perilous confidence in the flesh."[49] Deep down we know that the song of myself must give way to the song of Moses:

> I will sing to the Lord, for he has triumphed gloriously;
>   horse and rider he has thrown into the sea.
>
> The Lord is my strength and my might,
>   and he has become my salvation;
> this is my God, and I will praise him,
>   my father's God, and I will exalt him.
>
>   Exodus 15:1–2 NRSV

Notes

Introduction

1. Dorothy Sayers, *Creed or Chaos?* (New York: Harcourt, Brace and Company, 1949), 3.

2. Ibid., 7.

3. Sally Morgenthaler and Robb Redman, "New Paradigms for Worship and Ministry with Single Adults," *Worship Leader* (May/June 1999): 30.

4. Ibid., 31.

5. Ibid., 32.

6. Ibid., 34.

7. This metaphor has a long and distinguished career in theology. John Calvin, for instance, drew on this analogy in many places, such as the following from his commentary on Psalms: "The Church is a distinguished theatre on which the divine glory is displayed" (Ps. III:194); "The Church, which God has selected as the great theatre where his fatherly care may be manifested" (Ps. III:12); "The state or kingdom of the Church constitutes the principal and august theatre where God presents and displays the tokens of his wonderful power, wisdom, and righteousness" (Ps. IV: 335); "The whole world is a theatre for the display of the goodness, wisdom, justice, and power, but the Church is the orchestra . . . the most conspicuous part of it" (Ps. V:178).

8. The Heidelberg Catechism (1563), Lord's Day 35, Question 98, in *Ecumenical Creeds and Reformed Confessions* (Grand Rapids: CRC Publications, 1987), 56.

9. Cited by David Wells, *God in the Wasteland: The Reality of Truth in a World of Fading Dreams* (Grand Rapids: Eerdmans, 1994), 118.

10. Ann Douglas, *The Feminization of American Culture* (New York: Alfred A. Knopf, 1977), 7.

11. Philip Rieff, *The Triumph of the Therapeutic* (New York: Harper & Row, 1968), x–xii.

12. Sayers, *Creed or Chaos?* 24.

Chapter 1

1. For a full development of this theme, see Meredith Kline, *Treaty of the Great King* (Grand Rapids: Eerdmans, 1963).

2. Randy Rowland, "The Focus and Function of Worship: Music as a Medium to Connect Us to God," *Worship Leader* (May/June 1999): 14.

3. Donald Bruggink and Carl Droppers, *Christ and Architecture: Building Presbyterian/Reformed Churches* (Grand Rapids: Eerdmans, 1965), 285.

Chapter 2

1. Neal Gabler, *Life the Movie, Starring Everyone: How Entertainment Conquered Reality* (New York: Alfred A. Knopf, 1999), 8.
2. David Di Sabatino, "The Power of Music: What to Keep in Mind While under Its Influence," *Worship Leader* (May/June 1999): 22.
3. Cited in *Theological Digest and Outlook* (March 1999): 5.
4. Paul Ricoeur, *Figuring the Sacred* (Minneapolis: Fortress, 1995), 56.

Chapter 3

1. Robert Jay Lifton "The Protean Self," in *The Truth about the Truth*, ed. Walter Truett Anderson (New York: Putnam, 1995), 130–35.
2. Ibid., 132.
3. Peter Berger, *The Heretical Imperative* (New York: Doubleday, 1979), 78.
4. Ibid.
5. Lifton, "The Protean Self," 133.
6. Ibid., 135.
7. George Barna, *The Barna Report 1992–93* (Ventura, Calif.: Regal Books, 1992), 94.
8. Richard Lints, "Vinyl Narratives: The Metanarrative of Postmodernity and the Recovery of a Churchly Theology," in *A Confessing Theology for Postmodern Times*, ed. Michael Horton (Westchester, Ill.: Crossway, 2000), 119.
9. Stanley Hauerwas, "Preaching as Though We Had Enemies," *First Things* 53 (May 1995): 45–49.
10. John Updike, *A Month of Sundays* (New York: Fawcett Crest, 1975), 33.
11. See especially Alisdair MacIntyre's "The Virtues, the Unity of a Human Life and the Concept of a Tradition," in *After Virtue* (Notre Dame: University of Notre Dame, 1981), 190–209; and "Epistemological Crises, Dramatic Narrative, and the Philosophy of Science," *Monist* 60, no. 4 (October 1977): 435–72.
12. Mark C. Taylor, *Erring: A Postmodern A/Theology* (Chicago: University of Chicago Press, 1984).
13. H. Richard Niebuhr, *The Meaning of Revelation* (New York: Macmillan, 1941), 44–45.
14. Ibid.

Chapter 4

1. Charles Finney, in his *Systematic Theology* (Minneapolis: Bethany, 1976), railed against "the anti-scriptural and nonsensical dogma of a sinful constitution" (i.e., human depravity) (179), denied "that the atonement was a literal payment of a debt" (217) in favor of the governmental and moral example theory (209), adding, "It is true, that the atonement, of itself, does not secure the salvation of any one" (217) but rather provides the best incentive for our own obedience (209). Concerning the doctrine of justification, he wrote, "But for sinners to be forensically pronounced just, is impossible and absurd. . . . As has been already said, there can be no justification in a legal or forensic sense, but upon the ground of universal, perfect, and uninterrupted obedience to law. . . . The doctrine of an imputed righteousness, or that Christ's obedience to the law was accounted as our obedience, is founded on a most false and nonsensical assumption. . . . But if Christ owed personal obedience to the moral law, then his obedience could no more than justify himself. It can never be imputed to us" (320–21). Thus, ". . . representing the atonement as the ground of the sinner's justification, has been a sad occasion of stumbling to many" (322). Instead of Christ's obedience, "We shall see that perseverance in obedience to the end of life is also a condition of justification," and that viewing faith alone as the

condition of justification is "antinomian" (326). "Present sanctification, in the sense of present full consecration to God, is another condition, not ground, of justification" (327). His comments on the "old school" (orthodox) Presbyterian view are telling: "The relations of the old school view of justification to their view of depravity is obvious. They hold, as we have seen, that the constitution in every faculty and part is sinful. Of course, a return to personal, present holiness, in the sense of entire conformity to the law, cannot with them be a condition of justification. They must have a justification while yet at least in some degree of sin. This must be brought about by imputed righteousness. The intellect revolts at a justification in sin. . . . Constitutional depravity or sinfulness being once assumed, physical [supernatural] regeneration, physical sanctification, physical divine influence, imputed righteousness and justification, while personally in the commission of sin, follow of course" (338).

2. Charles G. Finney, *Revivals of Religion* (Old Tappan, N.J.: Revell, n.d.), 5.

3. Ibid., 4–5.

4. Ibid., 321.

5. See Keith J. Hardman, *Charles Grandison Finney: Revivalist and Reformer* (Grand Rapids: Baker, 1990), 380–94.

6. See, for instance, Whitney R. Cross, *The Burned-Over District: The Social and Intellectual History of Enthusiastic Religion in Western New York, 1800–1850* (Ithaca, N.Y.: Cornell University Press, 1982).

7. B. B. Warfield, "A Review of Lewis Sperry Chafer's *He That Is Spiritual*," in *Christ the Lord*, ed. Michael Horton (Grand Rapids: Baker, 1992), 212; reprinted from the *Princeton Theological Review* 17 (April 1919): 322–27.

8. William James, *Pragmatism* (1907; reprint, New York: Meridian Books, 1943), 192.

9. Louis Berkhof, *Systematic Theology* (Grand Rapids: Eerdmans, 1941), 612.

10. Karl Barth, *The Gottingen Dogmatics: Instruction in the Christian Religion*, vol. 1 (Grand Rapids: Eerdmans, 1991), 35.

11. James, *Pragmatism*, 192.

12. Katherine A. Kersten, "To Hell with Sin: When 'Being a Good Person' Excuses Everything," *The Wall Street Journal*, Friday, 17 September 1999, p. W15.

13. John Murray, "Law and Grace" (chap. 8), *Principles of Conduct: Aspects of Biblical Ethics* (1957; reprint, Grand Rapids: Eerdmans, 1991), 181.

14. Ibid., 185–86.

15. John Calvin, *Institutes of the Christian Religion*, 3.2.29 (575).

16. Calvin, *Institutes*, 2.11.23.

Chapter 5

1. For an excellent treatment, see Edmund P. Clowney, *The Unfolding Mystery: Christ in the Old Testament* (Colorado Springs: NavPress, 1988).

2. For more detailed description and analysis from this perspective, see Geerhardus Vos, *Redemptive History and Biblical Interpretation*, ed. Richard B. Gaffin Jr. (Phillipsburg, N.J.: Presbyterian and Reformed, 1980); Herman Ridderbos, *Paul: An Outline of His Theology*, trans. John R. De Witt (Grand Rapids: Eerdmans, 1975); *Redemptive History and the New Testament Scriptures*, trans. H. De Jongste (Phillipsburg, N.J.: Presbyterian and Reformed, 1963); and Richard Gaffin Jr., *Resurrection and Redemption: A Study in Paul's Soteriology* (Phillipsburg, N.J.: Presbyterian and Reformed, 1987).

3. Edmund P. Clowney, "Preaching Christ from All the Scriptures," in *Preaching and Preachers*, ed. Samuel T. Logan Jr. (Phillipsburg, N.J.: Presbyterian and Reformed, 1986).

4. From a personal conversation.

Chapter 6

1. Johannes Wollebius, *Compendium Theologiae Christianae*, in *Reformed Dogmatics*, ed. and trans. John W. Beardslee III (New York: Oxford University Press, 1965), 135.
2. Louis Berkhof, *Systematic Theology* (1941; reprint, Grand Rapids: Eerdmans, 1971), 604–5.
3. *The Oxford Desk Dictionary and Thesaurus, American Edition* (New York: Berkley Books, 1997), 813.
4. Meredith Kline, *By Oath Consigned* (Grand Rapids: Eerdmans, 1968), chaps. 3 and 4 especially.

Chapter 7

1. John Calvin, *Institutes of the Christian Religion*, 4.17.32.

Chapter 8

1. Stanley Hauerwas, "Preaching as Though We Had Enemies," *First Things* 53 (May 1995): 48.
2. Meredith Kline, *Images of the Spirit* (self-published, 1986 edition), 99.

Chapter 9

1. For expansion on this point, see John M. Frame, *The Doctrine of the Knowledge of God: A Theology of Lordship* (Phillipsburg, N.J.: Presbyterian and Reformed, 1987), especially 13–15.
2. The quotes on absolution are taken from John Calvin, *Institutes of the Christian Religion*, 3.4.1–14.
3. *The Book of Common Order of the Church of Scotland and the Directory for the Public Worship of God* (Edinburgh and London: William Blackwood and Sons, 1868), 69.
4. John Calvin, "The Form of Church Prayers," in *Liturgies of the Western Church*, selected and introduced by Bard Thompson (Philadelphia: Fortress, 1961), 198.
5. I am grateful to Rev. Danny Hyde for bringing this to my attention in Thompson's *Liturgies of the Western Church*, 191.
6. Ibid., 294.
7. Calvin, *Institutes*, 3.4.14.
8. V. Palachovsky and C. Vogel, *Sin in the Orthodox Church and the Protestant Churches*, trans. Charles Schaldenbrand (New York: Desclee Co., 1960), 39.

Chapter 10

1. Neil Postman, *Technopoly: The Surrender of Culture to Technology* (New York: Alfred A. Knopf, 1993), 164.
2. Ibid.
3. Ibid., 166.
4. Ibid., 170.
5. Immanuel Kant, "An Answer to the Question: What Is Enlightenment?" in *Kant's Political Writings*, trans. H. B. Nixbet, ed. Hans Reiss (Cambridge: Cambridge University Press, 1970), 54–55.
6. Postman, *Technopoly*, 179.
7. Rev. Brian Norkatis, in Oliver Libaw, "God on a Grand Scale," ABCNEWS.com, June 13. The subtitle of the article reads, "Bigger Is Better in America—Apparently Even When It Comes to God."
8. Postman, *Technopoly*, 171.

9. Cited in ibid., 189.

10. Ibid., 115.

11. Jaroslav Pelikan, *The Vindication of Tradition* (New Haven: Yale, 1984), 65.

12. John Updike, *A Month of Sundays* (New York: Fawcett Crest, 1975), 30–33.

13. Peter Berger, *The Heretical Imperative* (New York: Doubleday, 1980).

14. David Di Sabatino, "The Power of Music: What to Keep in Mind While under Its Influence," *Worship Leader* (May/June 1999): 22.

15. Ibid., 26.

16. Donald C. Boyd, *The Asbury Herald* (winter 1999): 6.

17. Kenneth Myers, "Is Popular Culture Either?" *Modern Reformation* 6, no. 1 (January/February 1997): 10.

Chapter 11

1. John Seabrook, *Nobrow: The Culture of Marketing—The Marketing of Culture* (New York: Alfred A. Knopf, 2000), 5.

2. Ibid., 43.

3. Ibid., 22.

4. Ibid.

5. Ibid., 28–29.

6. Ibid., 57–58.

7. Ibid., 96.

8. Ibid., 64.

9. Ibid., 65.

10. Ibid., 77.

11. Ibid., 170.

12. Cited in ibid., 151.

13. Gerhard Sauter, *What Dare We Hope? Reconsidering Eschatology* (Harrisburg, Pa.: Trinity Press International, 1999), 208.

14. Joseph A. Pipa, *The Lord's Day* (Ross-shire, Scotland: Christian Focus, 1997), 11.

15. Ibid.

16. It must be acknowledged that not everyone within the Reformed tradition would have agreed with this consensus. Calvin and the other Reformers were able to distinguish between a binding (moral) and obsolete (ceremonial) aspect of the fourth commandment. Nevertheless, theologians such as Francis Gomarus (1563–1641)—the leading opponent of the Arminian party in the Dutch Church—and Johannes Cocceius (1603–69)—father of the discipline known as "biblical theology" and a leading advocate of covenant theology—regarded the fourth commandment as abrogated in its entirety. A peculiar gift under the Mosaic economy, the commandment in toto was ceremonial. This is, however, an extreme view and need not be held by those who nevertheless do not regard the Lord's Day as the Christian Sabbath.

17. Anyone who is familiar with Meredith Kline's work on this subject (see especially *Kingdom Prologue* [privately published lectures], vol. 1, 26ff.) will easily see its influence on my brief summary here.

18. Ibid., 26.

19. Wendell Berry, *A Timbered Choir* (New York: Counterpoint, 1998).

20. B. B. Warfield and John E. Meeter, eds., *The Sabbath in the Word of God, Selected Shorter Writings—I* (Nutley, N.J.: Presbyterian and Reformed, 1970), 319.

21. Ibid., 320.

22. Richard Gaffin Jr., "The Sabbath: A Sign of Hope," Orthodox Presbyterian Church Position Paper, 5.

23. Ibid., 6.

24. Dorothy C. Bass, "Receiving the Day the Lord Has Made," *Christianity Today* (6 March 2000): 67.

25. Richard Bauckham and Trevor Hart, *Hope against Hope: Christian Eschatology in Contemporary Context* (London: Darton, Longman and Todd Ltd, 1999), 178.

26. Richard R. Osmer, "The Case for Catechism," *Christian Century* (23–30 April 1997): 408.

27. Ibid.

28. Ibid., 409.

29. Ibid., 411.

30. Ibid., 412.

Chapter 12

1. Sociologist Wade Clark Roof notes, "A surprising number of them [born-again Christians] actually identify themselves as 'seekers,' saying they believe in God but are not sure about organized religion (meaning churches as they have known them), or raise serious questions about the truthfulness of Christianity itself. By far, most self-proclaimed Evangelical seekers are of the first type: they hold to some core religious beliefs, may even say their 'Born-again' experience was a turning point in their lives, but for the most part they reject conventional churches and know very little about Christian doctrine and practice" (*Spiritual Marketplace: Baby Boomers and the Remaking of American Religion* [Princeton: Princeton University Press, 1999], 189).

2. Even George Barna, advocate of seeker-driven approaches to church growth, concedes, "The proportion of the unchurched has been slowly rising since the late eighties" (*The Index of Leading Spiritual Indicators* [Dallas: Word, 1996], 34).

3. Robert B. Reich, "The Choice Fetish: Blessings and Curses of a Market Idol," *Civilization* (August/September, 2000): 66.

4. Deborah Stone, "The People Who Won't Commit," in ibid., 74.

5. Ibid., 74.

6. David Brooks, *Bobos in Paradise: The New Upper Class and How They Got There* (New York: Simon & Schuster, 2000).

7. Ibid., 226.

8. Ibid., 239–40.

9. Ibid., 242.

10. Ibid., 246–47.

11. William Willimon, "Been There, Preached That," *Leadership Journal* (fall 1995): 75.

12. William Willimon, *Peculiar Speech: Preaching to the Baptized* (Grand Rapids: Eerdmans, 1992), 12.

13. Ibid., 13.

14. Lee Strobel in "An Interview with Gardner Taylor and Lee Strobel," *Leadership Journal* (fall 1995): 24.

15. Ibid., 21.

16. Ibid., 22.

17. Ibid., 23.

18. The Heidelberg Catechism (1563), Lord's Day 35, Question 98, in *Ecumenical Creeds and Reformed Confessions* (Grand Rapids: CRC Publications, 1987).

19. David Lyle Jeffrey, cited by Lynn Smith, *FaithToday* (September/October 1999): 23.

20. Stanley Hauerwas, "Preaching as Though We Had Enemies," *First Things* 53 (May 1995): 46.

21. Ibid., 49.

22. C. Peter Wagner, "Another New Wineskin," *Next* 5, no. 1 (January–March 1999): 3.

23. George Barna, *Marketing the Church* (Colorado Springs: NavPress, 1988), 145.

24. Walter Lippman, quoted in Ned Gabler, *Life the Movie, Starring Everyone: How Entertainment Conquered Reality* (New York: Alfred A. Knopf, 1999), 78.

25. Steiner Kvale, "Themes of Postmodernity," in *The Truth about the Truth: De-confusing and Re-constructing the Postmodern World,* ed. Walter Truett Anderson (New York: Putnam, 1995), 25.

26. Sally MacDonald, "New Church Changes to Fit Modern Society," *Seattle Times,* 18 October 1998, B1.

27. George Barna, news release from the Barna Research Group (February 1999).

28. Cited by Smith, *FaithToday,* 20.

29. Ibid.

30. Ibid., 22.

31. Cited in ibid., 23.

32. Robert Webber, "Culture Watch: Millennials on the Rise: Is Society on the Verge of Rediscovering the Past?" *Worship Leader* (May/June 1999): 12.

33. Christina Shankar, "Letters to the Editor," *New Yorker* (January 1999): 6.

34. Sarah E. Hinlicky, "Talking to Generation X," *First Things* (February 1999): 10–11.

35. Ibid., 11.

36. Eric Felton, "Data Divining," *The Wall Street Journal,* 28 April 2000, 12.

37. Ibid.

38. Willimon, "Been There, Preached That," 78.

39. "Brain Scan of America: A Conversation with Marketing Consultant Michael Sack," *Leadership Journal* (fall 1995): 30.

40. Ibid.

41. John C. LaRue Jr., "Special Report: Current Research Data on Churches," *Your Church* (January/February 2001): 96.

42. Ibid.

43. Ibid., 31.

44. Ibid.

45. *Current Thoughts and Trends* (June 1999): 14–15. James Troop's article is titled "Preaching's Plight," in *Sharing the Practice* 21, no. 4 (1999): 6–9.

46. Ibid., 15.

47. Gerhard Forde, "On Being a Theologian of the Cross," *Christian Century* (22 October 1997): 947–49.

48. John Calvin, *Institutes of the Christian Religion,* 3.8.1.

49. Ibid., 3.8.3.

The Rev. Michael S. Horton (Ph.D.) is associate professor of historical theology and apologetics at Westminster Theological Seminary in California. He is also president of the Alliance of Confessing Evangelicals, editor of *Modern Reformation* magazine, and the author of numerous books and articles, including *Covenant and Eschatology* (Westminster John Knox). A minister in the United Reformed Churches in North America (URCNA), Michael has served two churches in Southern California and now resides with his wife, Lisa, and son, James, in Escondido, California.